When God Speaks for Himself

I0540699

He Uses Words You'll _Never_ Hear in Church or Sunday School

- ➤ **God gave Moses the Ten Commandments:** Yes...but they're not the Ten Commandments you think you know. *(Page 110.)*

- ➤ **Noah's Ark and the Flood:** How the Bible's own words completely contradict this well-known story. *(Page 132.)*

- ➤ **Jesus' Divine Origin:** Affirmed by the Gospels of Matthew, Luke and John; not mentioned at all in the Gospel of Mark; and specifically denied in all the Epistles of St. Paul. *(Pages 34 & 98.)* (Or: possibly due to the mistranslation of a *single* Hebrew word? *Page 72.)*

- ➤ **Jonah and the Whale:** *Is* there a whale that could swallow a human whole? Yes, but... *(Page 142.)*

- ➤ **David killed Goliath with a slingshot** — or did he? *(Page 45.)*

- ➤ **Jesus gave his "Sermon on the Mount" on the mount?** "Yes!" — The Gospel of Matthew. "No!" — The Gospel of Luke. *(Page 13.)*

- ➤ **"Thou Shalt Honor Thy Father and Thy Mother":** Does Jesus obey this Commandment himself? *(Page 30.)*

- ➤ **And many more...**

WARNING!

This book contains lewd and graphic scenes of sex, incest, violence, murder, rape, cannibalism (including the eating of babies), and massacres that some people may find offensive. But they're all from the Holy Bible, so it's okay to share them with your children.

Also by Mark Tier

NON-FICTION
Understanding Inflation
The Nature of Market Cycles
How To Get A Second Passport
The Winning Investment Habits of
*   Warren Buffett & George Soros*
Ayn Rand's 5 Surprisingly Simple
*   Rules for Judging Political Candidates*
How to Make More Money By
*   Sitting On Your Butt*

FICTION
Give Me Liberty (co-edited with Martin H. Greenberg)
Visions of Liberty (co-edited with Martin H. Greenberg)
Freedom! (co-edited with Martin H. Greenberg)
Trust Your Enemies

Also by George Forrai

Russian Express: Don't Leave Home

When God Speaks for Himself

The Words of God You'll _Never_ Hear in Church or Sunday School

Mark Tier
George Forrai

inversebooks HONG KONG

CONTENTS

A Note From the Authors: This book is the result of a collaboration — but is written in the first person ("I" instead of "we") as Mark Tier is the writer of the team. Nevertheless, the opinions expressed herein are those of *both* authors.

When God Speaks
for Himself

Have you read the Bible?

From cover to cover? From Genesis to Revelation?

It would seem that few of us have.

Even those you'd think would be *required* to read the whole Bible haven't — as I discovered, to my surprise, when a nun happened to see a proof copy of the back WARNING! cover of this book. Horrified, she burst out:

"That's not true!

Those verses aren't in the Bible!"

To prove it, she opened the Bible — only to discover that she was *wrong.*

How can this be?

As kids in Sunday School, we hear the stories of Adam and Eve and the creation of the world, Jesus in the Manger and the Three Wise Men, Jonah and the Whale, and how Noah saved the animals from the flood.

These are, naturally enough, edited into an engaging style appropriate to five and ten year olds. Eve ate the apple, Jonah was swallowed by a whale, and Noah took the animals "two by two."

But how many of us have actually opened the Bible to read the *original* texts of these stories and found that:

➢ We don't know *what* kind of fruit Eve ate. Genesis 2:16-17 merely says: "...the LORD God commanded the man [Adam], saying, Of every tree of the garden thou mayest freely eat: But of the *tree of the knowledge of good and evil,* thou shalt not eat of it: for in the day that thou eatest thereof thou shalt surely die."

➤ The *kind* of fish that swallowed Jonah is not specified: "the LORD had prepared *a great fish* [a whale, of course, is not a fish but a mammal] to swallow up Jonah" [Jonah 1:17].

➤   "Noah took the animals, *two by two,...*" is actually *not* what God instructed: "Of every clean beast [that can be eaten according to Jewish dietary laws] thou shalt take to thee by *sevens,* the male and his female: and of beasts that are not clean by two, the male and his female. Of fowls also of the air by *sevens,* the male and the female;..." [Genesis 7:2-3].

These innocuous edits improve the story value but don't change the meaning. But even if we've read the Bible, it's the *edited* versions of the stories that stick in our minds — which we treat as the "Word of God."

This does not explain why, as adults, few of us know that Moses *does* command:

"Now therefore kill every male among the little ones, and kill every woman that hath known man by lying with him. But all the women children that have not known man by lying with him, ***keep alive for yourselves***" (Got your Bible handy? It's in Numbers 31, verses 17-18.)

Quite understandably, *that's* a passage you'll never hear in a sermon, any more than you'll be instructed in the finer points of boiling and eating your children (Deuteronomy 28:53), the God-given procedures for selling your daughter into slavery (Exodus 21:7-8) or His recommended treatment for stubborn or rebellious sons (death by stoning: Deuteronomy 21:18-21) — though, come to think of it, they're pretty good threats for keeping unruly kids in line!

How come even devout Christians, like the nun I mentioned above, are *mortified* to learn that these and, hundreds of similar passages, *are* the "Word of God"?

Because such passages are almost never heard in church!

Of the three to four Bible passages to be read in Catholic Church services each day, just *one every other week* contains a *few* verses, like those above, that the average person will find offensive.[*]

Those verses are, for the most part, buried in the middle of the reading: unless you're paying close attention, you'll miss them completely.

"Spin"

In politics this is called "spin": exaggerate the positive, downplay the negative — or ignore it and hope no one notices.

While politicians *may* be telling you the truth (a proposition that should automatically be doubted), you can be sure they aren't telling you the *whole* truth.

Similarly, what most people "know" about God, Jesus and what the Bible says is the abridged, saccharine version of the "Word of God."

No wonder, then, that most Christians are astonished to learn that, "When God Speaks for Himself," he uses words you'll *never* hear in church or Sunday School — as you

---

[*] For a detailed analysis of the Catholic Church's "Liturgical Guide" see Appendix II, page 312.

can discover for yourself in the following pages which contain:

➢ Gruesome, bloodthirsty massacres *ordered by God* — Bible passages that will make your stomach churn;

➢ Bible passages that say the exact opposite of another Bible passage, *sometimes in two consecutive verses!*

➢ Bible passages that contradict what you "know": *was* Jesus born in Bethlehem? (Page 39). And he gave his Sermon on the Mount on the mount, right? (Page 13);

➢ Obvious inconsistencies about the Virgin Birth, Original Sin, and other central tenets of Christianity — to which the churches' only possible answer is: "have faith";

➢ Simple questions about such Bible favorites as the Creation, the Flood and Noah's Ark that make *Cinderella* and *The Three Little Pigs* seem far more realistic;

Plus: extracts from official church documents — some kept hidden for centuries — including the actual words of the Inquisition's reasoning and verdict on Galileo, a collection of pointed and often hilarious quotes and comments from skeptics and believers from all over the world...and much more.

In sum, in your hands you hold the answers to dozens of questions you simply would not have been allowed to ask in church or Sunday School.

1

The Word
of God?

"A thorough reading and understanding of
the Bible is the surest path to atheism."
— *Donald Morgan*

"Most people are bothered by those
passages of Scripture they do not understand,
but the passages that bother me are those I do
understand."
— *Mark Twain*

"Properly read, the Bible is the most potent
force for atheism ever conceived."
— *Isaac Asimov*

"All scripture is given by inspiration of God, and is profitable for doctrine, for reproof, for correction, for instruction in righteousness:"

— *2 Timothy Chapter 3:16*

But the Bible is replete with contradictions and inconsistencies. A few examples...

Jesus gives his sermon on the mount...

From Matthew Chapter 5*
¹ And seeing the multitudes, he went up into a mountain: and when he was set, his disciples came unto him:

...or on the plain?...

From Luke Chapter 6
¹⁷ And he came down with them, and stood in the plain, and the company of his disciples, and a great multitude of people out of all Judaea and Jerusalem, and from the sea coast of Tyre and Sidon, which came to hear him, and to be healed of their diseases;

Or did he?...

*Neither Mark nor John mention
any such sermon at all.*

---

* All excerpts from the Holy Bible, King James Version, [Cambridge: Cambridge University Press].

God tempts man to be evil...

From Isaiah Chapter 45
⁷ I form the light, and create darkness: I make peace, and create evil: I the Lord do all these *things*.

From Genesis Chapter 12
¹ And it came to pass after these things, that God did ***tempt*** Abraham....

Or does he?...

From James Chapter 1
¹³ Let no man say when he is tempted, I am tempted of God: for God cannot be tempted with evil, neither tempteth he any man.

God's anger is fleeting...

From Psalms Chapter 30

5 For his anger endureth but a moment; in his favour is life: weeping may endure for a night, but joy cometh in the morning.

From Jeremiah Chapter 3

12 Go forth and proclaim these words towards the north, and say, Return, thou backsliding Israel, saith the LORD; *and* I will not cause mine anger to fall upon you: for I *am* merciful, saith the LORD, *and* I will not keep *anger* for ever.

From Micah Chapter 7

18 Who is a God like unto thee, that pardoneth iniquity, and passeth by the transgression of the remnant of his heritage? he retaineth not his anger for ever, because he delighteth in mercy.

...or eternal?...

From Jeremiah Chapter 17

4 And thou, even thyself, shalt discontinue from thine heritage that I gave thee; and I will cause thee to serve thine enemies in the land which thou knowest not: for ye have kindled a fire in mine anger, which shall burn for ever.

From Matthew Chapter 25

46 And these shall go away into everlasting punishment: but the righteous into life eternal.

Happy is the man that findeth wisdom...

From Proverbs Chapter 3
[13] Happy is the man that findeth wisdom, and the man that getteth understanding.

From Proverbs Chapter 4
[7] Wisdom is the principal thing; therefore get wisdom: and with all thy getting get understanding.

From Proverbs Chapter 19
[8] He that getteth wisdom loveth his own soul: he that keepeth understanding shall find good.

From Luke Chapter 2
[40] And the child grew, and waxed strong in spirit, filled with wisdom: and the grace of God was upon him....
[52] And Jesus increased in wisdom and stature, and in favour with God and man.

...or is he?...

From 1 Corinthians Chapter 1
[19] For it is written, I will destroy the wisdom of the wise, and will bring to nothing the understanding of the prudent.

From 1 Corinthians Chapter 3
[18] Let no man deceive himself. If any man among you seemeth to be wise in this world, let him become a fool, that he may be wise.

From Matthew Chapter 6
[34] Take therefore no thought for the morrow: for the morrow shall take thought for the things of itself. Sufficient unto the day is the evil thereof.

From Matthew Chapter 11
[25] At that time Jesus answered and said, I thank thee, O Father, Lord of heaven and earth, because thou hast hid these things from the wise and prudent, and hast revealed them unto babes.

God is love...

From John Chapter 4
8 He that loveth not knoweth not God; for God is love.
16 And we have known and believed the love that God hath to us. God is love; and he that dwelleth in love dwelleth in God, and God in him.

From Galatians Chapter 5
22 But the fruit of the Spirit is love, joy, peace, longsuffering, gentleness, goodness, faith,

...or is he?...

From Deuteronomy Chapter 4
24 For the LORD thy God is a consuming fire, even a jealous God.

From Psalms Chapter 7
11 God judgeth the righteous, and God is angry with the wicked every day.

From Psalms Chapter 78
49 He cast upon them the fierceness of his anger, wrath, and indignation, and trouble, by sending evil angels among them.

From Nahum Chapter 1
2 God is jealous, and the LORD revengeth; the LORD revengeth, and is furious; the LORD will take vengeance on his adversaries, and he reserveth wrath for his enemies.
6 Who can stand before his indignation? and who can abide in the fierceness of his anger? his fury is poured out like fire, and the rocks are thrown down by him.

From Exodus Chapter 15
3 The LORD is a man of war: the LORD is his name.

See God and die...

From Exodus Chapter 33
²⁰ And he [the LORD] said [to Moses], Thou canst not see my face: *for there shall no man see me, and live.*

From John Chapter 1
¹⁸ No man hath seen God at any time, the only begotten Son, which is in the bosom of the Father, he hath declared him.

...yet they lived...

From Exodus Chapter 24
⁹ Then went up Moses, and Aaron, Nadab, and Abihu, and seventy of the elders of Israel:
¹⁰ *And they saw the God of Israel*:...

From Genesis Chapter 32
³⁰ And Jacob called the name of the place Peniel: for I have seen God face to face, *and my life is preserved.*

God sees and knows *everything...*

From Proverbs Chapter 15

³ The eyes of the Lord are in every place, beholding the evil and the good.

From Jeremiah Chapter 16

¹⁷ For mine eyes are upon all their ways: they are not hid from my face, neither is their iniquity hid from mine eyes.

Abraham bargains with the Lord:

From Genesis Chapter 18:20-32

The Lord decided to destroy the wicked cities of Sodom and Gomorrah, because their sin is very grievous.

But Abraham stood yet before the Lord, and said, "Wilt thou also destroy the righteous with the wicked? Peradventure there be fifty righteous within the city: wilt thou also destroy and not spare the place for the fifty righteous that are therein?... Shall not the Judge of all the earth do right?

The Lord: "If I find in Sodom fifty righteous within the city, then I will spare all the place for their sakes."

Abraham: "Peradventure there shall lack five of the fifty righteous: wilt thou destroy all the city for lack of five?"

The Lord: "If I find there forty and five, I will not destroy it."

Abraham: "Peradventure there shall be forty found there."

...or does he?...

From Exodus Chapter 12

13 For I will pass through the land of Egypt this night, and will smite all the firstborn in the land of Egypt, both man and beast...: I am the LORD.

13 And the blood shall be to you for a token upon the houses where ye are: and when I see the blood, I will pass over you, and the plague shall not be upon you to destroy you, when I smite the land of Egypt.

If God is all-knowing, why did he require the Israelites to mark their homes with blood so he could "pass over" them? Presumably, God massacred the firstborn Jews whose parents didn't get the message along with all the others.

The LORD: "I will not do it for forty's sake."

Abraham: "Oh let not the LORD be angry, and I will speak: Peradventure there shall thirty be found there."

The LORD: "I will not do it, if I find thirty there."

Abraham: "And he said, Behold now, I have taken upon me to speak unto the LORD: Peradventure there shall be twenty found there."

The LORD: "I will not destroy it for twenty's sake."

Abraham: "Oh let not the LORD be angry, and I will speak yet but this once: Peradventure ten shall be found there."

The LORD: "I will not destroy it for ten's sake.

*But if God knows everything, he already **knows** how many "righteous" there are in Sodom and Gomorrah. Yet, quite clearly from this exchange, he obviously **doesn't know**.*

Christ's Ascension took place at dinner in Jerusalem...

From Mark Chapter 16

[14] Afterward he appeared unto the eleven as they sat at meat, and upbraided them with their unbelief and hardness of heart, because they believed not them which had seen him after he was risen....

[19] So then after the LORD had spoken unto them, he was received up into heaven, and sat on the right hand of God

...or near Mt. Olivet...

From Acts Chapter 1

[9] And when he had spoken these things, while they beheld, he was taken up; and a cloud received him out of their sight. [10] And while they looked stedfastly toward heaven as he went up, behold, two men stood by them in white apparel; [11] Which also said, Ye men of Galilee, why stand ye gazing up into heaven? this same Jesus, which is taken up from you into heaven, shall so come in like manner as ye have seen him go into heaven.

[12] Then returned they unto Jerusalem from the mount called Olivet, which is from Jerusalem a sabbath day's journey.

...or outdoors, near Bethany...

From Luke Chapter 24

⁵⁰ And he led them out as far as to Bethany, and he lifted up his hands, and blessed them.

⁵¹ And it came to pass, while he blessed them, he was parted from them, and carried up into heaven.

...or (maybe) near a mountain in Galilee?...

From Matthew Chapter 28

¹⁶ Then the eleven disciples went away into Galilee, into a mountain where Jesus had appointed them.

¹⁷ And when they saw him, they worshipped him: but some doubted.

¹⁸ And Jesus came and spake unto them, saying, All power is given unto me in heaven and in earth.

¹⁹ Go ye therefore, and teach all nations, baptizing them in the name of the Father, and of the Son, and of the Holy Ghost:

²⁰ Teaching them to observe all things whatsoever I have commanded you: and, lo, I am with you always, even unto the end of the world. Amen.

*That is where the book of Matthew
ends — without mentioning the
Ascension at all!*

God forbids usury...

From Leviticus Chapter 25

[37] Thou shalt not give him thy money upon usury, nor lend him thy victuals for increase.

From Psalms Chapter 15

[1] Lord, who shall abide in thy tabernacle? who shall dwell in thy holy hill?

[5] He that putteth not out his money to usury, nor taketh reward against the innocent. He that doeth these things shall never be moved.

...or does he?...

From Matthew Chapter 25

[27] Thou oughtest therefore to have put my money to the exchangers, and then at my coming I should have received mine own with usury.

From Luke Chapter 19

[23] Wherefore then gavest not thou my money into the bank, that at my coming I might have required mine own with usury?

Intriguingly, it would appear that the Old Testament forbids usury, while the New Testament permits it.

Yet, paradoxically, in the Middle Ages New Testament Christians were forbidden to lend money at interest, while Old Testament Jews became moneylenders!

God damns incest...

From Leviticus Chapter 20

17 And if a man shall take his sister, his father's daughter, or his mother's daughter, and see her nakedness, and she see his nakedness; it is a wicked thing; and they shall be cut off in the sight of their people: he hath uncovered his sister's nakedness; he shall bear his iniquity.

From Deuteronomy Chapter 27

20 Cursed be he that lieth with his father's wife; because he uncovereth his father's skirt. And all the people shall say, Amen.
21 Cursed be he that lieth with any manner of beast. And all the people shall say, Amen.
22 Cursed be he that lieth with his sister, the daughter of his father, or the daughter of his mother. And all the people shall say, Amen.

...or does he?...

From Genesis Chapter 17

15 And God said unto Abraham, As for Sarai thy wife, thou shalt not call her name Sarai, but Sarah shall her name be.
16 And I will bless her, and give thee a son also of her: yea, I will bless her, and she shall be a mother of nations; kings of people shall be of her.

From Genesis Chapter 20

11 And Abraham said, Because I thought, Surely the fear of God is not in this place; and they will slay me for my wife's sake.
12 And yet indeed she is my sister; she is the daughter of my father, but not the daughter of my mother; and she became my wife.

Thou Shalt Not Kill...
Thou Shalt Not Steal...

From Exodus Chapter 20

[13] Thou shalt not kill.

[15] Thou shalt not steal.

[17] Thou shalt not covet thy neighbour's house, thou shalt not covet thy neighbour's wife, nor his manservant, nor his maidservant, nor his ox, nor his ass, nor any thing that is thy neighbour's.

From Leviticus Chapter 19

[31] Thou shalt not defraud thy neighbour, neither rob him: the wages of him that is hired shall not abide with thee all night until the morning.

...or Thou Shalt?...

"My advice [to the poor], as a Christian priest, is to shoplift. I do not offer such advice because I think that stealing is a good thing, or because I think it is harmless, for it is neither. I would ask that they do not steal from small family businesses but from large national businesses.... I would ask them not to take any more than they need, for any longer than they need.... My advice does not contradict the Bible's Eighth Commandment because God's love for the poor and despised outweighs the property rights of the rich.**"**

— *the Reverend Tim Jones,* in his Sunday sermon at the Church of St Lawrence, York, UK *[The Times, 22 Dec 2009]*[1]

...except, of course, at God's order...

From Deuteronomy Chapter 20

16 But of the cities of these people, which the LORD thy God doth give thee for an inheritance, thou shalt save alive nothing that breatheth:

17 But thou shalt utterly destroy them; namely, the Hittites, and the Amorites, the Canaanites, and the Perizzites, the Hivites, and the Jebusites; as the LORD thy God hath commanded thee:

From Leviticus Chapter 26

7 And ye shall chase your enemies, and they shall fall before you by the sword.

8 And five of you shall chase an hundred, and an hundred of you shall put ten thousand to flight: and your enemies shall fall before you by the sword.

From Joshua Chapter 10

40 So Joshua smote all the country of the hills, and of the south, and of the vale, and of the springs, and all their kings: he left none remaining, but utterly destroyed all that breathed, as the LORD God of Israel commanded.

From Judges Chapter 14

19 And the Spirit of the LORD came upon him, and he went down to Ashkelon, and slew thirty men of them, and took their spoil,...

From Ezekiel Chapter 9

7 And he [the LORD] said unto them, Defile the house, and fill the courts with the slain: go ye forth. And they went forth, and slew in the city.

The origin of a great religious tradition.

Thou Shalt Love Thine Enemies...

From Matthew Chapter 5

[39] But I say unto you, That ye resist not evil: but whosoever shall smite thee on thy right cheek, turn to him the other also.

[44] But I say unto you, Love your enemies, bless them that curse you, do good to them that hate you, and pray for them which despitefully use you, and persecute you;

From Luke Chapter 6

[29] And unto him that smiteth thee on the one cheek offer also the other; and him that taketh away thy cloak forbid not to take thy coat also.

...or Curse, Hate and Slay them?...

From Luke Chapter 11

[23] He that is not with me [Jesus] is against me: and he that gathereth not with me scattereth.

From Deuteronomy Chapter 7

[9] Know therefore that the LORD thy God, he is God, the faithful God, which keepeth covenant and mercy with them that love him and keep his commandments to a thousand generations;

10 And repayeth them that hate him to their face, to destroy them: he will not be slack to him that hateth him, he will repay him to his face.

From Luke Chapter 11

44 Woe unto you, scribes and Pharisees, hypocrites! for ye are as graves which appear not, and the men that walk over them are not aware of them.

46 And he [Jesus] said, Woe unto you also, ye lawyers! for ye lade men with burdens grievous to be borne, and ye yourselves touch not the burdens with one of your fingers.

From Deuteronomy Chapter 6

15 (For the LORD thy God is a jealous God among you) lest the anger of the LORD thy God be kindled against thee, and destroy thee from off the face of the earth.

From Deuteronomy Chapter 29

20 The LORD will not spare him, but then the anger of the LORD and his jealousy shall smoke against that man, and all the curses that are written in this book shall lie upon him, and the LORD shall blot out his name from under heaven.

From Luke Chapter 19

27 But those mine [Jesus'] enemies, which would not that I should reign over them, bring hither, and slay them before me.

Thou shalt honor thy father and thy mother...

From Exodus Chapter 20

[12] Honour thy father and thy mother: that thy days may be long upon the land which the LORD thy God giveth thee.

From Luke Chapter 18

[20] Thou knowest the commandments, Do not commit adultery, Do not kill, Do not steal, Do not bear false witness, Honour thy father and thy mother.

From Matthew Chapter 15

[4] For God commanded, saying, Honour thy father and mother: and, He that curseth father or mother, let him die the death.

...unless you believe in Jesus...

From Matthew Chapter 10

[35] For I am come to set a man at variance against his father, and the daughter against her mother, and the daughter in law against her mother in law.

[36] And a man's foes shall be they of his own household.

[37] He that loveth father or mother more than me is not worthy of me: and he that loveth son or daughter more than me is not worthy of me.

From Luke Chapter 12

[52] For from henceforth there shall be five in one house divided, three against two, and two against three.

[53] The father shall be divided against the son, and the son against the father; the mother against the daughter, and the daughter against the mother; the mother in law against her daughter in law, and the daughter in law against her mother in law.

From Luke Chapter 14

26 If any man come to me, and hate not his father, and mother, and wife, and children, and brethren, and sisters, yea, and his own life also, he cannot be my disciple.

...and follow *his* example...

From Matthew Chapter 12

46 While he [Jesus] yet talked to the people, behold, his mother and his brethren stood without, desiring to speak with him.

47 Then one said unto him, Behold, thy mother and thy brethren stand without, desiring to speak with thee.

48 But he answered and said unto him that told him, Who is my mother? and who are my brethren?

49 And he stretched forth his hand toward his disciples, and said, Behold my mother and my brethren!

On the Other Hand...

From John 19:25-27:

Now there stood by the cross of Jesus his mother, and his mother's sister, Mary the wife of Cleophas, and Mary Magdalene. When Jesus therefore saw his mother, and the disciple standing by, whom he loved, he saith unto his mother, Woman, behold thy son! Then saith he to the disciple, Behold thy mother! And from that hour that disciple took her unto his own home.

Matthew, Mark, and Luke also list the women who stood by the cross, **but do not include Jesus' mother,** *suggesting this passage is a later addition, not to be found in the original texts.*

Children shall suffer for the sins of their fathers...

From Numbers Chapter 14

[18] The LORD is longsuffering, and of great mercy, forgiving iniquity and transgression, and by no means clearing the guilty, visiting the iniquity of the fathers upon the children unto the third and fourth generation.

From Deuteronomy Chapter 5

[9] Thou shalt not bow down thyself unto them [other gods], nor serve them: for I the LORD thy God am a jealous God, visiting the iniquity of the fathers upon the children unto the third and fourth generation of them that hate me,

From Isaiah Chapter 14

[21] Prepare slaughter for his children for the iniquity of their fathers; that they do not rise, nor possess the land, nor fill the face of the world with cities.

...or must *not?*...

From Deuteronomy Chapter 24

[16] The fathers shall not be put to death for the children, neither shall the children be put to death for the fathers: every man shall be put to death for his own sin.

From Ezekiel Chapter 18

[20] The soul that sinneth, it shall die. The son shall not bear the iniquity of the father, neither shall the father bear the iniquity of the son: the righteousness of the righteous shall be upon him, and the wickedness of the wicked shall be upon him.

From 2 Kings Chapter 14

[6] But the children of the murderers he slew not: according unto that which is written in the book of the law of Moses, wherein the LORD commanded, saying, The fathers shall not be put to death for the children, nor the children be put to death for the fathers; but every man shall be put to death for his own sin.

Jesus was the "seed of David" [via Joseph]...

From Romans Chapter 1
³ Concerning his Son, Jesus Christ our Lord, which was made of the seed of David according to the flesh;
⁴ And declared *to be* the Son of God with power, according to the spirit of holiness, by the resurrection from the dead:

From Mark Chapter 6
³ Is not this the carpenter, the son of Mary, the brother of James, and Joses, and of Juda, and Simon? and are not his sisters here with us?

Was Mary Jesus' Mother?

Mary is venerated, especially in the Catholic Church (where, to paraphrase Douglas Adams, she is the fourth member of the Trinity), as the mother of Jesus.

But was she?

A human being results from the fusion of a sperm and an ovum.

If God's "holy sperm" united with Mary's ovum, then Jesus was half man and half God...making the Nicene Creed *wrong*.

For Jesus to be "of the same substance" as God, the Holy Ghost must have implanted a fertilized egg in Mary's womb (making Jesus a test-tube baby...before there were test tubes). In which case Mary was just the host mother — and wasn't Jesus' real mother any more than Joseph was his real father.

...or the Son of God?...

From Matthew Chapter 1

18 Now the birth of Jesus was on this wise: When as his mother Mary was espoused to Joseph, before they came together, she was found with child of the Holy Ghost.

19 Then Joseph her husband, being just a *man,* and not willing to make her a publick example, was minded to put her away privily.

20 But while he thought on these things, behold, the angel of the Lord appeared unto him in a dream, saying, Joseph, thou son of David, fear not to take unto thee Mary thy wife: for that which is conceived in her of the Holy Ghost.

From Luke Chapter 1

26 ...the angel Gabriel was sent from God unto a city of Galilee, named Nazareth,

27 To a virgin espoused to a man whose name was Joseph of the house of David; and the virgin's name *was* Mary.

30 And the angel said unto her, Fear not, Mary: for thou hast found favour with God.

31 And, behold, thou shalt conceive in thy womb, and bring forth a son, and shalt call his name JESUS.

34 Then said Mary unto the angel, How shall this be, seeing I know not a man?

35 And the angel answered and said unto her, The Holy Ghost shall come upon thee, and the power of the Highest shall overshadow thee: therefore also that holy thing which shall be born of thee shall be called the Son of God.

Jesus' Genealogy

The authors of the Gospels of Luke and Matthew were both keen to establish Jesus' descent from King David, which would fulfill the Jewish belief, based on various passages of the Old Testament, that the Messiah would be descended from the House of King David [Isaiah 9:7].

But — as the table opposite shows — there is significant disagreement between the two Gospels as to Jesus' actual descent from Abraham. Luke counts 56 generations between Abraham and Jesus (omitting David's son Solomon!), while Matthew only counts 41. And while both agree on David's descent from Abraham (if you grant that "Juda" and "Judas" are different spellings of the same name), only *four* of Jesus' supposed forefathers after Abraham are the same: Jorim, Salathiel, Zorobabel and, of course, Joseph.

So: are *either* of these genealogies correct?

In a further contradiction, as we have already seen (page 30) both Luke [1:26-35] and Matthew [1:18-20] are *also* keen to fulfill *another* Old Testament prophecy: that the Messiah would be born of a virgin [Isaiah 7:14].

But if Mary was visited by the Holy Spirit, then Joseph was *not* Jesus' father — and Jesus was *not* descended from the House of David.

An interesting aside: Luke begins his genealogy with Adam, saying "which was the son of God" [Luke 3:38]. If so, this implies we're *all,* like Jesus, great-great-great-grandsons and granddaughters of God.

Luke	Matthew	Luke	Matthew
Abraham		Er	Achaz
Isaac		Elmodam	Ezekias
Jacob		Cosam	Manasses
Juda	Judas	Addi	Amon
Phares		Melchi	Josias
Esrom		Neri	Jechonias
Aram		**Salathiel**	
Aminadab		**Zorobabel**	
Naasson		Rhesa	Abiud
Salmon		Joanna	
Booz		Juda	Eliakim
Obed		Joseph	
Jesse		Semei	Azor
David [King]		Mattathias	
Nathan		Maath	Sadoc
Mattatha	Solomon [King]	Nagge	
Menan		Esli	Achim
Melea	Roboam	Naum	
Eliakim		Amos	Eliud
Jonan	Abia	Mattathias	
Joseph		Joseph	Eleazar
Juda	Asa	Janna	
Simeon		Melchi	Matthan
Levi	Josaphat	Levi	
Matthat		Matthat	Jacob
Jorim		Heli	
Eliezer	Ozias	**Joseph**	
Jose	Joatham	**Jesus**	

The names in **bold** indicate the agreement of Luke and Mark. From Luke Chapter 3, verses 23-38, and Matthew, Chapter 1, verses 2-16.

To get to Heaven, Jesus said you must: Love the Lord thy God with all thy heart?...

From Luke Chapter 10

[25] And, behold, a certain lawyer stood up, and tempted him, saying, Master, what shall I do to inherit eternal life?

[26] He said unto him, What is written in the law? how readest thou?

[27] And he answering said, Thou shalt love the Lord thy God with all thy heart, and with all thy soul, and with all thy strength, and with all thy mind; and thy neighbour as thyself.

[28] And he said unto him, Thou hast answered right: this do, and thou shalt live.

...OR: Believe in the Son?...

From John Chapter 3

[36] He that believeth on the Son hath everlasting life: and he that believeth not the Son shall not see life; but the wrath of God abideth on him.

From John Chapter 3

[17] For God sent not his Son into the world to condemn the world; but that the world through him might be saved.

[18] He that believeth on him is not condemned: but he that believeth not is condemned already, because he hath not believed in the name of the only begotten Son of God.

...OR: Just do good?...

From John Chapter 5

[28] Marvel not at this: for the hour is coming, in the which all that are in the graves shall hear his voice,

[29] And shall come forth; they that have done good, unto the resurrection of life; and they that have done evil, unto the resurrection of damnation.

Was Jesus born in Bethlehem...

From Matthew Chapter 2
[1] Now when Jesus was born in Bethlehem of Judæa in the days of Herod the king, behold, there came wise men from the east to Jerusalem.

From Luke Chapter 2
[15] ...the shepherds said one to another, Let us now go even unto Bethlehem, and see this thing which is come to pass, which the Lord has made known to us.

> *ONLY Matthew says directly that Jesus was born in Bethlehem, though Luke 2:15 implies that he was. Neither Mark nor John mention where Jesus was born, but the following verses imply it was NOT Bethlehem but Galilee (Nazareth is in Galilee)*

...or Galilee?...

From Mark Chapter 1
[9] And it came to pass in those days, that Jesus came from Nazareth of Galilee and was baptized of John in Jordan.

From John Chapter 7
[41] Others said, This is the Christ. But some said, Shall Christ come out of Galilee?
[42] Hath not the scriptures said, That Christ cometh of the seed of David, and out of the town of Bethlehem, where David was?
[43] So there was a division among the people because of him.

Jesus came in peace...

From John Chapter 16

[33] These things I have spoken unto you, that in me ye might have peace. In the world ye shall have tribulation: but be of good cheer; I have overcome the world.

...or did he?...

From Luke Chapter 12

[49] I am come to send fire on the earth; and what will I, if it be already kindled?

[50] But I have a baptism to be baptized with; and how am I straitened till it be accomplished!

[51] Suppose ye that I am come to give peace on earth? I tell you, Nay; but rather division:

> **"**If Christ, in fact, said "I came not to send peace, but a sword," it is the only prophecy in the New Testament that has been literally fulfilled.**"**
> — *Robert G. Ingersoll*

From Matthew Chapter 10

[34] Think not that I am come to send peace on earth: I came not to send peace, but a sword.

> **"**After Jesus Christ we have no need of speculation, after the Gospel no need of research. When we come to believe, we have no desire to believe in anything else; for we begin by believing that there is nothing else which we have to believe.... My first principle is this. Christ laid down one definite system of truth *which the world must believe without qualification.***"**
> — *Tertullian,* The Prescriptions Against the Heretics

And a few other things...

After Jesus was born...

Joseph and Mary flee to Egypt from Herod's slaughter of male infants
Matthew 2:13-16

OR they went to Jerusalem for about forty days to Present the newborn male to the Temple according to the Law; and then return to Nazareth without ever going anywhere near Egypt
Luke 2:22-40
There is no mention of Herod's slaughter of infants in Luke!.

Jesus will be called...

Emmanuel
Matthew 1:23

OR Jesus
Luke 1:31

At Jesus' Baptism...

Jesus saw the Spirit descending
Matthew 3:16, Mark 1:10

OR John saw the Spirit descending
John 1:32

After Jesus' Baptism...

He immediately went for 40 days into the wilderness to resist the temptations of the devil
Matthew 4:1-11, Mark 1:12-13

OR He went to a wedding in Cana three days later where he turned water into wine
John 2:1-11
There is no mention of Jesus' 40 days and forty nights in the desert in Luke!

Jesus curses the fig tree...

From Matthew Chapter 21	From Mark Chapter 11
One morning, as Jesus left Bethany for Jerusalem he hungered and came upon a fig tree... *Matthew 18-19; Mark 12-13*	
... with nothing theron except leaves only and said unto it, Let no fruit grow on thee henceforth and for ever. And presently the fig tree withered away! *Matthew 19*	...and when he came to it, he found nothing but leaves; for the time of figs was not *yet*. And Jesus answered and said unto it, No man eat fruit of thee hereafter for ever. And his disciples heard it.... *Mark 13-14*
And when the disciples *saw it,* they marvelled, saying, *How soon is the fig tree withered away!* *Matthew 20*	...And *in the* [next] *morning* as they passed by, they saw the fig tree dried up from the roots. And Peter calling to remembrance saith unto him, Master, behold, the fig tree which thou cursedst is withered away. *Mark 20-22*

What does this little incident reveal about Jesus' character?
Here's the man who can supposedly heal the sick, turn water into wine, and feed thousands with a single basket of loaves and fishes.
So what does he do? Wave his magic wand so the tree suddenly sprouts fresh, juicy figs?
Turn stones into bread?
NO! He gets angry with the fig tree for Heaven's sake! He uses his magic powers to curse it!
Which just proves the truth of the saying: like Father, like Son.
Oh...and he's still hungry. Serves him right, I say.

Jesus and God are the same...

From John Chapter 10
30 I and my Father are one.

...or God is greater than Jesus...

From John Chapter 14
28 Ye have heard how I said unto you, I go away, and come again unto you. If ye loved me, ye would rejoice, because I said, I go unto the Father: for my Father is greater than I.

...or Jesus was just an ordinary man?

From Acts Chapter 2
22 Ye men of Israel, hear these words; Jesus of Nazareth, a man approved of God among you by miracles and wonders and signs, which God did by him in the midst of you, as ye yourselves also know: *(See also Romans 1:3-4, page 30.)*

A bitter controversy over this issue was "settled" in 325CE when the Emperor Constantine stacked an ecumenical council in Nicea. The resulting "Nicene Creed" states that God and Jesus are of the same "substance," and it became a heresy punishable by law to say differently.

The previous contradictions came (mostly) from different books of the Bible.

The examples that follow come from the SAME book.

David slew Goliath with a slingshot...

From 1 Samuel Chapter 17

[50] So David prevailed over the Philistine with a sling and with a stone, and smote the Philistine, and slew him; but there was no sword in the hand of David.

...or with a sword?...

From 1 Samuel Chapter 17

[51] Therefore David ran, and stood upon the Philistine, and took his sword, and drew it out of the sheath thereof, and slew him, and cut off his head therewith. And when the Philistines saw their champion was dead, they fled.

These two completely conflicting accounts of Goliath's death come from two consecutive verses of the same book!

God created man last...

From Genesis Chapter 1

²⁵ And God made the *beast* of the earth after his kind, and the *cattle* after their kind, and everything that creepeth upon the earth after his kind: and God saw that it was good.

²⁶ And God said, Let us make man in our image, after our likeness: and let them have dominion over the fish of the sea, and over the fowl of the air, and over the cattle, and over all the earth, and over every creeping thing that creepeth upon the earth

²⁷ So God *created man* in his own image, in the image of God created he him; male and female created he them.

...or did he?...

From Genesis Chapter 2

¹⁸ And the LORD God said, It is not good that the *man* should be alone; I will make him an help-meet for him.

¹⁹ And out of the ground the LORD God formed *every beast* of the field, and *every fowl* of the air, and *brought them unto Adam* to see what he would call them: and whatsoever Adam called every living creature, that was the name thereof.

God created man and woman *together*...

From Genesis Chapter 1
²⁷ So God *created man* in his own image, in the image of God created he him; male and female created he them.

...or did he?...

From Genesis Chapter 2
⁷ And the LORD God formed man of the dust of the ground, and breathed into his nostrils the breath of life; and man became a living soul.
²¹ And the LORD God caused a deep sleep to fall upon Adam, and he slept: and he took one of his ribs, and closed up the flesh instead thereof;
²² And the rib, which the LORD God had taken from man, made he a woman, and brought her unto the man.

And God was pleased with creation...

From Genesis Chapter 1

³¹ And God saw every thing that he had made, and, behold, it was very good. And the evening and the morning were the sixth day.

...or was he?...

From Genesis Chapter 6

⁵ And God saw that the wickedness of man was great in the earth, and that every imagination of the thoughts of his heart was only evil continually.

⁶ And it repented the LORD that he had made man on the earth, and it grieved him at his heart.

> *Grieving with displeasure at his creation, God proceeds to massacre the human race [not to mention the plants and animals too: were they also born with Original Sin?] by drowning — with the exception of Noah and his family. I guess this is the meaning of "Divine Justice."*

Jesus judges not...

From John Chapter 8
15 Ye judge after the flesh; I judge no man.

From John Chapter 12
47 And if any man hear my words, and believe not, I judge him not: for I came not to judge the world, but to save the world.

...yet he is God's judge...

From John Chapter 5
22 For the Father judgeth no man, but hath committed all judgment unto the Son:

From John Chapter 5
30 I can of mine own self do nothing: as I hear, I judge: and my judgment is just; because I seek not mine own will, but the will of the Father which hath sent me.

From John Chapter 9
39 And Jesus said, For judgment I am come into this world, that they which see not might see; and that they which see might be made blind.

Jesus commanded his disciples to preach *only* to Jews...

From Matthew Chapter 10
⁵ These twelve Jesus sent forth, and commanded them, saying, Go not into the way of the Gentiles, and into any city of the Samaritans enter ye not:
⁶ But go rather to the lost sheep of the house of Israel
⁷ And as ye go, preach, saying, The kingdom of heaven is at hand.

From Matthew Chapter 19
²⁸ And Jesus said unto them [the twelve disciples — *including Judas!*], Verily I say unto you, That ye which have followed me, in the regeneration when the Son of man shall sit in the throne of his glory, ye also shall sit upon twelve thrones, judging the twelve tribes of Israel *[i.e.,* only Jews].

From John Chapter 4
²² Ye worship ye know not what: we know what we worship: for salvation is of the Jews.

...or to all nations?

From John Chapter 3

16 For God so loved the world, that he gave his only begotten Son, that *whosoever believeth in him* should not perish, but have everlasting life.

From Matthew Chapter 28

18 And Jesus came and spake unto them [the disciples], saying, All power is given unto me in heaven and in earth; 19 Go ye therefore, and teach all nations, baptizing them in the name of the Father, and of the Son, and of the Holy Ghost:

This last verse is NOT found in the earliest extant copies of Matthew. They were added later — with the clear purpose of softening Jesus' earlier command in Matthew to preach only to the "lost sheep of Israel" — i.e., other Jews.

According to Jesus, Peter is a "rock"...

From Matthew Chapter 16

[18] And I say also unto thee, That thou art Peter, and upon this rock I will build my church; and the gates of hell shall not prevail against it.

...or Satan?...

From Matthew Chapter 16

[23] But he turned, and said unto Peter, Get thee behind me, Satan: thou art an offence unto me: for thou savourest not the things that be of God, but those that be of men.

Jesus says you should display your good works...

From Matthew Chapter 5

[16] Let your light so shine before men, that they may see your good works, and glorify your Father which is in heaven.

...or hide them?...

From Matthew Chapter 6

[1] Take heed that ye do not your alms before men, to be seen of them: otherwise ye have no reward of your Father which is in heaven...

[4] That thine alms may be in secret: and thy Father which seeth in secret himself shall reward thee openly.

The Passion Week Story Stories...

Jesus enters Jerusalem...

on a colt *Mark 11:2-7; Luke 19:30-35; John 12:14*

which he tells the disciples to get *[Mark 11:2-7; Luke 19:30-35]*
OR did he get it himself? *John 12:14*

OR on an ass *and* a colt which he tells the disciples to get
Matthew 21:2-7

Jesus Cleanses the Temple...

at the beginning of Passion Week *Mark 11:15-17*

OR during Passion Week, near the end of his "career"
Matthew 21:12-13, Luke 19:45-46

OR near the beginning of his career well before his Passion
John 2:13-16

Jesus is anointed with oil...

at the house of leper named Simon in Bethany
Mark 14:3; Matthew 26:6-13

OR by a woman in a Pharisee's house in Galilee
Luke 7:36-38

and it was poured over his head *Mark 14:3; Matthew 26:7*
OR and it was poured over his feet *Luke 7-38; John 12:3*

The overall sequence of Passion Week events was:

Triumphal Entry, Cleansing the Temple, Anointing at Bethany
Mark 11:11; 1:15;14:3; Matthew 21:10;21:12; 26:7

OR Triumphal Entry, Cleansing the Temple, Teaching in the
Temple *Luke 19:37-44; 19:45;19:47*

OR Cleansing the Temple (*long before* Passion Week),
Anointing at Bethany, Triumphal Entry *John 2:15; 12:3;12:16-17*

The Last Supper was held on...

the first day of Passover *Mark 14:12, Matthew 6:17, Luke 22:7*
OR the day *before* Passover *John 19:14*

Jesus predicts his own betrayal...

before the communion portion of the Last Supper
Mark 14:17-21, Matthew 26:20-25, John 13:21-30
OR *after* the communion portion of the Last Supper
Luke 22:21-23

Judas betrayed Jesus due to Satan affecting him...

before the Last Supper *Luke 22:3-6*
OR *during* the Last Supper *John 13:27*
Not mentioned by either Mark or Matthew!

Judas bargained with the Priests to betray Jesus...

before the Last Supper
Mark 14: 10-11, Matthew 26:14-16, Luke 22:3-6
OR *after* the Last Supper *John 13:21-30*

The thirty pieces of silver were...

thrown away by Judas as he walked away from the priests
Matthew 27:5
OR used by Judas to buy some property *Acts 1:18*
Not mentioned by either Mark, Luke, or John!

Judas died...

by hanging himself *Matthew 27:5*
OR by falling down and splitting open, with his guts spilling
out *Acts 1:18*
No mention in Mark, Luke, or John of Judas killing himself!

Jesus' arrest and "trial"...

Jesus is arrested and taken to...

Caiphas, the High Priest *Mark 14:53, Matthew 26:57, Luke 22:54*

OR first to Annas, the son-in-law of Caiphas, and then later to Caiphas *John 18:13-24*

Jesus has his first hearing...

on Passover morning *Luke 22:13-15, 54-66*

OR on the day before Passover *John 18:28, 19:14*

OR in the morning, Jesus is taken before Pilate, after being charged on Passover eve
Mark 14:53-72, 15:1, Matthew 26:18-20,57-68, 27:1-2

Jesus' first trial is before...

the whole Sanhedrin *Mark 14:55-6, Matthew 26:59-66*

OR the Sanhedrin holds an inquiry but not a trial
Luke 22:66-71

OR the Sanhedrin holds no official inquiry, and Jesus appears before Annas and Caiphas *John 18:13-24*

When the High Priest asks Jesus if he's...

the "Son of the Blessed" Jesus answers: "I am" *Mark 14:61*

OR the "Son of God" Jesus answers: "Ye say that I am"
Matthew 26:63, Luke 22:70

There's no such interrogation in the Gospel according to John!

Jesus was interrogated by Herod...

when Pilate, hearing he was a Galilean, sent Jesus to Herod
Luke 23:7-11

But neither Mark, Matthew, or John mention any interrogation by Herod!

When Pilate asked if Jesus was King of the Jews...

Jesus answers: "Thou sayest it" — and does not answer any of the charges *Mark 15:2, Matthew 27:11, Luke 23:3*

OR he answers: "Sayest thou these things of thyself, or did others tell it thee of me" — and answers all the charges *John 18:33-34*

Barabbas is released because...

the Priests urge the people to demand it, though he is accused of insurrection and murder *Mark 15:11*

OR the priests and elders urge people to demand it, and his crimes are unknown *Matthew 27:20*

OR the people demand it, though he is accused of insurrection and murder *Luke 23:18-23*

OR The people demand it, though he is accused of being a robber *John 18:40*

Jesus carries the cross...

by himself the whole way *John 19:17*

OR with help from Simon of Cyrene *Mark 15:21, Matthew 27:32, Luke 23:26*

The inscription on Jesus' cross was...

"The King of the Jews" *Mark 15:26*

OR "This is Jesus the King of the Jews" *Matthew 27:37*

OR "This is the King of the Jews" *Luke 23:38*

OR "Jesus of Nazareth, the King of the Jews" *John 19:19*

...and Crucifixion...

Jesus was crucified along with two thieves...

who made no conversation *Mark*

OR who both taunt Jesus *Matthew 27:44*

OR one taunts Jesus — and is criticized by the other *Luke 23:39-42*

OR they are not described as thieves *John*

While on the cross, Jesus is given a drink of...

wine, mixed with myrrh, but he does not drink it *Mark 15:23*

OR vinegar, but he does not drink it *Matthew 27:48, Luke 23:36*

OR vinegar, which he drinks *John 19:29-30*

The centurion guarding the cross said...

"Truly this man was the son of God" *Mark 15:39*

OR "Truly this was the son of God" *Matthew 27:54*

OR "Certainly, this was a righteous man" *Luke 23:47*

OR Nothing at all *John*

The women who watched the crucifixion were...

watching from *afar Mark 15:40, Matthew 27:55, Luke 23:49*

OR *close*, so Jesus could speak to his mother *John 19:25-26*

Jesus was crucified...

on the "third hour" *Mark 15:25*

OR on the "sixth hour" *John 19:14-15*

Neither Matthew nor Luke state when it started, but in their accounts the "sixth hour" occurred during the crucifixion

Jesus' last words were:

"My God, my God, why hast thou forsaken me?"
Mark 15:34, Matthew 27:46
OR "Father, into thy hands I commend my spirit." *Luke 23:46*
OR "It is finished." *John 19:30*

The earthquake and influx of risen dead is...

mentioned at the moment of Jesus' death *Matthew 27:51-53*
Not mentioned in Mark, Luke, OR John — nor is there any historical record of any such momentous event!

After his crucifixion, Jesus said he will:

be "three days and three nights in the heart of the earth"
Matthew 12:40
OR rise again on the third day *Mark 10:34 [i.e., after just TWO nights "in the heart of the earth"]*
None of the resurrection stories state that Jesus was in the tomb for either of those periods!

A Roman guard is...

stationed outside the tomb *Matthew 27:62-66*
Not mentioned at all: Mark, Luke, and John

Jesus' body is anointed before burial by...

a group of women who had witnessed the crucifixion
Mark 16:1-3, Luke 23:55-56
OR Joseph of Arimathea *John 19:39-40*
OR No one (Joseph wraps the body) *Matthew*

...and Resurrection...

Jesus' tomb is visited by...

THREE women, Mary Magdalena, another Mary and Salome
Mark 16:1

OR TWO women, Mary Magdalena and another Mary
Matthew 28:1

OR At least SIX women: Mary Magdalena, Mary mother of James, Joanna and "other women" *Luke 24:10*

OR ONE woman, Mary Magdalena, who later fetches Peter and another disciple *John 20:1*

When the women arrived at the tomb, the rock at the entrance...

had been rolled away *Mark 16:4, Luke 24:2, John 20:1*

OR was still in place and would be rolled away later
Matthew 28:1-2

When the women enter the tomb...

they meet ONE young man in there *Mark 16:5*

OR TWO men suddenly appear *Luke 24:2-4*

OR an angel arrives during an earthquake, rolls away the stone and sits on it outside, while Pilate's guards are also there
Matthew 28:2

OR they do not enter but two angels are sitting inside
John 20:12

The women reacted by...

keeping quiet, despite being told to spread the word *Mark 16:8*

OR going to tell the disciples *Matthew 28:8*

OR telling "the eleven and all the rest" *Luke 24:9*

OR Mary stays to cry while the two disciples go home
John 20:10-11

Jesus' first resurrection appearance was...

to Mary Magdalena, but not clear where *Mark 16-14-15*
OR near his tomb *Matthew 28:8-9*
OR near Emmaus, several miles from Jerusalem *Luke 24:13-15*
OR at his tomb *John 20:13-14*

Jesus was first seen by...

Mary Magdalena, then two others, then the "eleven" *Mark 16:9-14*
OR Mary Magdalena and the other Mary, then the "eleven" *Matthew 28:1-18*
OR two men, then Simon, then the "eleven" *Luke 24:15-36*
OR Mary Magdalena, then the disciples without Thomas, then the disciples with Thomas, then the eleven disciples again *John 20:14-21:1*

After his resurrection, Jesus...

commissions the "eleven" to teach the gospel *Mark 16:14-15*
OR lets Mary Magdalena and the other Mary hold his feet *Matthew 28:9*
OR forbids Mary to touch him because he had not ascended to heaven yet, but a week later lets Thomas touch him anyway *John 20:17*

Jesus ascended to heaven...

while he and his disciples are seated at a table in or near Jerusalem *Mark 16:14-19*
OR outside, after dinner, at Bethany on the same day as his resurrection *Luke 24:50-51*
OR at Mt. Olivet, at least 40 days after his resurrection *Acts 1:19-20*
But neither John nor Matthew mention his Ascension at all!

"Thou shalt not kill"?...

The sixth commandment is not one that Christians or their churches have been very religious about obeying. Think of the Crusades or the Inquisition for just two examples of killing "in the name of the Lord."

And then there's the spectacle of the soldiers of two armies preparing for battle with each other being blessed by their chaplains so they'll all believe they have "God on their side."

Even so, "thou shalt not kill" is generally interpreted as meaning "thou shalt not kill *other people.*"

But "people" is not specified.

If Christians take "Thou shalt not kill" *literally,* shouldn't they be vegetarians?

...or "Thou shalt not murder"?...

The Hebrew for the Sixth Commandment (fifth in the Catholic version of the Bible...isn't that meddling with God's Word?) — לא תרצח — can be translated as "thou shalt not kill" *or,* more commonly, "thou shalt not murder."

Indeed, while Catholic and older Protestant translations use "kill," Jewish and newer Protestant versions use "murder."

In common parlance, we rarely make a distinction between "killing" or "murdering" a human being. These two words do, however, have distinctly different meanings: soldiers, for example, kill but do not (according to law) commit *murder.*

During boot camp (I was drafted into the army) an entire day from the four weeks was spent with two army chaplains (whose denominations I do not recall). They spent most of that day trying to convince us that

"Thou shalt not kill" had been mistranslated and it should read "Thou shalt not murder." For a soldier — especially a Christian one — this is clearly a crucial distinction which, if accepted, means he can go out and massacre the enemy with a clear conscience.*

"Murder," as the chaplains pointed out, is also a *legal term,* defined by the government, meaning it's okay to kill anyone the government says it's okay to kill.

It inevitably follows that since killing Jews was legal in Hitler's Germany, under German law (at that time) participants in the Holocaust did not transgress this Commandment.

...or "Thou shalt not murder *Jews*"?...

To the Rabbis of the Talmud — known as "The Sages" — it was clear that this commandment *only* refers to the murder of other Israelites — *God's chosen people.*

As Maimodines wrote in the 12th century:
If one slays a single Israelite, he transgresses a negative commandment, for Scripture says, Thou shalt not murder. If one murders willfully in the presence of witnesses, he is put to death by the sword.... **Needless to say, one is not put to death if he kills a heathen**. *[Emphasis added.]*

In which case, it's quite okay for Christians (and Muslims, Hindus, Buddhists, Zoroastrians, etc.) to kill each other...just so long as they don't kill any Jews.

---

* The chaplains failed miserably, by the way.

On the other hand,
the Bible is "without error":

"The Books of the Old and New Testament, whole and entire, with all their parts, as enumerated in the decree of the same Council (Trent) and in the ancient Latin Vulgate, *are to be received as sacred and canonical.*

And the Church holds them as sacred and canonical, not because, having been composed by human industry, they were afterwards approved by her authority; nor only because they contain revelation *without error*; but because, having been written under the inspiration of the Holy Ghost, *they have God for their author.*"

— *Pope Leo XIII in his Papal Encyclical: Providentissimus Deus, On The Study Of Holy Scripture, 13 November 1893*[2]

Lost in Translation

A good translator does not translate *literally*, word for word, from one language to another, but tries to convey the *meaning* of the original.

As the example of "kill" or "murder" shows, translators often have to make a difficult choice between different meanings of the same word. Whenever they make such a choice the result is no longer *literally* the same.

The language of Palestine at the time of Jesus was Aramaic. Paul took Christianity to the Greek-speaking world, and eventually, under Constantine, it became the official religion of Rome — where the language was Latin.

Kill or Murder?

The classic mistranslation of the fifth (or sixth?) commandment, from Exodus 20:13-16:

King James Version:
Thou shalt not kill.

New International Version:
You shall not murder.

The New Testament was written in Greek, so Jesus' Aramaic words were translated (from memory!) into Greek while the Old Testament was translated from Hebrew. And then the Bible was translated from Greek into Latin.

In 1611, King James of England was presented with a Bible translated into English from Greek and Hebrew. This translation, today, remains one of the most popular versions of the Bible in English.

But it's far from the only English-language edition. There's the Quaker Bible (1764), Webster's Revision (1830), the American Standard Version (1901), The Living Bible (1971), The New International Version (1978, modified [*Why?*] in 1984), The Good News Bible (1979), the New King James Version (1991), the Modern King James Version (1999), and the New Authorized [*by God?*] Version (2006).

That's not counting Bibles in *other* languages — let alone the Bibles of the Greek Orthodox, Russian Orthodox,

Macedonian Orthodox, Ukrainian Orthodox, Coptic, Nestorian, or Lutheran churches...not to mention the editions of their various sects *(22,000* of them, according to the *Encyclopedia Britannica!)*

Which one is the Word of God?

Well...none of them.

If the original "Words of God" were spoken in [archaic] Hebrew and [by Jesus] in Aramaic, a translation of a translation of a translation cannot be taken as the *literal truth.*

To appreciate the problem, consider a few examples from different *English-language* versions of the Bible:

Servant or Slave?

For example, in Exodus 21:7 the *King James Version* tells us:

And if a man sell his daughter to be a **maidservant**, she shall not go out as the **menservants** do.

But in the *New King James Version* this is changed to:

And if a man sells his daughter to be a **female slave**, she shall not go out as the **male slaves** do.

When Saul became King, was he one, thirty, forty, or forty-two years old?

The first verse of 1 Samuel 13, in the *King James Version* reads:

1 Saul reigned one year; and when he had reigned two years over Israel,

But when we turn to other English versions of the Bible we find *seven more* renderings of the same verse — all *different:*

Version		Age	Reigned for		
American Standard	Saul was	40	years old when he began to reign; and when he had reigned	2	years over Israel
Young's Literal Translation	A son of	a	year [is] Saul in his reigning, yea,	2	years he hath reigned over Israel,
New American Standard	Saul was	30	years old when he began to reign, and he reigned	42	years over Israel,
The Message	Saul was a	young man	when he began as king. He was king over Israel for	many	years.
Contemporary English	Saul was a	young man[1]	when he became king, and he ruled Israel for	2	years
1. *young man:* One possible meaning for the difficult Hebrew text; several manuscripts of one ancient translation have "thirty years old."					
Amplified Bible	Saul was	[forty][2]	years old when he began to reign; and when he had reigned	2	years over Israel.
2. The complete numbers in this verse are missing in the Hebrew. The word "forty" is supplied by the best available estimate.					
English Standard	Saul was	[Blank][3]	years old when he began to reign, and he reigned	[blank] and 2[4]	years over Israel.
3. The number is lacking in Hebrew and Septuagint; 4. *Two* may not be the entire number; something may have dropped out **NOTE:** the footnotes are those accompanying the texts at www.biblegateway.com					

What about the Torah? It's different *again:*

[1] Saul was ---- years old when he began to reign; and two

years he reigned over Israel[3]

The "----" number of years indicates that the number is unknown.

Who Killed Goliath?
(or his brother?)

For example, in 2 Samuel 21:19 we learn, according to the *King James Version:*

And there was again a battle in Gob with the Philistines, where **Elhanan** the son of Jaareoregim, a Bethlehemite, **slew the brother of Goliath** the Gittite, the staff of whose spear was like a weaver's beam.

But according to the *Contemporary English Version** of the Bible:

There was still another battle with the Philistines at Gob. A soldier named **Elhanan killed Goliath** from Gath, whose spear shaft was like a weaver's beam. Elhanan's father was Jari from Bethlehem.

Of course, in Sunday School we learn that *David,* not *Elhanan,* killed Goliath.

And, just to confuse matters further, *another* edition, *The Message,* says Goliath's spear "was as big as a flagpole," not "like a weaver's beam."

Mill's variations:

In 1707, John Mill, a fellow of Queens College, Oxford, published the results of his thirty-year study of the New Testament: he identified over thirty thousand places where different manuscripts, citations, and versions had different readings for passages of the New Testament.[4]

At that time, Mill could consult only 100 Greek manuscripts of the New Testament. Today, "more than 5,700 Greek manuscripts have been discovered and catalogued."[5]

---

* The source of texts for all versions of the Bible (except for the King James Version) is www.biblegateway.com

In summary, not only do the translators disagree on the correct numbers, from the four footnotes in the table on the previous page it's clear that those Hebrew texts which have survived *also* differ!

If the originals were written under the guidance of the Holy Spirit, one can't help but wonder why he didn't also inspire the translators (not to mention the copyists) to make sure they all got "the Words of God" right.

But then, as Bart D. Ehrman put it in his book *Misquoting Jesus:*

> **"**Even if God had inspired the original words [of the Bible], we don't have the original words.[6]**"**

"The problem with fundamentalists insisting on a literal interpretation of the Bible is that the meaning of words change. A prime example is "Spare the rod, spoil the child." A rod was a stick used by shepherds to guide their sheep to go in the desired direction. Shepherds did not use it to beat their sheep. The proper translation of the saying is "Give your child guidance, or they will go astray." It does not mean "Beat the shit out of your child or he will become rotten" as many fundamentalist parents seem to believe.**"**
— *Author Unknown*

Was Mary a "Virgin"?
Or just a "Young Woman"?

Most English editions of the Bible translate verse 27 from the first chapter of Luke the same way as the **King James Version:**

27 To a *virgin* espoused to a man whose name was Joseph of the house of David; and the virgin's name *was* Mary.

But in the **Worldwide English New Testament** we read:

27 The angel was sent to a *young woman* there. Her name was Mary. She was promised to a man named Joseph, to be his wife. He was of David's family line.

And the **Wycliffe New Testament** can't make up its mind:

27 to a *maiden* (to a *virgin*), wedded [**promised** or **espoused** in other versions!] to a man, whose name was Joseph, of the house of David; and the name of the maiden *was* Mary.

Which is right? "Virgin" — or "young woman/maiden"?

That's a good question, and it points to a far deeper issue.

In the book of Matthew, Chapter 1:23 **[King James Version]** we find this verse:

Behold, a *virgin* shall be with child, and shall bring forth a son, and they shall call his name Emmanuel, which being interpreted is, God with us.

Many Biblical scholars believe that Matthew was quoting from the book of Isaiah 7:14 which, in the **King James Version,** reads:

Therefore the Lord himself shall give you a sign; Behold, a *virgin* shall conceive, and bear a son, and shall call his name Immanuel.

Writing in Greek, Matthew was relying on a *Greek* translation of the Septuagint, which uses the word "παρθένος," or *parthenos*, which means "virgin."

However, the original Hebrew of this passage uses "העלמה" (almah) which, in today's Hebrew, has only *one* meaning: "young woman." (Of course, two and a half thousand years ago it may have *also* meant "virgin.")

And sure enough, when we turn to the English translation of the **Torah**, we find *this* rendering of Isaiah 7:14:
Therefore the Lord Himself shall give you a sign: behold, the *young woman* shall conceive, and bear a son, and shall call his name Immanuel.[7]

It's quite possible that the central feature of Christianity — Jesus' divine origin — is based on the mistranslation of a single word!

"No man ever believes that the Bible means what it says: He is always convinced that it says what he means.**"**
— *George Bernard Shaw*

2

"Would You Let Your 9-Year-Old Daughter Read this Filth?"

"Now therefore kill every male among the little ones, and kill every woman that hath known man by lying with him. But all the women children that have not known a man by lying with him, keep alive for yourselves"
— *Numbers 31, verses 17-18*

"And thou shalt eat the fruit of thine own body, the flesh of thy sons and of thy daughters, which the LORD thy God hath given thee..."
— *Deuteronomy 28, verse 53*

"But Rabshakeh said unto them...*Hath he* [my master] not *sent me* to the men which sit on the wall, that they may eat their own dung, and drink their own piss with you?"
— *2 Kings 18, verse 27*

"Would You Let Your 9-Year

"Early one Sunday morning a pair of Jehovah's Witnesses knocked on my door. I resented the wakeup and decided to get back at them. So I rounded up my Torah and said, pleasantly, and without the least hint of hostility: "The Bible? Would you let your nine-year-old daughter read this *filth?*"

They were floored. "Huh? What do you mean?"

"Abraham married Sarah, his *half-sister,* and when she couldn't conceive she told Abraham to take her slave maid, Hagar, and 'conceive on' her. Hagar, a maiden as well as a maid, didn't want to lie with Abraham. So he had her whipped until she gave in. Is this the type of story you want daughter to read — a wife giving a virgin slave to her husband to rape?"*

No response.

So I continued. "Lot's daughters got him drunk so they could lie with him and get his baby. They both succeeded. This is sick stuff," I said, and continued:

"When Moses sent the Israelites to war against the Midianites, he tells his men to slay *everyone,* even the

---

* This story was embellished in the telling compared to the passages in the Bible, where Sarah abused Hagar *after* Abraham got her pregnant, not before. But "God's door-knockers" really weren't familiar enough with the product they were selling to dispute this account.

Old Daughter Read this Filth?"

babies — and to spare only the virgins. So innocent boys and babies were murdered. The virgins were forced into slavery to satisfy the sexual whims of the same men who had just murdered their fathers, mothers and brothers. Again, is this sort of story you want your 9-year-old daughter to read?"

They had no answer, but their body language showed much discomfort.

"And in Genesis," I said, "God created Adam and Eve, and that was the end of creation." I showed them where it said that, right in the Old Testament.

"If that was the end of creation, *who did Adam's and Eve's sons Cain and Abel marry?* The only woman available was their mother Eve. So Cain and Abel were bonking their mother."

I asked them again: "This is filth. Would you let your nine-year-old daughter read it?

They parlayed quietly among themselves, they packed their copies of *Awake* and other publications and left without a word.**"**

— *Dan Rosenthal*[8]

Do you want your sons and daughters to read about cannibalism...

From 2 Kings Chapter 6

[29] So we boiled my son, and did eat him: and I said unto her on the next day, Give thy son, that we may eat him: and she hath hid her son.

...the sacrifice of *children*...

From 2 Kings Chapter 3

[27] Then he took his eldest son that should have reigned in his stead, and offered him for a burnt offering upon the wall. And there was great indignation against Israel: and they departed from him, and returned to their own land.

...semi-veiled pornography?...

From Song of Solomon Chapter 4

[1] Behold, thou art fair, my love; behold, thou art fair; thou hast doves' eyes within thy locks: thy hair is as a flock of goats, that appear from mount Gilead.

[2] Thy teeth are like a flock of sheep that are even shorn, which came up from the washing; whereof every one bear twins, and none is barren among them.

[3] Thy lips are like a thread of scarlet, and thy speech is comely: thy temples are like a piece of a pomegranate within thy locks.

⁴ Thy neck is like the tower of David builded for an armoury, whereon there hang a thousand bucklers, all shields of mighty men.

⁵ Thy two breasts are like two young roes [young deer, or fawns] that are twins, which feed among the lilies.

⁶ Until the day break, and the shadows flee away, I will get me to the mountain of myrrh, and to the hill of frankincense.

From Song of Solomon Chapter 7

⁶ How fair and how pleasant art thou, O love, for delights!

⁷ This thy stature is like to a palm tree, and thy breasts to clusters of grapes.

⁸ I said, I will go up to the palm tree, I will take hold of the boughs thereof: now also thy breasts shall be as clusters of the vine, and the smell of thy nose like apples;

⁹ And the roof of thy mouth like the best wine for my beloved, that goeth down sweetly, causing the lips of those that are asleep to speak.

¹⁰ I am my beloved's, and his desire is toward me.

¹¹ Come, my beloved, let us go forth into the field; let us lodge in the villages.

¹² Let us get up early to the vineyards; let us see if the vine flourish, whether the tender grape appear, and the pomegranates bud forth: there will I give thee my loves.

...learn that the "God of Love" seems to love DEATH...

From Exodus Chapter 32

[27] And he said unto them, Thus saith the LORD God of Israel, Put every man his sword by his side, and go in and out from gate to gate throughout the camp, and slay every man his brother, and every man his companion, and every man his neighbour.

From Deuteronomy Chapter 7

[2] And when the LORD thy God shall deliver them before thee; thou shalt smite them, and utterly destroy them; thou shalt make no covenant with them, nor shew mercy unto them:

From Deuteronomy Chapter 13

[15] Thou shalt surely smite the inhabitants of that city with the edge of the sword, destroying it utterly, and all that is therein, and the cattle thereof, with the edge of the sword.

From 2 Kings Chapter 19

[35] And it came to pass that night, that *the angel of the LORD* went out, and smote in the camp of the Assyrians an hundred fourscore and five thousand: and when they arose early in the morning, behold, they were all dead corpses.

From Deuteronomy Chapter 21

[18] If a man have a stubborn and rebellious son, which will not obey the voice of his father, or the voice of his mother, and that, when they have chastened him, will not hearken unto them:

¹⁹ Then shall his father and his mother lay hold on him, and bring him out unto the elders of his city, and unto the gate of his place;

²⁰ And they shall say unto the elders of his city, This our son is stubborn and rebellious, he will not obey our voice; he is a glutton, and a drunkard.

²¹ And all the men of his city shall stone him with stones, that he die: so shalt thou put evil away from among you; and all Israel shall hear, and fear.

...orders non-believers be tortured or put to death...

From 2 Chronicles Chapter 15

¹² And they entered into a covenant to seek the LORD God of their fathers with all their heart and with all their soul;

¹³ That whosoever would not seek the LORD God of Israel should be put to death, whether small or great, whether man or woman.

From Exodus Chapter 22

²⁰ He that sacrificeth unto any god, save unto the LORD only, he shall be utterly destroyed.

From Revelation Chapter 9

¹ And the fifth angel sounded, and I saw a star fall from heaven unto the earth: and to him was given the key of the bottomless pit.

² And he opened the bottomless pit; and there arose a smoke out of the pit, as the smoke of a great furnace; and the sun and

the air were darkened by reason of the smoke of the pit.

[3] And there came out of the smoke locusts upon the earth: and unto them was given power, as the scorpions of the earth have power.

[4] And it was commanded them that they should not hurt the grass of the earth, neither any green thing, neither any tree; but only those men which have not the seal of God in their foreheads.

[5] And to them it was given that they should not kill them, but that they should be tormented five months: and their torment was as the torment of a scorpion, when he striketh a man.

[6] And in those days shall men seek death, and shall not find it; and shall desire to die, and death shall flee from them.

Apologia

An **Apologia** is "a defence."
Apologetics is the branch of theology concerned with the defence or proof of Christianity.

These two words spring from the same root as **Apology** (Greek: απολογία, "apologia," via Latin: apologia and French: apologie). The original meaning of "apology" is "a justification or defence"; only in the eighteenth century did the primary meaning become the one we use today, "an expression of regret or remorse" — usually accompanied by some kind of justification (as in: "I'm sorry. I didn't mean to do that").

In this respect, the Bible and the Koran are the same!

...and orders *children* to be massacred...

From Isaiah Chapter 13

[15] Every one that is found shall be thrust through; and every one that is joined unto them shall fall by the sword.

[16] Their children also shall be dashed to pieces before their eyes; their houses shall be spoiled, and their wives ravished....

[18] Their bows also shall dash the young men to pieces; and they shall have no pity on the fruit of the womb; their eyes shall not spare children.

From Hosea Chapter 13

[16] Samaria shall become desolate; for she hath rebelled against her God: they shall fall by the sword: their infants shall be dashed in pieces, and their women with child shall be ripped up.

Apologia

Numbers 31:17-18

Now therefore kill every male among the little ones, and kill every woman that hath known man by lying with him. But all the women children that have not known man by lying with him, keep alive for yourselves.

From *Matthew Henry's Commentary on the Whole Bible* (1708-10):

The sword of war should spare women and children; but the sword of justice should know no distinction, but that of guilty or not guilty. This war was the execution of a righteous sentence upon a guilty nation, in which the women were the worst criminals. The female children were spared, who, being brought up among the Israelites, would not tempt them to idolatry.

Matthew Henry (1662-1714), was an English non-conformist clergyman.

...and *eaten!*...

From Jeremiah 19

⁹ And I will cause them to eat the flesh of their sons and the flesh of their daughters, and they shall eat every one the flesh of his friend in the siege and straitness, wherewith their enemies, and they that seek their lives, shall straiten them.

...and massacres millions HIMSELF...

From Genesis Chapter 6

⁶ And it repented the LORD that he had made man on the earth, and it grieved him at his heart.

⁷ And the LORD said, I will destroy man whom I have created from the face of the earth; both man, and beast, and the creeping thing, and the fowls of the air; for it repenteth me that I have made them.

Biologists estimate that around thirty million humans were alive at the (supposed) time of Noah...five times the number of Jews killed in the Holocaust! — for which Hitler and the Nazis were justly condemned.

And if God made man in his own image, and was so displeased with what he saw that he killed them all but eight (Noah, his wife, his three sons and their wives), what does that say about the nature of God?

...advocates the subjugation of women...

From Genesis Chapter 3
[16] Unto the woman [Eve] he [God] said, I will greatly multiply thy sorrow and thy conception; in sorrow thou shalt bring forth children; and thy desire shall be to thy husband, ***and he shall rule over thee.***

From Deuteronomy Chapter 25
[11] When men strive together one with another, and the wife of the one draweth near for to deliver her husband out of the hand of him that smiteth him, and putteth forth her hand, and taketh him by the secrets:
[12] Then thou shalt cut off her hand, thine eye shall not pity her.

From 1 Timothy Chapter 2
[11] Let the woman learn in silence with all subjection.
[12] But I suffer not a woman to teach, nor to usurp authority over the man, but to be in silence.

From 1 Corinthians Chapter 14
[34] Let your women keep silence in the churches: for it is not permitted unto them to speak; but they are commanded to be under obedience as also saith the law.
[35] And if they will learn any thing, let them ask their husbands at home: for it is a shame for women to speak in the church.

...and rape...

From Judges Chapter 19

[22] ...behold, the men of the city, certain sons of Belial, beset the house round about, *and* beat at the door, and spake to the master of the house, the old man, saying, Bring forth the man that came into thine house, that we may know him.

[23] And the man, the master of the house, went out unto them, and said unto them, Nay, my brethren, nay, I pray you, do not so wickedly; seeing that this man is come into mine house, do not this folly.

[24] Behold, here is my daughter a maiden, and his concubine; them I will bring out now, and humble ye them, and do with them what seemeth good unto you: but unto this man do not so vile a thing.

[25] But the men would not hearken to him: so the man took his concubine, and brought her forth unto them; and they knew her, and abused her all the night until the morning: and when the day began to spring, they let her go.

[26] Then came the woman in the dawning of the day, and fell down at the door of the man's house where her lord was, till it was light.

From 2 Samuel Chapter 12

[11] Thus saith the LORD, Behold, I will raise up evil against thee out of thine own house, and I will take thy wives before thine eyes, and give them unto thy neighbour, and he shall lie with thy wives in the sight of this sun.

...and incest!...

From Genesis Chapter 19

[31] And the firstborn said unto the younger, Our father *[Lot]* is old, and there is not a man in the earth to come in unto us after the manner of all the earth:

[32] Come, let us make our father drink wine, and we will lie with him, that we may preserve seed of our father.

[33] And they made their father drink wine that night: and the firstborn went in, and lay with her father; and he perceived not when she lay down, nor when she arose.

[34] And it came to pass on the morrow, that the firstborn said unto the younger, Behold, I lay yesternight with my father: let us make him drink wine this night also; and go thou in, and lie with him, that we may preserve seed of our father.

[35] And they made their father drink wine that night also: and the younger arose, and lay with him; and he perceived not when she lay down, nor when she arose.

[36] Thus were both the daughters of Lot with child by their father.

...and slavery...

From Leviticus Chapter 25

[44] Both thy bondmen,* and thy bondmaids,* which thou shalt have, shall be of the heathen that are round about you; of them shall ye buy bondmen and bondmaids.

[45] Moreover of the children of the strangers that do sojourn among you, of them shall ye buy, and of their families that are with you, which they begat in your land: and they shall be your possession.

---

* Translated as "slave" in other English editions of the Bible.

[46] And ye shall take them as an inheritance for your children after you, to inherit them for a possession; they shall be your bondmen for ever...

From Exodus Chapter 21

[7] And if a man sell his daughter to be a maidservant [slave], she shall not go out as the menservants do.

[8] If she please not her master, who hath betrothed her to himself, then shall he let her be redeemed: to sell her unto a strange nation he shall have no power, seeing he hath dealt deceitfully with her.

From Deuteronomy Chapter 20

[10] When thou comest nigh unto a city to fight against it, then proclaim peace unto it.

[11] And it shall be, if it make thee answer of peace, and open unto thee, then it shall be, that all the people that is found therein shall be tributaries unto thee, and they shall serve thee.

Apologia

1 Corinthians 11:7-10

The man indeed ought not to cover his head: because he is the image and glory of God. But the woman is the glory of the man. For the man is not of the woman: but the woman of the man. For the man was not created for the woman: but the woman for the man. Therefore ought the woman to have a power over her head, because of the angels.

From the *Catholic Encyclopedia*[9]:

A power...that is, a veil or covering, as a sign that she is under the power of her husband: and this, the apostle adds, because of the angels, who are present in the assemblies of the faithful.

---

[12] And if it will make no peace with thee, but will make war against thee, then thou shalt besiege it:

13 And when the LORD thy God hath delivered it into thine hands, thou shalt smite every male thereof with the edge of the sword:

14 But the women, and the little ones, and the cattle, and all that is in the city, even all the spoil thereof, shalt thou take unto thyself; and thou shalt eat the spoil of thine enemies, which the LORD thy God hath given thee.

...and turning your virgin daughters into sex slaves...

From Genesis Chapter 19

1 And there came two angels to Sodom at even: and Lot... seeing *them* rose up to meet them...

2 And he said, Behold now, my lords, turn in, I pray you, into your servant's house, and tarry all night...

4 But before they lay down, the men of the city, *even* the men of Sodom, compassed the house round, both old and young, all the people from every quarter:

5 And they called unto Lot, and said unto him, Where *are* the men which came in to thee this night? bring them out unto us, that we may know *[i.e., Sodomize]* them,

6 And Lot went out at the door unto them, and shut the door after him,

7 And said, I pray you, brethren, do not so wickedly.

8 Behold now, I have two daughters which have not known man; let me, I pray you, bring them out unto you, and do ye to them as is good in your eyes...

> *And Lot was the "righteous man" God saved when he razed Sodom and Gomorrah!*

...demands the sacrifice of *innocent* loved ones...

From Judges Chapter 11

[29] Then the Spirit of the LORD came upon Jephthah,...

[30] And Jephthah vowed a vow unto the LORD, and said, If thou shalt without fail deliver the children of Ammon into mine hands,

[31] Then it shall be, that whatsoever cometh forth of the doors of my house to meet me, when I return in peace from the children of Ammon, shall surely be the LORD's, and I will offer it up for a burnt offering.

[32] So Jephthah passed over unto the children of Ammon to fight against them; and the LORD delivered them into his hands.

[33] And he smote them from Aroer, even till thou come to Minnith, even twenty cities, and unto the plain of the vineyards, with a very great slaughter. Thus the children of Ammon were subdued before the children of Israel.

[34] And Jephthah came to Mizpeh unto his house, and, behold, his daughter came out to meet him with timbrels and with dances: and she was his only child; beside her he had neither son nor daughter.

If God is omniscient, then he knew EXACTLY who Jephthah had agreed to offer up for a "burnt offering" when he made the "deal"!

And unlike Abraham's son Isaac, Jephthah's daughter didn't get a last-minute reprieve from the Heavenly Executioner.

....loves the smell of "burnt offerings"...

From Leviticus Chapter 1

¹ And the LORD called unto Moses, and spake unto him out of the tabernacle of the congregation, saying,

² Speak unto the children of Israel, and say unto them, If any man of you bring an offering unto the LORD, ye shall bring your offering of the cattle, even of the herd, and of the flock....

⁵ And he shall kill the bullock before the LORD: and the priests, Aaron's sons, shall bring the blood, and sprinkle the blood round about upon the altar that is by the door of the tabernacle of the congregation....

⁸ And the priests, Aaron's sons, shall lay the parts, the

Apologia

Matthew 5:9

Blessed are the peacemakers: for they shall be called the children of God.

From *Commentary on the Gospel of Matthew* by Origen[10]:

To the man who is a peacemaker in either sense there is in the Divine oracles nothing crooked or perverse, for they are all plain to those who understand. And because to such a one there is nothing crooked or perverse, he sees therefore abundance of peace in all the Scriptures, even in those which seem to be at conflict and in contradiction with one another.... He demonstrates that that which appears to others to be a conflict in the Scriptures is no conflict, and exhibits their concord and peace, whether of the Old Scriptures with the New, or of the Law with the Prophets, or of the Gospels with the Apostolic Scriptures, or of the Apostolic Scriptures with each other.

head, and the fat, in order upon the wood that is on the fire which is upon the altar:

⁹ ...and the priest shall burn all on the altar, to be a burnt

sacrifice, an offering made by fire, **of a sweet savour unto the LORD.**

[10] And if his offering be of the flocks, namely, of the sheep, or of the goats, for a burnt sacrifice; he shall bring it a male without blemish....

[13] ...and the priest shall bring it all, and burn it upon the altar: it is a burnt sacrifice, an offering made by fire, **of a sweet savour unto the LORD.**

[14] And if the burnt sacrifice for his offering

Apologia

Psalm 137:9

Happy shall he be, that taketh and dasheth thy little ones against the stones.

From the *Catholic Encyclopedia*[11]:

Dash thy little ones, etc... In the spiritual sense, we dash the little ones of Babylon against the rock, when we mortify our passions, and stifle the first motions of them, by a speedy recourse to the rock which is Christ.

Just one thing: Psalm 137 was written long before Christ was born.

---

to the LORD be of fowls, then he shall bring his offering of turtledoves, or of young pigeons.

[17] ...and the priest shall burn it upon the altar, upon the wood that is upon the fire: it is a burnt sacrifice, an offering made by fire, **of a sweet savour unto the LORD.**

From Leviticus Chapter 2

[1] And when any will offer a meat offering unto the LORD, his offering shall be of fine flour; and he shall pour oil upon it, and put frankincense thereon:

[2] And he shall bring it to Aaron's sons the priests...and the priest shall burn the memorial of it upon the altar, to be an offering made by fire, **of a sweet savour unto the LORD...**

⁴ And if thou bring an oblation of a meat offering baken in the oven, it shall be unleavened cakes of fine flour mingled with oil, or unleavened wafers anointed with oil....

⁹ And the priest shall...burn it upon the altar: it is an offering made by fire, **of a sweet savour unto the LORD.**

If God is omnipotent (all-powerful) then he can "savour" the smell of "burnt offerings" any time he likes. And not just as a memory — which is all we can do — but in living 3-D color with sound effects.

Or, if God is omni-present (everywhere) then all he needs to do is hang around the cooking fires, as the smell of cooking meat is the same.

So the prime attraction can't *really* be the "aroma" of a burnt offering but the abject fear and grovelling that *accompanies* a sacrifice.

If a human being exhibited this kind of sadistic behavior, it would get him a one-way ticket to the insane asylum. Unless, of course, his name was Lenin, Stalin, Hitler, Mao, or Pol Pot.

...and is just plain disgusting...

From 2 Chronicles Chapter 21

¹⁸ And after all this the LORD smote him in his bowels with an incurable disease.

¹⁹ And it came to pass, that in process of time, after the end of two years, his bowels fell out by reason of his sickness: so he died of sore diseases. And his people made no burning for him, like the burning of his fathers.

And if you think the morality of the Old Testament has been superseded by the New...

From Matthew Chapter 5

¹⁷ Think not that I [Jesus] am come to destroy the [Jewish Old Testament] law, or the prophets: I am not come to destroy, but to fulfil.

From Mark Chapter 7

²⁵ For a certain woman, whose young daughter had an unclean spirit, heard of him [Jesus], and came and fell at his feet:
²⁶ The woman was a Greek, a Syrophenician by nation; and she besought him that he would cast forth the devil out of her daughter.
²⁷ But Jesus said unto her, Let the children [of Israel] first be filled: for it is not meet to take the children's bread, and to cast it unto the dogs [*e.g.,* Greeks &c].

From Luke Chapter 16

¹⁷ And it is easier for heaven and earth to pass, than one tittle of the law to fail.

And God hasn't changed much either...

From Luke Chapter 12

⁵ But I will forewarn you whom ye shall fear: Fear him [God], which after he hath killed hath power to cast into hell; yea, I say unto you, Fear him

Gotcha!

From Matthew Chapter 5

28 But I say unto you, That whosoever looketh on a woman to lust after her hath committed adultery with her already in his heart.

Don't imagine a pink elephant.

I said DON'T...but the moment I mention it, you *have to* think of a pink elephant, if only for an instant, right?

The only way to NOT think of a pink elephant is to think of something else...say, a purple hippopotamus with yellow zebra stripes.

There! The pink elephant's gone (oops...it just came back, didn't it?)

It's biologically impossible for a male of the species *homo sapiens* to NOT "commit adultery in his heart" the moment he sees an attractive woman, especially as a teenager. [Even if he isn't married! Jesus said *"whosoever looketh on a woman to lust...hath committed adultery,"* not *"whosoever is married...."*]

According to Matthew, Jesus has condemned *every* human male to hell *by his nature as a human being!*

As a Christian you can only hope to live to a ripe old age when your testosterone or estrogen levels have dropped to the point where sex is merely a faded memory...and pray that God will forgive you for your youthful (mental) indiscretions.

Ban the Bible?

HONG KONG, WEDNESDAY 16 MAY 2007

A Chinese-language website exhorted its readers to pressure Hong Kong's Television and Entertainments Licensing Authority — Tela, which oversees the publishing industry — to reclassify the Bible as an indecent publication.

Tela received 208 complaints which reputedly claimed that passages in the Old and New Testaments referring to acts of violence, rape and cannibalism were indecent.

"The thrust of the complaints," said a Tela spokeswoman, "was that the Bible was obscene, that different parts of the Bible were offensive to readers."

It appears that the sudden flurry of messages to Tela came amid a row in Hong Kong when the Obscene Articles Tribunal classified, as indecent, a sex survey in a student journal which questioned respondents on bestiality and incest.

"The only difference between *The Da Vinci Code* and the gospels is that the gospels are ancient fiction while *The Da Vinci Code* is modern fiction."
— *Richard Dawkins*

And The Da Vinci Code *had a better editor*

3

The Virgin Birth and the Many "Sons of God"

"Isn't it enough to see that a garden is beautiful without having to believe that there are fairies at the bottom of it too?"
— *Douglas Adams*

"Faith may be defined briefly as an illogical belief in the occurrence of the improbable."
— *H.L. Mencken*

"The same people who wrote the bible thought that the world was flat."
— *Unknown*

The "Virgin Birth" and the Many "Sons of God"

Of the four Gospels — Matthew, Mark, Luke, and John — only Matthew and Luke tell of Jesus' virgin birth; John merely calls Jesus *(and* John the Baptist) a "Son of God"; while Mark — which, most scholars conclude, was the first of the Gospels to be written — doesn't mention Jesus' birth at all.

Nor is there any mention of the Virgin Birth in Corinthians, Thessalonians 1, Philippians, Galatians, or Romans — the books of the New Testament attributed to Paul's authorship and reputedly written *before* any of the four Gospels.

Indeed, Paul repeatedly stressed the very opposite, referring on multiple occasions to Jesus as "the seed of David,"

So either Paul and the author of Mark:

➢ Didn't know about (or believe in) the Virgin Birth of Jesus; or

➢ they did know about it — and forgot to mention it.

In the context of the Greek-speaking world of the time — the second possibility is highly improbable.

When Paul began preaching to the Gentiles, his converts came from the Greek and Roman religions of Zeus and Jupiter, Mithraism, Zoroastrianism, and many other creeds and sects where virgin birth stories were common. A few examples:

➢ *Perseus* was the mythic Greek hero who killed the Medusa. His mother, Danaë, was impregnated by Zeus

➢ Cyebele (or Nana), the mother of *Attis* — a semi-diety of Phrygia (eastern Turkey) — was impregnated by an almond or pomegranate tossed away by the gods

➢ *Ra*, the Egyptian sun god, had no father. His mother, Net, conceived by parthenogenesis. *Horus* was another Egyptian god conceived parthenogenically by Isis

➢ Other pre-Christian figures believed to have been born of a virgin include **Sargon** (Babylon), **Adonis** (Syria), **Osiris** (Egypt), and **Dionysus** (Greece)

➢ Even **Apis**, the sacred bull of Memphis, was believed

The Four Main Views of Jesus Christ:

In the first two centuries following the crucifixion there were dozens of different "Christianities" that we know of, and quite probably hundreds more that have left no traces. The four main ones:

Jewish Christians who viewed Jesus as a *Jewish* prophet or rabbi, but not a deity. They followed Mosaic Law and Jewish dietary and other practices. Effectively wiped out by the Romans' sacking of Jerusalem in 70 CE.

Pauline Christians: followers of Paul, who laid the foundation of Christian (especially Catholic) theology as we know it today and spread it through the Graeco-Roman world. Became a semi-official religion of the Roman Empire under Constantine (313 CE), and the monopoly religion under Theodosius (380 CE).

Gnostics, who believed the story of Jesus' divine origin was *allegorical* and claimed, like Mithraism and other "mystery" religions of the time, to have secret knowledge of God and the universe. Despite being deemed "heretical" by the official Christian church of Rome many Gnostic elements are incorporated in the Gospels, especially in John.

Marcionites, who believed that the God who sent Jesus was NOT the God of the Jews, but Yahweh's *successor.* This sect was the Paulines' main competitor for converts.

to have been fathered by a god striking a cow with a ray of moonlight

So common, indeed, was this belief in the Graeco-Roman world that many mortals were elevated retroactively to the status of Virgin Births: Romulus and Remus, the mythical founders of Rome, Pythagoras, Plato, Apollonius, Alexander the Great, the Roman emperor Augustus, the Roman general who defeated Hannibal, Scipio the Elder, all Egyptian Pharaohs — even Buddha.

Some scholars believe that, at the time, a virgin birth was widely thought (except by Jews) to be a *prerequisite* for divinity. Whether true or not, Paul's *Gentile* audience was primed to accept a Virgin Birth as clear "proof" of the arrival of a messenger from God. So why didn't he use it?

Paul's clearest statement on Jesus' origin is in Romans 1:3-4: "Concerning his Son, Jesus Christ our Lord, **which was made of the seed of David according to the flesh;** And **declared to be the Son of God** with power, according to the spirit of holiness, by the resurrection from the dead."

In other words: Joseph was Jesus' father, and by resurrecting him, God *later* elevated Jesus to the status of a "Son of God."

> **"**The chief of the fathers [of Mithraism], a sort of pope, *who always lived at Rome,* was called "Pater Patrum" or "Pater Patratus."**"**
>
> — *The Catholic Encyclopedia*[12]

So by the time the second Gospel, Matthew, was written (sometime between 70 and 100 CE) the idea of Jesus' Virgin Birth had crept into Christianity. The obvious source is the Virgin Birth stories of all Christianity's pagan competitors.

This is hardly a new hypothesis. Justin Martyr, writing in

his *The First Apology of Justin* (2nd century) claims that devils went back in time and planted stories similar to Christ's miracles *(e.g.,* that Bacchus was the son of Jupiter and ascended to heaven after being torn to pieces, and the virgin birth of Perseus) merely to muddy the waters when Jesus came along (chapter 54). But in chapter 22 of the same work he says: "And if we even affirm that He was born of a virgin, accept this in common with what you accept of Perseus,"[13] in effect positioning Jesus as just one of many "Sons of God."

Other early writers claimed that Christianity was the source of Virgin Birth stories in contemporaneous pagan religions — contradicted by the evidence

Origins of Christian doctrines

Christian doctrines with no Jewish roots:

Virgin Birth [probable sources: Old Testament mistranslation of Hebrew word for "maiden/young unmarried woman" as "virgin"; Gnosticism and/or Pagan "Mystery Religions"]

Trinity [most probable sources: Greek/Platonist concept of "Logos" ("Word"); Greek polytheism]

Christian doctrines with Jewish/Old Testament roots — but not part of Jewish doctrine:

Original Sin [most probable sources: similar view held by a minority of Jewish scholars; Paul's reinterpretation of Adam and Eve's ejection from the Garden of Eden; Gnosticism which, unlike Graeco-Roman religions and Judaism, held that man and the earth were evil and/or fallen]

Purgatory

Christian doctrines with no Biblical or Jewish basis:

Limbo

Immaculate Conception

Assumption of Virgin Mary

Papal Infallibility

of the New Testament itself (if scholars are right that Mark was the first Gospel written, and *all* the Gospels were written after Paul's epistles had been committed to papyrus), and the fact that most other Virgin Birth stories pre-dated Christ — some by many centuries.

Ultimately, the only refuge for Christians is, in the words of Dr. Dan Hayen:

> The virgin birth of Jesus Christ is not something we believe because we can prove it by some scientific explanation. We believe in the virgin conception because the Word of God says that that is how it happened. It is a matter of revelation, not a matter of reason. God said so, and that settles it for us."[14]

The "Holy Stork Theory"

In Sunday School in the West we learn that Jesus was born in a manger where he was visited by the three wise men.

But in some countries (the Philippines being one example), there's a different twist to the story children learn: rather than Jesus emerging from Mary's womb, the Holy Ghost flies in like a "Holy Stork" with the baby Jesus in his arms.

Of course, this variation contradicts the Bible where the angel Gabriel clearly tells Mary: And, behold, thou shalt conceive in thy womb, ***and bring forth a son,*** and...that holy thing which shall be born of thee shall be called the Son of God. *(Luke Chapter 1:31,33).*

You'd think the nuns and priests who teach it would know better.

But...based on the "Holy Stork Theory," there is, of course, absolutely no doubt about Mary's virginity.

Except — as we saw above — God (well, the Bible) *also* said the *opposite*.

This matter was "settled" by *decree* of the Lateran Council held in the time of Pope Martin I in 649 CE, where "the virginity of our Blessed Lady was defined under anathema" *(i.e.,* threat of excommunication).[15]

Mary's "Assumption" and her "Immaculate Conception"

While one can (selectively) call on biblical support for the Virgin Birth, the same can't be said of the other doctrines that surround Jesus' mother: her veneration (and effective elevation to the "fourth member of the Trinity"), her "Immaculate Conception," Assumption, and its corollary: absolute purity and *"perpetual* virginity."

In the Bible itself, Mary receives no special reverence, not even from her son [*see Matthew 12:46-49,* page 34]; and even the *Catholic Encyclopedia*[16] admits that "we do not meet with any clear traces of the cultus of the Blessed Virgin in the first Christian centuries," and that the veneration of Mary "is not contained, at least explicitly, in the earlier forms of the Apostles' Creed" — which *now* includes the words: "Hail Mary, full of grace...."

The early Church Fathers, like Origen, St. Basil, Justin and Tertullian, writing in the second and third centuries, agreed that Mary had a special place, but debated just how "pure" she was. The consensus of the time was probably best summarized by St. Epiphanius (died 403 CE) when, denouncing the Collyridians (an "obscure sect") for "their sacrificial offering of cakes to Mary," he "laid down the rule": "Let Mary be held in honour. Let the Father, Son, and Holy Ghost be adored, *but let no one adore Mary."*

The first *documentary* evidence that Mary *was* being adored, despite St. Epiphanius, is found in a Syrian manuscript from the sixth century, according to the *Catholic Encyclopedia*.

By the early Middle Ages, the "cult of Mary" was firmly established — with feast days in her honor; churches dedicated to her memory; and various popular, poetic, *and* ecclesiastical writings venerating her including, of course, the Apostles' Creed. The veneration of Mary was, it would appear, a popular groundswell from the laity who prayed to her to put in a good word for them to her son.

While the doctrine of the Virgin Birth was decreed in 649 CE, the others came *more than a millennium* later!

Mary's **Immaculate Conception**, that Mary was born *without* Original Sin, was decreed only by Pope Pius IX in *1854.*[17]

The Assumption, the doctrine that Mary was received bodily into Heaven *(because* she was without Original Sin) came even later: it was declared official dogma by Pius XII in *1950.*[18]

The Immaculate Conception means that Mary joins Adam, Eve, and Jesus as the only humans born without Original Sin.

One rationale for its adoption was that unless Mary was free from Original Sin, how could *Jesus* have been born without having "Fallen from Grace"? Logically, of course, Mary's "Immaculate Conception" is an unnecessary extra step: If *Mary* could be born without Original Sin without *her* mother *also* being "immaculately conceived," so could Jesus.

According to the doctrine of the Assumption, Mary ascended *bodily* to heaven (not just her soul like ordinary folks) *because,* like Jesus, she was also without Original Sin.

A Question of Virginity

In common parlance, a "virgin" is someone who has never had sexual intercourse. But the *Catholic Encyclopedia* defines "virginity" very differently:

> "Morally, virginity signifies the reverence for bodily integrity which is suggested by a virtuous motive. Thus understood, it is common to both sexes, and *may exist in a woman even after bodily violation committed upon her against her will.*"

Here, the church is echoing Augustine: who wrote chastity is "a virtue of the mind, and is not lost by rape, but is lost by the intention of sin, even if unperformed." *[City of God, 14.17.]*

Virginity, in other words, is a *moral* not physical issue, defined by *motive*. Have sex from *lust* and you lose your virginity; but if sex is imposed upon you against your will, you're still a virgin.

So what happens to a nun, who has taken vows of chastity, who is raped *against her will?*

In some orders, nothing. But in stricter orders, like the Dominicans, she'll be thrown out. What's more, a woman can only become a Dominican sister *after* a physical examination: her hymen must be intact. No "excuses."

What about the *child* of a rape victim?

Although born with Original Sin, once baptized a child is "forgiven" for that. Whether he or she gets to heaven depends only on what, if any, sins are committed *after* baptism.

Nevertheless, in many Catholic countries the child of a rape victim *cannot become a nun.* The sins of the fathers (and mothers) are *definitely* visited upon the daughters — *by the church.*

As it happens, however, this attitude has a Biblical basis:

> *From* Deuteronomy 23
> [2] A bastard shall not enter into the congregation of the LORD; even to his tenth generation shall he not enter into the congregation of the LORD.

This, of course, is pure nonsense. The fact that *Eve* was born without Original Sin didn't stop her from eating the apple.*

A Question of Descent

If Original Sin was *acquired* by Adam and Eve, but was not in their original nature, how could it be passed to their children?

Either God altered Adam and Eve's genes as they were ejected from the Garden of Eden, so descent is *Darwinian* (only genetic traits are inheritable), or *acquired* traits can be passed on, making descent *Lamarckian* — a theory which is contradicted by the evidence.

But in defining the "divinely revealed dogma" that the "Immaculate Mother of God, the ever Virgin Mary, having completed the course of her earthly life, was assumed body and soul into heavenly glory," Pope Pius XII went further and confirmed, *inter alia,* the widely-held belief that Mary had attained a state of "absolute purity" — meaning, among other things, that while on earth she *never* sinned and must have remained a perpetual virgin.

This idea is contradicted by Biblical passages such as Mark 6:3: "Is not this the carpenter, the son of Mary, the **brother** of James, and Joses, and of Juda, and Simon? and are not his **sisters** here with us?"†

It's clear that Mary, as Jesus' mother, gained a special

---

* Was the "forbidden fruit" an apple? Genesis 3:3 doesn't specify, merely saying: "But of the fruit of the tree which is in the midst of the garden, God hath said, Ye shall not eat of it, neither shall ye touch it, lest ye die."

† The *Catholic Encyclopedia* tries to finesse this problem by suggesting that "brethren" could have meant half-brothers and -sisters, step-brothers and -sisters (though there is no evidence Mary was Joseph's second wife) or even cousins. Possibly, though it seems more like a *post hoc ergo propter hoc* argument.

place in the Christian pantheon. But in the end, as the *Encyclopedia Britannica* puts it:

> ➤ For neither of these [the Immaculate Conception and Assumption] is there any Biblical evidence; more significantly there is no evidence in tradition for either before the 6th century.[19]

Original Sin, Purgatory, and Limbo

Original Sin is primarily based on Paul's reinterpretation of Adam and Eve's story in Genesis [see Romans 5:12-21 and 1 Corinthians 15:22]. Original Sin is not part of Jewish doctrine, but was a minority opinion amongst Jewish scholars.

Adam and Eve were *not* born with Original Sin, but acquired it by eating the apple, and so passed it on to all their descendants. All of us, thanks to Adam and Eve's actions, "were made sinners" [Romans, 5:19], and henceforth *born sinful*.

Baptism is the only "cure" for Original Sin — though as we are still "sinners by nature" it can't be considered permanent (so it's more a forgiveness than a cure). Only people who have been baptized are candidates for heaven. Upon their death, they are then judged on whether they have sinned *after* baptism.

The doctrine of Original Sin was first put in something like its current form by Irenaeus, the Bishop of Lyon, in the second century, as part of the battle against the Gnostics. It became official Catholic doctrine at the Second Council of Orange in 529 CE where, following Augustine, it was declared that man *inherited* an utterly depraved nature, the only way out being divine grace. This position was later softened, after Aquinas, so that a child is now considered born only without God's "sanctifying grace."

The logical consequence of this doctrine is that all sinners, baptized or not, go straight to hell. This was Augustine's position.

While there is Biblical support for Original Sin, the same can't be said of Purgatory and Limbo.

Purgatory is a place of temporary punishment for souls who had committed venial (forgivable) sins, but not *mortal* sins *(e.g.,* denying God) severe enough to be sent straight to hell. After purification, they could enter heaven.

Only those who committed venial sins could enter Purgatory.

While such an intermediate state between heaven and hell was widely accepted, especially in the western church after the split with Byzantium in 1054, Purgatory as a place did not become official Catholic dogma until the First Council of Lyon in 1254. This was reaffirmed by later councils in Florence (1431-1445) and Trent (1545-1563).

Purgatory is the only one of these three doctrines with firm Jewish roots. The Jewish equivalent is a *process* rather than a place: some souls float up and down between heaven and hell until, if purified, they could enter heaven.

The idea of purgatory comes from the all but universal practice of praying for the souls of the dead, supported by Bible passages like 2 Timothy 1:16-18 that imply it's a good idea. The reasoning: if the dead go straight to heaven or hell, there's no point in praying for them. Since we're advised to pray for the dead, there must be some point in doing so: hence, the possibility of redemption — and Purgatory.

But...if God decides to redeem someone, what does he need Purgatory for?

Limbo. A question that bothered many people, lay and theologian alike, was what happened to unbaptized infants? Without baptism, they could not go to Purgatory. Yet, being free of all sin except Original Sin, sending them straight to hell

The Other Gospels

The first four books of the New Testament are the "canonical" *(i.e.,* "official") gospels of Christianity. But they are merely four of hundreds of gospels (meaning "good news") that circulated in the first three centuries CE. A partial list of others:

Gospel of Thomas
Gospel of Judas
Gospel of Truth
Coptic Gospel of the Egyptians
Greek Gospel of the Egyptians
Gospel of Nicodemus
Gospel of Barnabas
Gospel of Mary
Gospel of Philip
Gospel of Peter
Secret Gospel of Mark
The Egerton Gospel [a.k.a. the "Unknown Gospel"]
Gospel of the Ebionites
Gospel of the Nazareans
Gospel of the Hebrews
Gospel of James
Infancy Gospel of Thomas
Gospel of the Saviour
Gospel of Eve

Gospel of the Twelve
Oxyrhynchus Gospels
Dialogue of the Saviour
Gospel of Bartholomew
Gospel of Matthias
Gospel of the Seventy
Gospel of the Four Heavenly Realms
Gospel of Perfection

Alternate, edited or rewritten versions of the canonical Gospels (Matthew, Mark, Luke & John):

Gospel of Mani
*Gospel of Marcion**
Gospel of Appelles
Gospel of Bardesanes
Gospel of Basilides
Gospel of Cerinthus

---

*Some scholars suggest that rather than being based on Luke, Marcion may be the source of Luke.

Gospels (and *Epistles, Apocalypses,* and *Letters* not listed) were the early Christian equivalent of televangelism: anyone could write one, and hundreds (possibly thousands) did. As copies could only be made by hand, most of them did not circulate very widely. Non-canonical gospels were suppressed by the Roman church *and* state once Christianity gained a government-granted religious monopoly, and few have survived intact.

For a more complete list, plus commentary, see www.interfaith.org/christianity/apocrypha/, www.nag-hammadi.com/ (the Nag Hammadi Library) and www.newadvent.org/cathen/ 01601a.htm *(Catholic Encyclopedia).* Read some of these gospels at www.earlychristianwritings.com/apocrypha.html

Just How Bad *Is* Original Sin?

Limbo raises the question: just how bad *is* Original Sin?

Augustine's position that unbaptized infants would suffer only mild punishment suggests that Original Sin isn't that much of a transgression.

Aquinas' position that unbaptized infants would enjoy eternal happiness but, being tainted with Original Sin, never experience God's Grace, makes Limbo sound like an *atheist's* idea of heaven — preferable to heaven itself (an atheist is hardly likely to enjoy singing God's graces for the rest of eternity!). On Aquinas' view, Original Sin *is not serious enough to require punishment of any kind!* On this view it follows logically that Original Sin is nothing more than possessing the *ability* to sin — which a new-born infant has yet to exercise.

Augustine, however, undercuts his own position when he calls new-born infants "guileless." Surely, if Original Sin is everything it's cracked up to be, a new-born infant is full of it and looking for every opportunity to commit his or her first sin.

where they'd be punished forever just didn't seem fair. Hence: Limbo, a state where infants would suffer mild punishment (Augustine) or enjoy eternal happiness but, since tainted with Original Sin, would never experience God's grace (Aquinas).

Limbo was never, like Purgatory, *official* Catholic doctrine. The Catechism (1992 version, as in 1261) merely says: "the Church can only entrust them to the mercy of God." Even so, in 1794 Pope Pius VI condemned the dissident "Jansenists," saying their denial of Limbo was "false, rash, and injurious to Catholic education."

In October 2006, an International Theological Commission announced that "Limbo is no longer the common opinion of Catholic theology" — an opinion Pope Benedict concurred with while a Cardinal.

Which takes the church back to square one:

➢ If souls of the unbaptized *cannot* enter Heaven *or* Purgatory, where do they go?

Hell is the only place left.

"Well, You've sent them floods, earthquakes, famines, pestilence, plagues, wars, and hurricanes — of *course* they're fatalistic!"

The Ten[?] Commandments

In Sunday School we are told that Moses went up the mountain where God spoke to him, and gave him two stone tablets upon which were written the Ten Commandments.

However, the Ten Commandments, in the form we're so familiar with, simply *aren't to be found anywhere in the Bible.* Not only that, difference sects have different lists for the Ten Commandments!

What we are told are the Ten Commandments are actually extracted and edited from Chapter 20 of Exodus and/or Chapter 5 of Deuteronomy,* which explains why Judaism and the different Christian creeds do not agree *exactly* on what the Ten Commandments are — as shown on the table opposite.

But are these, in fact, the Ten Commandments that God gave to Moses?

Possibly.

Except...there are actually *fourteen* commandments (fifteen if you split coveting thy neighbour's house from coveting his wife — and if you accept that separation how should you treat the rest of verse 21 which also commands you not to covet thy neighbour's field, manservant, maidservant, ox, ass, "or any *thing* that *is* thy neighbour's"? Add another *six* commandments?).

Nevertheless, at least Deuteronomy states (twice: 4:13 and 10:4) that God wrote "ten commandments" on "two tables of stone" and gave them to Moses...except we're left completely in the dark as *what* "Ten Commandments" God actually wrote!

---

* To quote from the Catholic Encyclopedia: "There is *no numerical division* of the Commandments in the Books of Moses, but the injunctions *are distinctly tenfold*, and are found *almost identical* in both sources." *[Emphasis added.]*

Commandment [from Exodus, Chapter 20: 2-17 King James Version]	Jewish	Anglican, Reformed, and other Christian	Orthodox	Roman Catholic, Lutheran
Division of the Ten Commandments **by religion/denomination**				
I am the LORD thy God	1	Preface		
Thou shalt have none other gods before me	2	1	1	1
Thou shalt not make thee any graven image		2	2	
Thou shalt not take the name of the LORD thy God in vain	3	3	3	2
Remember the sabbath day to keep it holy	4	4	4	3
Thou shalt honour thy father and thy mother	5	5	5	4
Thou shalt not kill	6	6	6	5
Thou shalt not commit adultery	7	7	7	6
Thou shalt not steal	8	8	8	7
Thou shalt not bear false witness against thy neighbour	9	9	9	8
Thou shalt not covet thy neighbour's house*	10	10	10	9
Thou shalt not covet thy neighbour's wife*				10

* These two commandments (or should they be just one?) are taken from Exodus 20:17. But in Chapter 5, verse 21 of Deuteronomy which has a similar list, the order is reversed: Neither shalt thou desire thy neighbour's wife, neither shalt thou covet thy neighbour's house

Table adapted from Wikipedia (en.wikipedia.org/wiki/Ten_Commandments)

The Book of Exodus also tells the story of Moses and the Ten Commandments. But when we turn to it for enlightenment...we only end up more confused.

In Exodus, Chapter 20, Verses 2 to 17, you'll find a list very similar to Deuteronomy's...with the same *fourteen* (or more) Commandments.

But then God *continues,* in Verse 22, speaking to Moses, issuing a long list of further "commandments" which does not end until the last verse of *Chapter 23* — 105 verses in all! These cover a wide range of mostly minutiae, from detailed architectural plans for the altar the Israelites must build to their God and the nature of the sacrifices they must make, to the penalties for stealing your neighbour's ox, ass, sheep or raiment.*

But nowhere in Exodus is there any mention that any of these instructions are "The Ten Commandments."

So let us turn to Chapter 34 of Exodus. Here, at long last, we find a clear statement:

© 2010 baloocartoons.com

© 2010 www.baloocartoons.com / Reproduced by permission

Baloo

"Does this mean everything else is *optional?*"

²⁷ And the LORD said unto Moses, Write thou these words; for after the tenor of these words I have made a covenant with thee and with Israel.

²⁸ And he was there with the LORD forty days and forty nights; he did neither eat bread nor drink water. And he [Moses — see previous verse] wrote upon the tables the words of the covenant, the ten commandments.

But what words did *Moses* write "upon the tables"?

---

* The Jewish scholar Maimonides enumerated these as the "613 Mitzvot" ["mitzvot" means "commandments"]: that's *in addition* to the original ten!

Not the Ten Commandments we are familiar with:

1. Thou shalt worship no other god: for the Lord whose name *is* Jealous *is* a jealous God: Thou shalt make no covenant with the inhabitants of the land, nor take their daughters unto thy, but ye shall destroy their altars, break their images, and cut down their groves *Exodus 34:14-16*

2. Thou shalt make thee no molten idols *Exodus 34:17*

3. The Feast of Unleavened Bread thou shalt keep. Seven days thou shalt eat unleavened bread...in the month of Abib *Exodus 34:18*

4. Every firstling among thy cattle, whether ox or sheep, that is male...is mine *[i.e., sacrificed to Yahweh]* *Exodus 34:19*

5. Six days thou shalt work, but on the seventh day thou shalt rest *Exodus 34:21*

6. Thou shalt observe the feast of weeks, of the first-fruits of wheat harvest, and the feast of ingathering. Thrice in the year shall all your men children appear before the Lord GOD, the God of Israel *Exodus 34:22-23*

7. Thou shalt not offer the blood of my sacrifice with leaven[ed bread] *Exodus 34:25*

8. Neither shall the sacrifice of the feast of the passover be left unto the morning *Exodus 34:25*

9. The first of the first-fruits of thy land thou shalt bring unto the house of the LORD thy God *Exodus 34:26*

10. Thou shalt not seethe [cook] a kid in his mother's milk *Exodus 34:26*

These Commandments are known as "The Ritual Decalogue"—which is edited into this format from the original verses in Exodus. To distinguish them, the "traditional" Ten Commandments are called "The Ethical Decalogue."

For relief, let us turn to the *Catholic Encyclopedia* where we learn:

The system of numeration found in Catholic Bibles, based on the Hebrew text, was made by St. Augustine (fifth century) in his book of "Questions of Exodus" and was adopted by the Council of Trent.*

In other words, the Ten Commandments were *edited* from God's inspired text (on the assumption that the Bible is "The Word of God") but at the end of the day, as even the Catholic Church freely admits, *they are man made.*

If you're *still* confused, what to do?

It's really quite simple: follow the example of St. Augustine and the other great theologians and do as they did: *take your pick.*

"For I am a Jealous God"

From Exodus 20:5

³ Thou shalt have no other gods before me.

⁴ Thou shalt not make unto thee any graven image,† or any likeness *of any thing* that *is* in heaven above, or that *is* in the earth beneath, or that *is* in the water under the earth:

⁵ Thou shalt not bow down thyself to them, nor serve them: for I the LORD thy God am a jealous God, visiting the iniquity of the fathers upon the children unto the third and fourth generation of them that hate me;

These first three paragraphs of the Ten Commandments are perfectly clear — as is the punishment for disobedience.

But why does god feel it necessary to stress: "for I the LORD thy God am a jealous God"?

---

* The Council of Trent (1545-1563) was the 19th Ecumenical Council of the Catholic Church. It was called primarily to counter Martin Luther's "heresies."
† Considering that in just about every church you'll see graven images, paintings or stained-glass images of Jesus (not to mention Mary and even *God* in the Sistine Chapel!) this is a commandment that Christians *and the clergy* routinely ignore.

What (or Who) on earth could he be *jealous* of?

When a woman is jealous it's because her boyfriend or husband is making eyes (or more) at other girls. But such jealousy would be impossible if, like Eve, she was the *only* woman on earth.

So for Jehovah to be "a jealous God" there must be:

> ➤ *Other gods to worship.*

Which he admits by saying: "Thou shalt not bow down thyself to *them,* nor serve *them."*

But are "them" merely false, imaginary gods the ignorant heathens worship — or *actual* gods, in competition with Jehovah?

The evidence of the Bible suggests the latter.

After Adam and Eve had eaten from the tree of knowledge, "the LORD God said, The man has now become like *one of us,* knowing good and evil" (Genesis 3 :21-23).

In Exodus 15:11 we read: "Who *is* like unto thee, O LORD, *among the gods?"* Numbers 33:4 tells us that "the Egyptians buried all their firstborn, which the LORD had smitten among them: *upon their gods* also the LORD executed judgments."

Psalms 82:1 suggests Jehovah is merely one of many members of a *council of gods:* "God standeth in the congregation of the might; he judgeth among the gods," which he reaffirms in verse 6 by saying: "I have said, Ye *are* gods; and all of you *are* children of the most High."

But what happened to all these other gods? Verse 7 of that same psalm — "But ye shall die like men, and fall like one of the princes" — suggests that Jehovah knocked them off.

Hiding From God?

From Genesis Chapter 3

[8] And they [Adam and Eve] heard the voice of the LORD God walking in the garden in the cool of the day: and Adam and his wife hid themselves from the presence of the LORD God amongst the trees of the garden.
[9] And the LORD God called unto Adam, and said unto him, Where art thou?

How could Adam and Eve hide *from God? Why would God need to call: "Where art thou?"*

No one *can hide from an "all-knowing,"* omniscient god.

Clearly, when this passage of Genesis was written, Jehovah had yet to acquire the omniscience he has today — another example of how Jehovah evolved as Judaism slowly became monotheistic.

Most, but not all traces of other gods have been edited out. But "if you read the Hebrew Bible carefully," writes Robin Wright in *The Evolution of God,* "it tells the story of a god in evolution, a god whose character changes radically from beginning to end."[20] On this basis, the Israelites (like everyone else around them) were originally regular, polytheistic pagans. Jehovah was originally a "warrior god," one among many, slowly displacing the other gods until — only in the second century BCE — Judaism became monotheistic with Jehovah as the *only* god.

So when Jehovah said: "Thou shalt have no other gods *before* me" that's exactly what he meant — implying it's okay to have other gods *"after* me."

After all, if Jehovah was the *only* god, it would make more sense for him to say something like:

> There are no other gods but me, and upon those fools who worship imaginary beings of their own creation I shall visit the iniquity of the fathers upon the children unto the third and fourth generation of them that hate me.

Or simply laugh at them.

The Oldest Biblical Manuscripts

Oldest surviving Bible manuscripts: Dead Sea Scrolls, written 250 BCE to 65 CE. Books from the Old Testament, plus commentaries. *(See www.deadseascrollsfoundation.com)*

Oldest surviving New Testament manuscript: fragment of the Gospel of John, dated to ca. A.D. 125. *(See scriptorium.lib. duke.edu/papyrus/texts/manuscripts.html)*

Oldest surviving Bible: The Codex Sinaiticus, written in the fourth century around the time of the Emperor Constantine, hidden for some 1,500 years in St Catherine's Monastery in Sinai, came to light in 1844. It contains two extra books in the New Testament: the Shepherd of Hermas and the Epistle of Barnabas. It also omits some mentions of the ascension of Jesus into heaven, key references to the Resurrection, and the story of the woman taken in adultery and about to be stoned — until Jesus invited anyone without sin to cast the first stone. Nor are there words of forgiveness from the cross: Jesus does not say, "Father forgive them for they know not what they do." *(See more at www.codexsinaiticus.org)*

Books in the Catholic but not most Protestant Bibles: Tobit, Judith, 1 Maccabees, 2 Maccabees, Wisdom, Ecclesiasticus, Baruch. Portions of Esther and Daniel were also excised.

Heavenly Beings

A brief survey

The Christian cosmology is populated with a variety of divine, semi-divine, or damned characters: God, Jesus, the Holy Spirit, the Virgin Mary, the Apostles, nine orders of angels from Archangels like Gabriel to the lesser angels, fallen angels or devils and demons (including Satan), saints, and, of course, the souls of the dead in heaven, hell, Purgatory or Limbo.

All Christian sects agree that **God, Jesus,** and the **Holy Spirit** stand preeminent among all these heavenly beings. Their *relationship* is far from settled, despite the imposition of the "Trinitarian" orthodoxy by the Roman Emperor Constantine in 325 AD (Nicene Creed) which collapsed after the Protestant Reformation in the 16th century. The three main beliefs:

Trinity: Three beings (which are One — but *not* three-in-one) "of the *same substance.*"

Subscribed to by most Christians sects including Catholic, Anglican, Lutheran.

Triumvirate: three *separate* beings united in *purpose* — making *this* version of Christianity no longer monotheistic but *tri*theistic.

Currently held by Iglesia ni Cristo, Most Holy Church of God in Christ Jesus, the Unification Church. Jehovah's Witnesses, Christadelphians, The Church of Jesus Christ of Latter-day Saints (Mormons), and Unitarians. In the past: Cathars (a 13th century "heretical" movement which was violently suppressed), and Adoptionists, Arians, Ebionites, some Gnostics, and Marcionites in the early centuries of Christianity.

Oneness: One being who manifests himself as God, Jesus, the Holy Spirit, or any other way he chooses — as when he spoke to Moses from a burning bush.

Held by Pentecostals.

Whichever of these dogmas a believer accepts, in daily life the average Christian thinks of God, Jesus, and the Holy Spirit as three separate beings and prays to them as individuals.

On the next rung come the **Virgin Mary** and **Satan**.

Mary is the most *loved and revered* of all the heavenly entities, probably because she is the only heavenly being no one has any reason to *fear*. Indeed, Mary as the gentle and loving "Divine Mother"

The "**Mystery**" of the Trinity

From the *Catholic Encyclopedia:*

"In the words of the Athanasian Creed: "the Father is God, the Son is God, and the Holy Spirit is God, and yet there are not three Gods but one God."

In this Trinity of Persons the Son is begotten of the Father by an eternal generation, and the Holy Spirit proceeds by an eternal procession from the Father and the Son.

Yet, notwithstanding this difference as to origin, the Persons are co-eternal and co-equal: all alike are uncreated and omnipotent....

The Vatican Council has explained... that a mystery is a truth which we are not merely incapable of discovering apart from Divine Revelation, but which, even when revealed, remains "hidden by the veil of faith and enveloped, so to speak, by a kind of darkness"."

---

completes the "Holy Family": she counterbalances the fearful, angry Father, mirroring the earthly patriarchal family.

But, as in the family where the father rules with an iron fist, "Mother Mary" has *no heavenly power,* but may have *influence*. Although, given the way Jesus treated her (see Matthew 12:46-49, page 30) she probably has no heavenly influence either.

Satan's "job description" is to tempt us all away from God. As an archangel, Satan is second only to God, Jesus, and the Holy Spirit in power, though in the end he is trumped by another archangel, St. Michael, so ranking fifth in the hierarchy of heavenly power.

With the exception of the possibly apocryphal devil worshippers, no one actually *prays* to Satan. And despite the continual warnings to avoid his temptations, Christians have far more reason to fear God than they do to fear Satan.

Saints

In Judaism, "saintliness"* is considered "one of the attributes of God."[21] While the Rabbis styled some people as "saints," it was more a term of admiration and reverence than a formal "beatification" as in Christianity.

Saints also appear in the Bible, but with no clues as to where they came from, who created them, why, or what they can do. They are often mentioned only in passing, as in their first appearance in Deuteronomy 33:2: "The LORD came... with ten thousands of saints...."

In the early Christian church saints were acclaimed by local congregations. Only in 1634 did Pope Urban VII reserve the process of beatification and canonization of saints in the Catholic church for the Holy See.

Only the Catholic church has a formal process of canonization. Protestant, Orthodox and other Christian sects also recognize and create saints — though not always the *same* saints. To give just one example, Martin Luther King is considered a saint by the Anglican and Episcopal churches but not by the Catholic church (though many Catholics, no doubt, consider him "saintly").

---

* A higher state than holiness, "saintliness" is defined by the *Jewish Encyclopedia* as "a divine and lofty type of piety, and a higher morality."

Christianity's Monotheism: A Pantheon of Gods?

THE TRINITY

TRINITY   **OR**   **TRIUMVIRATE**   **OR**   **ONENESS**

Jesus — God — Holy Spirit

God — Jesus — Holy Spirit

God — Jesus — Holy Spirit
Or any way he likes

Virgin Mary
[Fourth member of the Trinity]

Satan
[Fallen Archangel]

SAINTS

Peter
*Patron of Fisherman
and Ship builders*

Paul
*Patron of Authors, Press,
Publishers and Writers*

The Other Apostles

Augustine
Patron of Theologians

Thomas Aquinas
Patron of Universities and Students

John the Baptist
*Patron of Baptism,
Conversion and Tailors*

Mary Magdalene
*Patron of Frail and
Penitent Women*

Francis of Assisi
*Patron of Animals, Birds, Fire,
Merchants and Solitary death*

Dominic Ignatius Loyola
*Patron of Jesuit Order
and Retreats*

Lesser Saints

*Over 10,000 saints have been beatified by the Vatican — but nobody's ever
done a headcount so the actual total is not known. Herewith, a selection:*

Agnes, Patron of Chastity and Girl Scouts
Alban, Patron of Refugees
Benedict, Patron of Monks and Poisoning
Bonaventura, Patron of Bowel disorders
Christina, Patron of Millers, Insanity and Psychiatrists
Christopher, Patron of Bachelors, Drivers, Travel and Travellers
Clare of Assisi, Patron of Television
Clement, Patron of Tanners and Mariners
Dominic Savio, Patron of Choir members
Dominic, Patron of Astronomers and Astronomy
Eustace, Patron of Hunters and those facing adversity
Florian, Patron of Austria, Firefighters and chimney sweeps
Germaine, Patron of Child abuse
Giles, Patron of the Disabled, Beggars and Lepers
Gregory the Great, Patron of Teachers, Students and Musicians

Helena, Patron of Archaeologists
Hippolytus, Patron of horses, prisons and prison officers
Hubert, Patron of Hunters and Mathematicians
Jude, Patron of Desperation and Hopeless causes
Lidwina, Patron of Skaters
Margaret, Patron of Homelessness
Mark, Patron of Venice, Glaziers and Stained glass workers
Martin de Porres, Patron of Negroes
Norbert, Patron of Peasants
Patrick, Patron of Ireland, Snake bites and Tooth ache
Peter the Martyr, Patron of Inquisitors and Midwives
Roch, Patron of Dogs, Plague and Pestilence
Theresa of Avila, Patron of Headache sufferers
Victor of Marseilles, Patron of Torture Victims
Winifred, Patron of Virgins

ANGELS

Gabriel
Archangel

St. Michael
Archangel

Plus an unknown number of "ordinary" angels and "guardian" angels, rarely named

FALLEN ANGELS

Satan, *also called Lucifer, Beezelbub and the Devil, and an unspecified
number of unnamed demons and lesser devils — Satan's assistants.*

The Catholic Church has beatified over 10,000 people* "whose lives have been marked by the exercise of heroic virtue" as saints. "The Church see[s] in the saints nothing more than friends and servants of God whose holy lives have made them worthy of His special love. She does not pretend to make gods."

So saints should be *venerated* for their holiness by laity and priest alike, and may be worshipped as "we can be helped by the prayers of the saints, and ask their intercession with humility."[22]

In practice, however, Christians pray *to* the saints as if they were minor deities — especially of course to Saint "Primus Inter Pares": the Virgin Mary.

But saints are no more than human, "a little less than the angels" (Psalm 8:6), so have no more heavenly power than we do (and there is no Biblical evidence that God has granted them such power).

"Osgood was a theologian back on Earth, and he thought all this stuff would be allegorical."

Even so, most Christians believe saints *can* intercede with God on their behalf — another belief with no Biblical support.

---

* The exact number of saints is unknown as no one has done a headcount.

To the contrary, the saints' relationship to God seems no different from man's:

From Psalm 89

[7] ***God is greatly to be feared*** in the assembly of the saints, and to be had in reverence of all them that are about him.

Even so, Christians pray more often to saints than to angels who *do* have heavenly power — *and* direct access to God.

Hierarchy of WORSHIP	Hierarchy of POWER
God / Jesus	God
Virgin Mary	Jesus
Holy Spirit	Holy Spirit
Saints	Michael
Angels	Satan
	Angels

NOTE: The "Hierarchy of Worship" is an estimated average, and will vary from one worshipper or sect to another. But considering the number of "Hail Marys" recited every day (as penance for Catholics and when saying the rosary) it's quite likely that the Virgin Mary is the most-prayed-to of all heavenly beings.

Angels

"Angels of the LORD" appear frequently in the Bible, mainly as messengers ("angel" comes, via Greek and Latin, from the Hebrew for "one going" or "one sent" — hence "messenger"[23]). They are usually unnamed, with three major exceptions:

Gabriel, who visited Mary to tell her she would give birth to a divine child;

Michael, who first appears in the Book of Daniel, and again in Revelation when he casts Satan out of heaven. Michael is considered the "prince of angels"; he is also a saint. He is also Israel's representative in heaven, according to the *Jewish Encyclopedia;*

Satan, a "fallen angel," who appears far more often than the other two combined.

Angels were created by God "between God and man." Thus, they are more powerful than man, and less powerful than God. Beings of pure spirit without material form, they can nevertheless act in the material world:

From 2 Kings Chapter 19

[35] And it came to pass that night, that the angel of the LORD went out, and smote in the camp of the Assyrians an hundred fourscore and five thousand: and when they arose early in the morning, behold, they were all dead corpses.

But *when* did God create the angels? The first "Angel of the LORD" appears in Genesis 16:7 — yet nowhere in the story of the creation (Genesis 1 & 2) is there any mention of how angels came into being.

© 2010 baloocartoons.com

Bʒlα

"All those things you say about Satan — isn't that negative campaigning?"

If, as is commonly believed, the serpent in the Garden of Eden was Satan in disguise (see *Fallen Angels),* then angels must have been created *before* man,* *and* Satan must have already decided to challenge God's rule of the universe.

---

* "Behind the disobedient choice of our first parents [Adam and Eve] lurks a seductive voice, opposed to God, which, out of envy makes them fall into death. Scripture and the Church's Tradition see in this being a fallen angel, called 'Satan' or the 'devil'." From the Catechism of the Catholic Church, www.vatican.va/archive/catechism/p1s2c1p7. htm#II.

Even though the angels' "heavenly power" is greater than man's, it appears that their primary role is as God's attendants, and (with the *possible* exception of "Fallen Angels") to strictly carry out God's instructions whether as messengers or agents of destruction.

There are, according to St. Gregory the Great, nine different orders of Angels (Angels, Archangels, Virtues, Powers, Principalities, Dominations, Throne, Cherubim and Seraphim), plus "Guardian Angels"* ["For he shall give his angels charge over thee, to keep thee in all thy ways" (Psalm 91:11)].

> ## Jesus and the Angels
>
> *From* Hebrews 1:6
>
> And again, when he bringeth in the firstbegotten into the world, he saith, **And let all the angels of God worship him.**
>
> *So Jesus is **higher** than the angels*
>
> *From* Hebrews 2:9
>
> But we see Jesus, who was made **a little lower than the angels**...
>
> *So the angels are **more powerful** than Jesus (so how can he be part of the Trinity?) Except that...*
>
> *From* 1 Peter 3:22
>
> Who is gone into heaven, and is on the right hand of God; angels and authorities and powers being made subject unto him.

"The dignity of a soul is so great," St. Jerome wrote, "that each [including "infidels"?] has a guardian angel from its birth."[24]

But, given the amount of sin in the world, these "guardian angels" clearly haven't been doing their job very well.

---

* Whether Guardian Angels constitute a *tenth* order, or is a role given to one or more of the other orders, is not clear.

Fallen Angels

Satan is, perhaps, the most intriguing character in the Christian pantheon. He appears in the first and last books of the Bible, and many times in between.

In Genesis he is assumed to be the serpent, the tempter of Eve: "In the story of the Fall, the original cause of evil is the serpent, which in later Jewish tradition is identified with Satan,"[25] with the following passage cited as evidence:

From Wisdom Chapter 2

[23] For God created man incorruptible, and to the image of his own likeness he made him.

[24] But by the envy of the devil [as the serpent], death came into the world:*[26]

...and in Revelation, the *last* book of the Bible, Satan appears as a dragon:

From Revelation Chapter 12

[7] And there was war in heaven: Michael and his angels fought against the dragon [Satan]; and the dragon fought....

[9] And the great dragon was cast out, that old serpent, called the Devil, and Satan, which deceiveth the whole world: he was cast out into the earth, and his angels were cast out with him.†

Since the Book of Revelation is often considered to be the "prediction" of Judgement Day and the End of the World, this would imply that *Satan will stay in heaven until God's Kingdom comes,* contradicting the general belief that Satan

---

* This view is flatly contradicted by Genesis 3:14: "And the LORD God said unto the serpent, Because thou hast done this, thou art cursed above all cattle, and above every beast of the field; ***upon thy belly shalt thou go, and dust shalt thou eat all the days of thy life.***" In other words: the serpent was a serpent, not Satan in disguise.

† "The similarity between scenes such as these and the early Babylonian accounts of the struggle between Merodach and the dragon Tiamat is very striking." *Catholic Encyclopedia.*

is now residing as the "prince of darkness" in hell. Indeed, in the Old Testament Satan often appears with "the LORD" in heaven...

From Job Chapter 1
⁶ Now there was a day when the sons of God came to present themselves before the LORD, and Satan came also among them.
...and even "preempts Jesus" at *God's right hand:*

From Zechariah Chapter 3
¹ And he shewed me Joshua the high priest standing before the angel of the LORD, **and Satan standing at his right hand** to resist him.

Satan and the "Problem of Evil"

Why was Satan welcome in heaven (even if, as the *Catholic Encyclopedia* insists, "on sufferance")?

To receive his instructions from God:

From Job Chapter 1
¹² And the LORD said unto Satan, Behold, all that he [Job] hath is in thy power; only upon himself put not forth thine hand. So Satan went forth from the presence of the LORD.
...and proceeded to destroy Job's crops, oxen, servants, sheep, camels. But, *obeying God,* "put not forth" his hand against Job.

All in all, there is considerable Biblical and theological confusion about Satan's place in God's scheme.
— Satan defied God (the "Fall") in time to make his first appearance as the serpent tempting Eve — yet (Revelation) he won't be thrown out of heaven until Judgement Day.

— Fallen angels were damned and banished from heaven — yet Satan appears there, even sitting at God's right hand.

— Satan (with his devils and demons) is assumed to be the instigator of evil in the world — yet at times Satan not only acts on God's explicit instructions, *he obeys them to the letter.*

— God's powers far exceed Satan's: God created Satan and could zap him at any moment. So why doesn't he?

One can only wonder whether God *approves* of what Satan is up to — and even that Satan is *always* acting at God's command.

As the Catholic Catechism puts it: "It is a great mystery that providence should permit diabolical activity" — a statement which conveniently ignores the inescapable Biblical evidence that God not only *permits* evil to exist, but *he kills, murders, and maims people himself — or sends plagues, fire, floods or "good" angels to do it for him.*

Ultimately, the "Problem of Evil" was best summarized by the Greek philosopher Epicurus some 2,500 years ago:

[If the gods] have the will to remove evil and cannot, then they are not omnipotent.

If they can but will not, then they are not benevolent.

If they are neither able nor willing, they are neither omnipotent nor benevolent.

Lastly, if they are both able and willing to annihilate evil, why does it exist?

4

Reason, Science
and the Church

"Nothing is to be accepted save on the authority
of scripture, since greater is the authority of
scripture than all the powers of the human mind."
— *St. Augustine in* De Genesi

"Before Adam's sin none of [the animals]
attempted to devour or in any wise hurt one
another; the spider was as harmless as the fly!"
— *John Wesley, founder of Methodism*

"[Stephen] Hawking is attempting [in his book *A
Brief History of Time*], as he explicitly states, to
understand the mind of God. And this makes all
the more unexpected the conclusion of the effort,
at least so far: a universe with no edge in space,
no beginning or end in time, and nothing for a
Creator to do."
— *Carl Sagan, in his Introduction*

"Your Highness, I have no need of this hypothesis."
— *Pierre Laplace to Napoleon on why his works
on celestial mechanics made no mention of God*

The Supremacy of Faith

When Christianity was declared Rome's monopoly religion in 380 CE by Emperor Theodosius, all competing religions — including Christian sects not obeying the doctrinal edicts of Rome — *and* Greek knowledge were violently suppressed by the combined forces of church and state. Books were burned, the library at Alexandria was pillaged, faith and revelation replaced reason and experimentation as the only sources of knowledge, literacy plunged, and Europe entered the "Dark Ages."

The Bible was in Latin, the language of Catholic services (a practice only discontinued in the 1960s). Access was, therefore, restricted to people who could speak *and read* Latin — mostly monks and nuns. So the populace at large was entirely dependent on their priests for their knowledge of what God and the Bible actually *said.*

> **"Unless witchcraft is true, nothing in the Bible is true."**
> — *John Wesley, founder of Methodism*

Christendom, in other words, was one enormous Sunday School.

Unsurprisingly in a context where the authority of the scriptures became absolute, they became the source of scientific pronouncements.

The Science of the Bible:

The Creation

The Bible begins [Genesis 1]:

¹ In the beginning God created the heaven and the earth.

² And the earth was without form, and void; and darkness was

upon the face of the deep. And the Spirit of God moved upon the face of the waters.

3 And God said, Let there be light: and there was light.

4 And God saw the light, that it was good: and God divided the light from the darkness.

5 And God called the light Day, and the darkness he called Night. And the evening and the morning were the first day.

God created light on the first day — but he doesn't get around to creating any *source* of light until the *fourth* day. And there's no known scientific basis for the existence of light *without* a source.

And what does it mean to "divide the light from the darkness"? Darkness, after all, is merely the *absence* of *light.*

On the third day, God created grass, herbs, fruits, and (presumably) the other plants which all flourished *before* the creation of a life-giving sun.

Eventually, on the *fourth* day, God gets around to creating the sun and the moon:

16 And God made two great lights; the greater light to rule the day, and the lesser light to rule the night: he made the stars also.

17 And God set them in the firmament of the heaven to give light upon the earth,

18 And to rule over the day and over the night, and to divide the light from the darkness: and God saw that it was good.

19 And the evening and the morning were the fourth day.

So God created *"two great lights":* the sun and the moon. But the moon, as we know, is not a light, it's a *reflector* of light. And why did he need to "set them in the firmament of the heaven to give light upon the earth" and "to divide the light from the darkness" when he's already created light and divided it from the darkness? Isn't he repeating himself?

At the end of the sixth day "God saw every thing that he had made, and, behold, it was very good" [Genesis 1:31].

But didn't take long for him to see the "error of his ways" "And it repented the LORD that he had made man on the earth, and it grieved him at his heart" [Genesis 6:6].

So he decides to destroy his creation by drowning everyone (and every thing).

The Flood

Why a flood? Since God created man why not simply strike all the evil people dead? And since his *rationale* for the flood is that he "saw that the wickedness of man was great in the earth" [Genesis 6:5] why does he *also* decide to destroy *every* animal — and why does "it repenteth me that I have made them"? [Genesis 6:7]. No reason is given.

And if he "repenteth" at his creation of the animals, why then enlist Noah's aid to *save them?*

Be that as it may, it's worth examining the story of the flood in some detail — and the details provided in the Bible are unusually clear.

The cause of the flood: rain. "And the rain was upon the earth forty days and forty nights" [Genesis 7:12]; "And the waters prevailed exceedingly upon the earth; and all the high hills, that were under the whole heaven, were covered" [Genesis 7:19].

So the entire world was covered with water — every patch of earth, no matter how high.

The results were predictable [Genesis 7:21-23]:

21 And all flesh died that moved upon the earth, both of fowl, and of cattle, and of beast, and of every creeping thing that creepeth upon the earth, and every man:

22 All in whose nostrils was the breath of life, of all that was in the dry land, died.

23 And ***every living substance was destroyed which was upon the face of the ground***, both man, and cattle, and the creeping

things, and the fowl of the heaven; and they were destroyed from the earth: and Noah only remained alive, and they that were with him in the ark.

That seems pretty straightforward...but Genesis 7:20 specifies exactly how *deep* the flood waters were:

20 Fifteen cubits upward did the waters prevail; and the mountains were covered.

Considering that the highest point of the earth is the tip of Mount Everest, 8,848 meters, *one* cubit must be a pretty long measure.

Except it isn't.

Like the foot, the cubit is a measurement based on the human body. If you bunch your fingers onto the tip of your thumb, the cubit is the distance from the tips of your fingers to your elbow.

Used as a unit of measurement in Babylon, Persia, Mesopotamia, Greece, Rome, Arabia and elsewhere in the ancient world, cubits varied considerably in length, from 428.1 mm (16.85 inches) in the First Temple period of Israel to 650.2 mm (25.6 inches), the Arab cubit.[27]

Which means the 15-cubit depth of the flood was somewhere between 6.42 and 9.75 *meters.*

Whichever cubit you use, it's way short of the 8,848 meter height of Mount Everest. Nor does it make much of a flood at the top of the somewhat closer Mount Sinai, 2,285 meters high.

Whichever way you look at it, God *didn't* achieve his aim of destroying "All in whose nostrils was the breath of life."

The Ark

Noah's Ark, according to God's instructions, was to carry "every living thing of all flesh, two of every *sort* shall thee bring into the ark, to keep *them* alive with thee; they shall be male and female" [Genesis 7:19] (but *seven* of "every clean beast*...[and] fowls also of the air" [Genesis 7:2-3]).

Exactly how many animals is "every *sort*"? Today, there are 1,250,000 *known* animal species (including insects, fishes, reptiles, amphibians, mollusks, and, of course, mammals) — and, perhaps, many more. Assuming Noah didn't need to take the 30,000-odd salt-water fishes, he "only" had to carry 1,220,000 species — or *2.4 million* insects and animals, with one of each sex. Plus the food to keep them all alive for 150 days.[†]

To put this in perspective, the San Diego Zoo is the world's largest. It covers 100 acres and employs 1,900 staff to look after just 4,000 animals from 800 species — 0.07% of the number of species Noah and his family had to contend with.

So exactly what sort of vessel was the ark?

God's instructions on the design and building of the ark are very clear [Genesis 6:14-15]:

[14] Make thee an ark of gopher wood;[‡] rooms shalt thou make in the ark, and shalt pitch it within and without with pitch.

[15] And this *is the fashion* which thou shalt make it *of:* The length of the ark *shall be* three hundred cubits, and the height of it thirty cubits.

Using the standardized measure of one cubit = .472 meters, the ark's length of 300 cubits is 141.6 meters or 464.5 feet; its height of thirty cubits is 14.2 meters or 46.5 feet.

God doesn't specify the beam (or width). So let's look at a similar ship, the six-masted schooner *Wyoming,* which

---

* That can be eaten according to Jewish dietary laws.
† "And the waters prevailed upon the earth an hundred and fifty days" [Genesis 6:24].
‡ What is "gopher wood"? Nobody knows. Various possibilities suggested include cypress, pine, cedar, "squared timber" or possibly even willow-branches and palm leaves woven together like basket-work with bitumen on the inside — this type of vessel was know as "kufa" (From the *Jewish Encyclopedia* [www.jewishencyclopedia.com/view. jsp?artid=365&letter=G]: "kufa" (Arabic, "kufr" = Hebrew "kofer" = "gofer")

is the largest wooden ship ever built in recorded history; it was completed in 1909 in Bath, Maine.

The *Wyoming* was 100.4 meters long (140 meters including the jib and spanker booms — about as long as a 30-storey building is high) and 15.3 meters wide; nearly as big as a modern-day US Navy frigate.

The *Wyoming*'s draft was 9.3 meters — so it needed a depth of 10 meters at the bare minimum or it would run aground. Given that God's flood covered

Couldn't Evolution Produce all the Species *After* the Flood?

But perhaps Noah took just a hundred-odd animals, and the rest evolved after the flood.

If God created the universe in 4004 BCE, as per the Biblical schedule, the flood must have happened some 5,000-5,500 years ago. That's just not long enough for more than a handful of species to have evolved.

In any case, creationists who might otherwise make this argument *don't believe evolution works.* So for creationists and evolutionists both, there's only *one* way for those 1,220,000 species to exist today: they *all* went with Noah on the Ark.

Oh...and one other thing: we haven't considered the millions of species of bacteria and viruses which would also have been made extinct by the death of their hosts. Noah must have carried them too.

the world only to a depth of 15 cubits, or *7.08 meters,* if the ark was anything like the *Wyoming* it would never have left the ground.

Of course the Ark, unlike the *Wyoming,* wasn't going anywhere. But if the tip of Mount Everest was covered at low tide, with no land to disperse storms the seas would have been ferocious — not to mention the blinding rain and icebergs (ice floats on water, so the polar icecaps would break up), some, no doubt, bigger than the *Titanic.* So the Ark would

And the Dinosaurs?

"All dinosaurs died out when they came out of Noah's Ark after the great flood. They were baby Dino's or even eggs, but as they grew older there was no lush vegetation too eat, because the climate was completely different to what it was before the flood.*"

*Hmm. Wonder how Noah managed to lasso a couple of Brontosauruses —
not to mention a pair of* Tyrannosaurus Rex *(even baby ones)? And then stop them from eating all the other animals on the Ark? What a guy!*

have *had* to have been a very strong ship — and Noah an excellent sailor.

The *Wyoming* had a cargo capacity of 8,600 cubic meters. If Noah's Ark had a similar capacity, the *two animals* of each *species* could be allocated an average space of just seven cubic *millimeters.* That's a tiny cube just 2.65 millimeters or about one inch *per side.* And that calculation doesn't allow for any storage space for the animals' food.

So the ark must have been *significantly* bigger than the *Wyoming* — bigger, at least than the world's largest supertanker!

The *Wyoming* was built in a shipyard by hundreds of experienced carpenters, shipwrights, and workmen using modern technology. Nevertheless, when the *Wyoming* put to sea it had a serious problem: due to the length of its wooden construction it *flexed* in high seas — and constantly *leaked.* Its crew of thirteen to fourteen had to continually pump water *out* to keep the *Wyoming* from sinking.

The Ark, by comparison, had a crew of just *eight people.* And while the crew of the *Wyoming* only had to sail their vessel, the crew of the Ark *also* had to look after two and a half *million* animals: not only feed them, but shovel their

---

* A comment on "Bang goes that theory: Dinosaur extinction due to volcano NOT asteroid" [A Flatroofer] at www.dailymail.co.uk/sciencetech/article-1173846/Bang-goes-theory-Dinosaur-extinction-volcano-NOT-asteroid.html

excrement over the side. (Think of hippopotami, giraffes, rhinos and elephants — just to start with!) In sum, the

> **"**The biblical account of Noah's Ark and the Flood is perhaps the most implausible story for fundamentalists to defend. Where, for example, while loading his ark, did Noah find penguins and polar bears in Palestine?**"**
> — *Judith Hayes*
> *And don't forget the piranhas, Noah!*

Ark had to have been a *far* bigger vessel than the *Wyoming* — and so far more complex. There's no mention in the Bible that God helped Noah build the Ark, or sail it — and nor is there any suggestion that Noah had any expertise as a shipwright.

There is just one clue to a possible solution, however: Genesis 5:32 tells us that "Noah was five hundred years old." The rains that caused the flood began on Noah's six hundredth birthday [Genesis 7:11]: perhaps because it took him a hundred years to build the monster Ark with the available, primitive, technology.*

One other thing: Genesis 7:4 tells us that God gave Noah just *seven days' notice* of the coming flood. Only *then* did Noah set out to

"I hope you don't mind — I just *had* to get some fresh air!"

collect the animals — all 2,440,000+ of them.

A super-human effort indeed!

---

* But if Noah was 600 years old, how come he had only *three children*?

After the Flood

After the flood "God blessed Noah and his sons, and said unto them, Be fruitful and multiply" [Genesis 9:1].

Reading the rest of Genesis chapter 9 and beyond, it's quite clear that's exactly what Noah and the animals did.

There's just one problem.

After being under water for 150 days, *all* vegetable life would die. The whole land would be a muddy desert. So after the flood, what did Noah and the animals he carried on the ark *eat*?

God's instructions to Noah do *not* include collecting the seeds of all *plant* species to re-vegetate the dead, post-flood earth — *or* carrying enough food to last until the first harvest came in.

The Earth: Flat or Round?

While not made explicit, the idea that the earth is flat is embedded in the Bible.

For example, Isaiah 48:13 tells us "Mine [God's] hand also **hath laid the foundation of the earth,**" implying that the earth was built like a house, the land standing on a solid foundation (or held up on pillars, if Job 9:6 is to be believed: "Which shaketh the earth out of her place, **and the pillars thereof tremble.**")

While Jesus is fasting in the desert for forty days and forty nights "the devil taketh him up into an exceeding high mountain, and sheweth him **all the kingdoms of the world**" [Matthew 4:8]. This view of the earth's size is repeated in Matthew 24:30: when Jesus is in heaven "then shall **all the tribes of the earth mourn,** and **they shall see** the Son of man coming in the clouds of heaven with power and great glory," and repeated in Revelation 1:7.

If, from the top of a high mountain Jesus can see *all* the "kingdoms of the world," and if *"all the tribes of earth... shall see"* him ascending to heaven, the earth must be a small, flat disc.

The Inhabitants of the Antipodes?

In the four hundred years before Christianity became the monopoly religion of the Roman empire, it existed as a "minnow" in the "sea" of Graeco-Roman thought and various concepts of Greek cosmology crept into Christian theology.

One was Aristotle's theory of the "heavenly spheres," with a *stationary* (and *round)* earth at the center, surrounded by spheres holding the moon, planets, sun and stars. This view is in harmony with passages stating "the world also shall be stable, that it be not moved" [1 Chronicles 16:30], "the world also is stablished, that it cannot be moved" [Psalm 93:1] and the story in Joshua 10:13 where, after Joshua spoke to God, God commanded the sun and moon to stay still:

> **"**It would evidently be absurd to argue with an atheist or a thoroughgoing agnostic as to the possibility of miracles. As he does not acknowledge the existence of God, to discuss whether God can work miracles would be a waste of time.... Unless miracles are acknowledged to be possible they cannot be adduced as evidential facts, so that the fundamental theses of Natural Theology and of Theism are presupposed by the discussion of miracle, and cannot be proved by it**"**
> — *R.P. Phillips,* Modern Thomistic Philosophy[28]

13 And **the sun stood still,** and **the moon stayed,** until the people had avenged themselves upon their enemies. Is not

this written in the book of Jasher? *So the sun stood still in the midst of heaven, and hasted not to go down about a whole day.*

In the ninth chapter of his *City of God,* "Whether We Are To Believe In The Antipodes," St. Augustine relies on *Aristotle's* cosmology when he writes:

> "But as to the *fable* that there are Antipodes, that is to say, men on the opposite side of the earth, where the sun rises when it sets to us, men who walk with their feet opposite ours, *that is on no ground credible."*

The reason?

> "For Scripture, which proves the truth of its historical statements by the accomplishment of its prophecies, *gives no false information;* and *it is too absurd to say,* that some men might have taken ship and traversed the whole wide ocean, and crossed from this side of the world to the other, and that thus even the inhabitants of that distant region are descended from that one first man."

In a similar vein, Father Procopius (c. 465-528 CE) claims that the Antipodeans are theologically impossible. "If there be men on the other side of the earth, Christ must have gone there and suffered a second time to save them; and therefore there must have been, as necessary preliminaries to his coming, a duplicate Adam, Eden, serpent, and Deluge!"

Christopher Columbus

When Columbus was trying to sell King Ferdinand of Spain on his idea of reaching India and even the Holy Land by sailing *west* instead of around the Cape of Good Hope, the King assembled a council of astronomers and cosmographers. Known as the Council of Salamanca, in 1487 it solemnly decided against Columbus's theory of the rotundity of the earth and the antipodes, declaring that texts of Scripture and "the Fathers" were opposed to such an idea; that, as Father St.

Augustine said, "If there were any antipodes, the Bible would have said so."*

The Bible and Medicine

The Bible was also a source of medical practice. Origen (c 185-c 254 CE), one of the early church fathers, advises that: "It is demons which produce famine, unfruitfulness, corruptions of the air, and pestilences; they hover concealed in clouds in the lower atmosphere, and are attracted by the blood and incense which the heathen offer to them as gods."

Augustine agrees: "All diseases of Christians are to be ascribed to these demons; chiefly do they torment fresh-baptized Christians, yea, even the guileless, new-born infants!"† And Father St. Bernard warned his monks that "to seek relief from disease in medicine was in harmony neither with religion nor with the honor and purity of their order." (This strain of thinking persists to this day in the misnamed sect of *Christian Science*.)

It could be argued that such misguided claims were merely a result of ignorance. If so, it was *willful ignorance,* as church and state combined to suppress all that was known before, and persecuted all "non-official" thought as "heresy."

> **"The Black Death** (the plague) is a "pestilence with which God is afflicting the Christian people."
> — *Pope Clement VI, Papal Bull issued September, 1348*[29]

---

* Five years later, Columbus persuaded Queen Isabella, Ferdinand's wife, to finance his expedition.
† Hmm. It was *Augustine* who codified the doctrine that humans were born with Original Sin — and that babies born unbaptized went to hell. Yet, they're "guileless"??

"Oh Jonah, he lived in de whale...
Well, it ain't necessarily so"

From *It Ain't Necessarily So,* by George Gershwin (from Porgy & Bess)

The story of Jonah and the whale is a Sunday School favorite.

God told Jonah to go to Nineveh "and cry against it; for their wickedness is come up before me" [Jonah 1:2]. Instead (the Bible doesn't say why) Jonah jumped on a ship heading "unto Tarshish,"* so God sent a great wind which whipped up "a mighty tempest in the sea, so that the ship was like to be broken" [Jonah 1:4].

When the sailors discovered that Jonah had aroused God's anger by disobeying his command, they threw him overboard where he was swallowed by the whale. Jonah prayed fiercely for three days, so God relented and "spake unto the fish, and it vomited out Jonah upon the dry land" [Jonah 2:10].

This story brings up rather obvious questions:

1. What kind of fish, if any, could swallow a man whole? and,

2. If there *is* such a fish, could a man live in its stomach for three days?

Whales are potentially large enough to be candidates (and, of course, whales aren't fish; they're mammals).

There are two main kinds of whales: *baleen* whales and *horned-tooth* whales. Baleen whales have enormous mouths and feed on krill, but their throats are only a few inches in diameter.

Horned-toothed whales *(odontocetous)* have slicing teeth and throats large enough to swallow chunks of fish and gigantic squid. Most, though, are too small to swallow a man whole, except for the sperm whale and the giant beaked whale.

---

* "Tarshish is either Tarsus, a village in Lebanon 1,400 meters above sea level, or simply means "somewhere far away." Another possibility: "ships of Tarshish" may have been a term for "trading ships" in general.

On "Interpreting" the Bible

If, as skeptics and atheists claim, the Bible was no more than a collection of ancient myths, legends and fairytales, mixed with a few grains of truth, then no one would bother analyzing the veracity of the stories of the Creation, Noah and the Flood, or Jonah and the Whale, just as nobody has ever cared to attempt to establish the truth (or fantasy) of *Jack and the Beanstalk, Rapunzel,* or *Goldilocks and the Three Bears.*

We all *know* they're fairytales — and present them to our children as such.

But if, as more than a billion people believe, the Bible is the Word of God, we must address these questions:

1. If the Bible *isn't* the *literal* Word of God, what *is* it?
2. If God speaks *metaphorically* through "divinely inspired" — but *fallible* — humans who wrote the books of the Bible, then God's meaning is hidden and his words are open to interpretation.
3. If the Bible requires interpretation, *whose* interpretation is the right one?

Two thousand years and 22,000+ disputing sects of Christianity later, these questions still remain unanswered.

So the approach of this book is to take the "fundamentalist" position: that the Bible is the *literal* and therefore True Word of God...and let the chips fall where they may.

On the Other Hand...

"St Augustine (354-430), a major authority for both Catholics and Protestants, insisted that if a biblical text contradicted reputable science, it must be interpreted allegorically.**"** — *Karen Armstrong*
Soooo...which part(s) of the Bible should NOT be interpreted allegorically?

As the giant beaked whale lives only in polar regions, the sperm whale, found anywhere in the seven seas including the eastern Mediterranean, is the primary candidate.

A sperm whale can be 20.5 meters (67 feet) long — 11 times the height of a tall man. Its jawbone is about 25% of its length — up to five meters (16½ feet), so its mouth is large enough to snap shut around Jonah without slicing off his feet or head; its throat is also large enough for Jonah to have slid down, so long as he's slightly built.

The sperm whales' favorite foods are the giant squid and the colossal squid, which live up to *three kilometers* (1.9 miles) *below* the ocean surface. These creatures can be up to 13 meters (42½ feet) long, but as most of their length is tentacles, their bodies are, at best, 4 meters (13 feet) long and 1½ meters (5 feet) in diameter. So it seems a sperm whale *could* swallow a man whole.

Other possibilities have been suggested, like the Great White Shark — but whale, shark, or something else there's an insuperable problem: once swallowed, "Jonah was in the belly of the fish three days and three nights" [Jonah 2:17], which raises the obvious question: *how did he survive without oxygen* which isn't to be found in *any* fish's or whale's stomach.

What's more, for those "three days and three nights" Jonah's only protection against stomach acids and digestive processes was "the weeds...wrapped about my head"
[Jonah 2:5]. They *may* have "protected" him just long enough for him to die of oxygen starvation. Or, more likely, drowning from gulping stomach acids (not a nice way to go).

"The sad thing is, Jonah's so afraid of the water now, he won't even take a *bath*."

But *"the LORD had prepared a great fish* to swallow up Jonah" [Jonah 1:17]: so it was a *fish,* not a *mammal,* especially prepared for Jonah so of no known species. A magical fish with a stomach full of oxygen and — who knows? — fresh water and a buffet banquet as well.

All in all, doesn't it sound like Hans Christian Andersen's *Little Red Riding Hood?* Remember, the Big Bad Wolf swallowed Little Red Riding Hood's grandmother *whole,* and when the kind hunter shot the wolf and sliced open its stomach, her grandmother appeared alive and well, no worse for her experience. Another miracle! ■

The Rediscovery of Reason: the "Handmaiden" of Faith

When Europeans invaded Muslim Spain the eleventh and early twelfth centuries — taking Toledo in 1085 — they stumbled upon a treasure trove: the "lost" writings of Plato, Aristotle, Pythagoras, Euclid, Galen, Hippocrates, and the other giants of Greek antiquity — along with the Arab and Jewish commentaries which built upon and extended the original Greek texts.

Between 1125 and 1200 CE, translations of the Greek legacy flooded into western Christendom. The new "pagan" learning was welcomed as a means of extending the knowledge, understanding and appreciation of God and the world he had created. This "invasion" was so complete "that by the sixteenth century Aristotle had taken on the appearance of a Christian saint."[30]

In retrospect, inviting Aristotle and his fellow rationalist thinkers into the bosom of the church was like asking the fox to set up residence *in* the henhouse. So why were these "pagan writings" so readily welcomed by western Christendom?

One reason: there was, then, little conception of a possible conflict between faith and reason; to virtually all concerned, it was quite clear that reason was merely another tool of investigation, a "handmaiden" of faith; and that faith would always triumph.

Just as importantly, Christianity had been "primed" to accept Greek learning, perhaps most significantly by St. Paul. In his *Epistles,* Paul introduced a Greek concept that is not found in Judaism or the Old Testament: *conscience,* an internal, self-regulating moral agent that judges your thoughts and actions. Paul used the Greek word *synteresis;* but St. Jerome (who was commissioned by Pope Damasus I in 382 CE to revise Latin translations of the Old and New Testaments, which were then incorporated in the official Vulgate edition of the Bible), translated *synteresis* with Latin word *conscientia,* "a very much broader and more indefinite [notion] than its Greek equivalent, if indeed, they are equivalents."[31]

Thus, thanks to Jerome's mistranslation, embedded in western Christianity was the idea of man as an independent moral being, a concept which came to full flower with Martin Luther's "95 Theses" (1517), which led to the Reformation. The Protestant creeds which split from Rome dispensed with the notion of church and priest as unnecessary intermediaries between man and God.

In addition, a very few Greek works had survived the collapse of the Roman Empire in Latin, the most significant being a single volume of Plato: the *Timaeus,* which was welcomed by theologians as early as Origen and Augustine. "What most impressed the European thinkers of the early modern period about the *Timaeus* was the image of nature as an orderly, integrated whole. The natural world was portrayed as a rational order of causes and effects, while man, as part of the rational order of things, was elevated by virtue of his reason."[32]

Timaeus was but a tantalizing taste of the wealth of

learning discovered in Muslim Spain; theologians across Europe eagerly studied and debated its meaning, and universities across western Christendom were established to teach "natural philosophy." Taught in the Arts faculty, "natural philosophy" (basically the works of Aristotle) became the prerequisite for progression to the faculties of law, medicine and theology. The new scientific attitude infected every realm of thought, *including* the effort to make theology the "queen of the sciences," a quest which culminated with St. Thomas Aquinas' (*c.*1225-1274) *Summa Theologica,* described by the *Catholic Encyclopedia* as "Christian doctrine in scientific form."

That Aquinas is, today, considered the most important *Aristotelian* philosopher since Aristotle himself shows how quickly — less than two centuries — Greek thought was absorbed into western thinking and theology.

But in the process, it wasn't long before scholars and students at the universities of Paris, Oxford, Toulouse, Bologna and elsewhere began questioning around the edges of Biblical doctrine.

Western universities had begun as clerical colleges, but by the thirteenth century, having formed into corporations (or *universitas)* they had gained significant independence from ecclesiastical and secular authorities. Nonetheless, their primary mission remained to train theologians, and many of the teachers were clerics.

Inevitably, scholars began to question the tenets at the heart of the scriptures. For example, William of Conches (d. 1154) wrote:

> And the divine page says, "He divided the waters which were under the firmament from the waters which were above the firmament." Since such a statement is contradictory to reason let us show how it cannot be thus.[33]

his unspoken implication being: if the conclusions of reason contradict the scriptures, it must be the *Bible* that is wrong.

And William of Ockham (*c.*1280-*c.*1343) effectively argued that faith and reason were separate realms (the doctrine of "Double Truth"):

Creation presents itself as a gift to us. The gift, however, bears no connection to the giver — except in the tautological sense that a gift must be given. Therefore, nature as creation can be unpacked. And since we are cut off from God except in the act of faith, we might as well unpack that gift and make ourselves at home here.[34]

A reaction from the church was not long in coming. In 1210 "the provincial synod of Sens decreed that the books of Aristotle on natural philosophy and all commentaries thereon were not to be read at Paris in public or secret, on penalty of excommunication."[35] This ban was repeated in 1215, targeted at the University of Paris (founded only in 1200!) — and was in effect for forty years; in 1231 the ban was sanctioned by Pope Gregory IX, who also ordered Aristotle's treatises to be "purged of error" (but the commission he appointed never produced a report); in 1245 Pope Innocent IV extended the ban to the University of Toulouse.

The apogee of the reaction came when Stephen Tempier, Bishop of Paris, issued the "Condemnation of Paris" in 1277.

The Condemnation of Paris, 1277

On March 7, 1277, Stephen Tempier, the Bishop of Paris condemned the works of Aristotle and others, saying:

"...some students of the arts in Paris are exceeding the boundaries of their own faculty and are presuming to treat and discuss, as if they were debatable in the schools, certain obvious and loathsome errors, or rather vanities and lying follies, which are contained in the roll joined to this letter....

Propositions "Thou Shalt Not Think"

A selection of the 219 propositions condemned by
Stephen Tempier, Bishop of Paris, March 1277

1. That there is no more excellent state than to study philosophy.

2. That the only wise men in the world are the philosophers.

4. That one should not hold anything unless it is self-evident or can be manifested from self-evident principles.

5. That man should not be content with authority to have certitude about any question.

6. That there is no rationally disputable question that the philosopher ought not to dispute and determine, because reasons are derived from things. It belongs to philosophy under one or another of its parts to consider all things.

89. That it is impossible to refute the arguments of the Philosopher [*i.e.*, Aristotle] concerning the eternity of the world unless we say that the will of the first being embraces incompatibles.

133. That the soul is inseparable from the body, and that the soul is corrupted when the harmony of the body is corrupted.

138. That there was no first man, nor will there be a last; indeed, the generation of man from man always was and always will be.

180. That the Christian law impedes learning.

181. That there are fables and falsehoods in the Christian law just as in others.

182. That one does not know anything more by the fact that he knows theology.

183. That the teachings of the theologian are based on fables.

188. That it is not true that something comes from nothing or was made in a first creation.

From "Selections from the Condemnation of 1277," www.fordham.edu/gsas/phil/klima/Blackwell-proofs/MP_C22.pdf.

"For they say that these things are true according to philosophy but not according to the Catholic faith, as if there were two contrary truths and as if the truth of Sacred Scripture were contradicted by the truth in the sayings of the accursed pagans....

"We pronounce the sentence of excommunication against those who shall have taught the said scrolls, books, and leaflets, or listened to them, unless they reveal themselves to us or to the chancery of Paris within seven days."

Attached to his proclamation was the "roll" of 219 propositions which:

"...we, having taken counsel with the doctors of Sacred Scripture and other prudent men, strictly forbid these and like things and totally condemn them. We excommunicate all those who shall have taught the said errors or any one of them, or shall have dared in any way to defend or uphold them, *or even to listen to them,* unless they choose to reveal themselves to us or to the chancery of Paris within seven days;"[36]

This Condemnation was not taken up by the church as a whole, so its effect was mainly confined to Paris, although milder restrictions were also imposed at the universities of Oxford and Toulouse. Certainly, the Condemnation cast a pall of suspicion at other universities; nevertheless, the study of Aristotle proceeded apace, enhanced by a debate over the Condemnation itself, and an exodus of masters and students from the university of Paris to other universities. One cause:

The Separation of State from Church

Although the separation of church and state appears to be an innovation enshrined for the first time in the Constitution of the United States, it has far deeper roots. Indeed, it began with the collapse of the Roman Empire — not as a matter of principle but as a matter of necessity. While the Catholic Church, centered in Rome, held a monolithic sway over the heavenly realm, secular power was divided into dozens of kingly states and petty principalities.

The church held an awesome — but one-off — power over kings and princes: excommunication, effective when it cost the king or prince his domestic support. But in his own territory the monarch ruled on a day-to-day basis and could resist (up to a point) encroachment on his authority whether by ecclesiastical power in Rome, or the secular power of a neighboring monarch.

But not even excommunication guaranteed Papal supremacy. A vicious dispute between Pope Boniface VIII and King Philip "the Fair" of France came to an abrupt end when Boniface excommunicated Philip in 1302. Philip responded by sending an army to Rome to unseat Boniface and appoint his own, tame, Pope instead.

"Saint Thomas Aquinas is all very well, but I get my best material from Spencer Tracy."

The Catholic Church had lost a power retained by its counterparts in the Byzantine Empire and the Islamic world, where the heavenly and secular powers were united: the ability to call on the police power of the state to forcibly suppress any dissent from the official theological opinion.

Into this mix of countervailing and disputatious powers was added the *universitas* which, as a separate legal entity, jealously guarded its own powers and was also able to resist (up to a point) encroachment on its authority from any outside source.

The prime ideological issues at stake in 1277 and the decades before included:

The eternity of the world: Aristotle's conclusion in his *On the Heavens* — "the world as a whole was not generated and cannot be destroyed, as some allege, but is unique and eternal, having no beginning or end of its whole life"[37] — quite obviously conflicts with the story of creation in Genesis. Twenty-seven of Tempier's 219 propositions "thou shalt not think" were devoted to "not thinking about" the eternity of the world.

Double Truth: the idea that there could be *two* truths: those of faith and those of reason.

Arts masters claimed they merely taught natural philosophy — "the nature of things." Nevertheless, conclusions from the study of "the nature of things" conflicted, more often than not, with the scriptures. The Arts masters would then simply affirm the superiority of revelation — but leave the conflict hanging. As Boethius of Dacia put it: "we incur foolishness by seeking a proof where none is possible or incur heresy by refusing to believe what ought to be held on faith."

This attitude infuriated the theologians, and was condemned by Tempier in his preamble: "For they say that these things are true according to philosophy but not according to the Catholic faith, *as if there were two contrary truths...."*

Limitations on the power of God: Tempier condemned various Aristotelian conclusions that limited God's power to do anything he wants, including that everything must have a cause [Proposition 23]; that God could not create several worlds [34] or create man "without an agent" *[i.e., parents,* 35].

But on top of the ideological conflicts were several others:

➤ *Radical Aristotelians vs. everybody else:* the appearance of a group of radical Aristotelians within the Arts faculty led by Siger de Brabant "taught a number of [Aristotelian] doctrines that seemed to contradict the fundamental teachings of Christianity"[38] which, the conservatives felt, threatened the hierarchy of church *and* university. The election for rector of the Arts faculty in 1272 resulted in defeat for the radicals' candidate Siger at the hands of the conservative Alberic of Rhiems. The radicals refused to recognize the election and elected a rector of their own. For three years — until the Pope intervened to settle the matter in favor of the conservatives — there were, in effect, *two* Arts faculties at the University of Paris.

➤ *Arts vs. Theology:* the Arts faculty sought equal status with Theology, which the faculty of Theology, convinced that revelation was superior to all other forms of knowledge, naturally resisted. In another apparent victory for the conservative forces, one of Alberic's first acts as rector was to adopt "new statutes forbidding the arts masters to either reach theological conclusions in their lectures or to 'teach against the faith' in philosophical matters."[39]

➤ *The Franciscans vs. the Dominicans.* Led by Bonaventure, the Franciscans attempted to place limits on the teaching of Aristotle and attacked Aquinas among others; the Dominicans rallied behind their most prominent thinker. Aquinas was accused of "drinking too deeply of Aristotelian wine,"[40] and of holding beliefs barely distinguishable from Siger and his radical followers. In an apparent victory for the Franciscans, Bishop Tempier pushed Aquinas' leading disciple, Giles of Rome, out of his position at the faculty of theology at the University of Paris.

In the 1280s, Archbishop Peckham, a Franciscan, "condemned a master of theology [at Oxford] for teaching Thomas' views on the soul,"[41] and was supported by the then-Pope, Nicholas IV — a former Franciscan. To all appearances, the conservatives had won.

Yet, in 1323, Aquinas was canonized, and two years later the Bishop of Paris withdrew the Condemnation.

Why? Aristotle was firmly entrenched at *other* universities — and even in the Catholic Church itself, which no longer had the power to enforce theological purity (however defined) across western Christendom. Ultimately, the Condemnation of Paris was a tactical (and local) victory, but a strategic defeat.

In the end, Aquinas (and Aristotle) prevailed over Augustine in both the universities and the church, while the "separation of powers" continued with the disintegration of the monolithic Roman church itself in the Reformation.

Galileo Galilei

> **"**To assert that the earth revolves around the
> sun is as erroneous as to claim that Jesus was
> not born of a virgin.**"**
> — *Cardinal Bellarmine (1615)*
> **"**I do not feel obliged to believe that the same
> God who has endowed us with sense, reason,
> and intellect has intended us to forgo their use.**"**
> — *Galileo Galilei*

The most famous example of the conflict between faith and reason is that of Galileo. Galileo held that it was the earth, not the sun, which moved. This assertion conflicted with the scriptures (see *The Earth: Flat or Round?,* page 138) but also with *Aristotle's* cosmology of the "heavenly spheres" which had become church dogma.

Galileo was condemned in 1616 and, in 1633, forced by the Inquisition to *recant* his (and Copernicus') conclusion that the earth moved around the sun under the threat of being declared a heretic. He was eventually — *359 years later* — "pardoned" by Pope John Paul II in 1992.

While certainly more famous than the Condemnation of Paris, the persecution of Galileo was, by comparison, an isolated event. Copernicus' writings — now spread rapidly thanks to Gutenberg's printing press — continued to be read and studied all over western Europe, and the church's efforts to suppress "Copernicanism" were feeble and ineffective.

Some excerpts from the official Vatican documents condemning Galileo:

24 February 1616:
Consultant's Report on Copernicanism
*Assessment made at the Holy Office, Rome,
Wednesday, 24 February 1616, in the presence
of the Father Theologians signed below.*

Proposition to be assessed:
1. The sun is the center of the world and completely devoid of local motion.

Assessment: *All said that this proposition is foolish and absurd in philosophy, and formally heretical since it explicitly contradicts in many places the sense of Holy Scripture, according to the literal meaning of the words and according to the common interpretation and understanding of the Holy Fathers and the doctors of theology.*

2. The earth is not the center of the world, nor motionless,

but it moves as a whole and also with diurnal motion.

Assessment: *All said that this proposition receives the same judgement in philosophy and that in regard to theological truth it is at least erroneous in faith.*[42]

Galileo's works were also added to the church's "Index of Prohibited Books."

22 June 1633:
Sentence of the Inquisition[43]

...by order of His Holiness and the Most Eminent and Most Reverend Lord Cardinals of this Supreme and Universal Inquisition, the Assessor Theologians assessed the two propositions of the sun's stability and the earth's motions as follows:

That the sun is the center of the world and motionless is a proposition which is philosophically absurd and false, and formally heretical, for being explicitly contrary to Holy Scripture;

That the earth is neither the center of the world nor motionless but moves even with diurnal motion is philosophically equally absurd and false, and theologically at least erroneous in the Faith....

Therefore...We say, pronounce, sentence, and declare that you, the above-mentioned Galileo...have rendered yourself according to this Holy Office vehemently suspected of heresy, namely of having held and believed a doctrine which is false and contrary to the divine and Holy Scripture: that the sun is the center of the world and does not move from east to west, and the earth moves and is not the center of the world, and that one may hold and defend as probable an opinion after it has been declared and defined as contrary to Holy Scripture...

Furthermore, so that this serious and pernicious error and transgression of yours does not remain completely unpunished, and so that you will be more cautious in the future and an example for others to abstain from similar crimes, we order that the book *Dialogue* by Galileo Galilei be prohibited by public edict....

Luther & Calvin agreed

Calling him "an upstart astrologer," **Martin Luther** said: "This fool wishes to reverse the entire science of astronomy; but sacred scripture tells us that Joshua commanded the sun to stand still, and not the earth."

"The world also is established, that it cannot be moved!" **John Calvin** declared, appealing to the authority of Psalm 18. "Who will put the authority of Copernicus above that of the Holy Spirit?"

This we say, pronounce, sentence, declare, order, and reserve by this or any other better manner or form that we reasonably can or shall think of.

So we the undersigned Cardinals pronounce.

Galileo — aged 69, in infirm health, and terrified of torture — recanted.

In **1664**, Pope Alexander VII condemned *all* works teaching the "heresy" that "the earth moved and the sun did not," and added them to the "Index of Prohibited Books."

Only in **1835** were Galileo's works *removed* from the "Index of Prohibited Books."

4th November, 1992
The Pope recants:

❝Thanks to his intuition as a brilliant physicist and by relying on different arguments, Galileo, who practically invented the experimental method, understood why only the sun could function as the centre of the world, as it was then known, that is to say, as a planetary system. The *error of the theologians of the time,* when they maintained the centrality of the Earth, was to think *that our understanding of the physical world's structure was, in some way, imposed by the literal sense of Sacred Scripture....* "

> **But in 1990, Cardinal Joseph Ratzinger (now Pope Benedict) said:**
> "At the time of Galileo the Church remained much more reasonable than Galileo himself. The process against Galileo was reasonable and just."

— *Pope John Paul II, L'Osservatore Romano N. 44 (1264)*[44]

The "Big Bang"

The church's retreat in the face of science continues to the present day. Consider just two recent examples.

In a 1951 address[45] Pope Pius XII seized on the then-new scientific hypothesis of the "big bang" as the origin of the universe as *scientific proof* for the existence of God:

"44. ...a mind enlightened and enriched with modern scientific knowledge...perceives and recognizes the work of creative omnipotence, whose power, set in motion by the mighty 'Fiat' pronounced billions of years ago by the Creating Spirit, spread out over the universe, calling into existence with a gesture of generous love matter bursting with energy. In fact, it would seem that present-day science, with one sweeping step back across millions of centuries, has succeeded in bearing witness to that primordial 'Fiat lux' uttered at the moment when, along with matter, there burst forth from nothing a sea of light and radiation, while the particles of chemical elements split and formed into millions of galaxies....

"50. It has, besides, followed the course and the direction of cosmic developments, and, just as it was able to get a glimpse of the term toward which these developments were inexorably leading, so also has it pointed to their beginning in time some five billion years ago. Thus, with that concreteness which is characteristic of physical proofs, it has confirmed the contingency of the universe and also the well-founded deduction as to the epoch when the cosmos came forth from the hands of the Creator.

"51. Hence, creation took place in time. Therefore, there is a Creator. Therefore, God exists! Although it is neither explicit nor complete, this is the reply we were awaiting from science, and which the present human generation is awaiting from it."

Evolution

In an opening address to a conference of scientists in 1996, Pope John Paul II endorsed the theory of evolution, saying:

"Taking into account the state of scientific research at the time as well as of the requirements of theology, the encyclical *Humani Generis* considered the doctrine of 'evolutionism' a serious hypothesis, worthy of investigation and in-depth study equal to that of the opposing hypothesis.... Today, almost half a century after the publication of the encyclical, new knowledge has led to the recognition of the theory of evolution as more than a hypothesis. It is indeed remarkable that this theory has been progressively accepted by researchers, following a series of discoveries in various fields of knowledge. The convergence, neither sought nor fabricated, of the results of work that was conducted independently is in itself a significant argument in favor of this theory."[46]

By endorsing the Big Bang and Evolution, even just as serious *hypotheses,* both Popes implicitly *reject* the scriptures.

According to the hypothesis, the big bang took mere milliseconds to create the foundation matter of the universe — and then *billions of years* (rather than six days) passed before our earth came into being. To accept the Big Bang, then, is to deny the "truth" of the book of Genesis which clearly states that God created the earth in just *six days.*

> ### Looking for the Virgin Mary
>
> "At least 50 people have lost their sight after staring at the sun hoping to see an image of the Virgin Mary," the *Daily Telegraph* (London) reported on 16 March 2008.
>
> Despite warnings, "believers are allegedly still flocking to a hotelier's house in Erumeli [in India's Kottayam district] near where the divine image is said to have appeared."

Once the earth coalesced into a planet, *another* several billion years passed before life appeared and *another* billion or so before *homo sapiens* evolved. Man, in other words, was *not* created on "the sixth day." Indeed, if man *evolved* he wasn't "created" — certainly not in the sense of the book of Genesis. And what happened to Eve and Adam's rib?

But the implications for Christian doctrine go far deeper. What happened to the Garden of Eden? If man evolved he wasn't thrown out of it — so how did he acquire Original Sin (and how do the snake and the apple enter the story?) And when (and how) did God decide to add a "soul" to the mix — or did *that* evolve too?

By accepting evolution and the "big bang," both Popes are *(inter alia)* totally rejecting Genesis, necessarily implying that the Bible is not *literally* the Word of God and is, in reality, little more than a collection of ancient fairy tales.

But then...neither of them were speaking *infallibly*...

A Note on Papal Infallibility

You might think that these errors and reversals of the church cast doubt on the Catholic doctrine of Papal Infallibility.

Well — no, they don't.

What exactly *is* "Papal Infallibility"? Turning once again to the *Catholic Encyclopedia*[47] we learn, first of all,

That the Church is infallible in her definitions on faith and morals is itself a Catholic dogma, which, although it was formulated ecumenically for the first time in the Vatican Council, had been explicitly taught long before and had been assumed from the very beginning without question down to the time of the Protestant Reformation.

The Vatican Council declared that:

"the doctrine of faith, which God has revealed, has not been proposed as a philosophical discovery to be improved upon by human talent, but has been committed as a Divine deposit to the spouse of Christ, to be faithfully guarded and infallibly interpreted by her";

Papal Infallibility refers only to a Pope speaking under certain circumstances:

...it is defined that the Roman pontiff when he teaches ex cathedra [literally, "speaking in his chair"] "enjoys, by reason of the Divine assistance promised to him in blessed Peter, that infallibility with which the Divine Redeemer wished His Church to be endowed in defining doctrine regarding faith and morals."

Furthermore:

> ➤ Infallibility means more than exemption from actual error; it means exemption from the *possibility* of error;
> ➤ it does not require holiness of life, much less imply impeccability in its organs; sinful and wicked men

may be God's agents in defining infallibly; *[Given the Borgias, Medicis and all the other corrupt and sinful Popes, this is clearly an essential requirement!]*

> and finally that the validity of the Divine guarantee is independent of the fallible arguments upon which a definitive decision may be based.... *[The reasoning can be full of holes, but that doesn't matter.]*

There's a problem here that neither the *Catholic Encyclopedia* nor the Vatican Council confronts *directly:* that if a doctrine is "infallible" *only* when the Pope speaks *ex cathedra,* then:

> Every *other* doctrine decreed by the Pope or lower church official is *fallible,* and so *potentially in error.*

Which is exactly the argument the *Catholic Encyclopedia* uses (implicitly) when considering whether the condemnation of Galileo cast doubt on the Pope's or the church's infallibility.

As to the Galileo affair, it is quite enough to point out the fact that ***the condemnation of the heliocentric theory was the work of a fallible tribunal.*** The pope cannot delegate the exercise of his infallible authority to the Roman Congregations, and whatever issues formally in the name of any of these, even when approved and confirmed in the ordinary official way by the pope, does not pretend to be ex cathedra and infallible. The pope, of course, can convert doctrinal decisions of the Holy Office, which are not in themselves infallible, into ex cathedra papal pronouncements, but in doing so he must comply with the conditions already explained — which neither Paul V nor Urban VIII did in the Galileo case.

Neat trick!

Never mind that Galileo was *forced* by the threat of excommunication (which, at the time, tended to be fatal) to recant. Never mind that the Inquisition tried, tortured, and executed thousands *fallibly.*

The *church* may have done all these things *by mistake.* But since the Pope didn't speak "ex cathedra" well...*c'est la vie!* Or more accurately, *c'est la mort!*

The *Catholic Encyclopedia* can conclude with, presumably a clear conscience:

> The broad fact, therefore, remains certain that no ex cathedra definition of any pope has ever been shown to be erroneous.

"Don't look now, but they just thought up a new heresy."

"The Four Windows of the Soul"

Prompted by a student who "asked too many questions," the Mother Superior in a Catholic girls' high school taught the class "The Four Windows of the Soul." Drawing a window with four panes on the blackboard, she wrote as follows:

Questions that can be answered...	
1. "Yes"	2. "No"
3. "Maybe"	4. Can't be answered

Saying that all questions fall into one of the four panes, she explained that questions in the first three panes could be answered truthfully.

But questions of faith, she said, fall into the window's fourth pane — and so are opaque to reason and should be "answered" not with the mind but with the heart and soul.

> "If we are going to teach "creation science" as an alternative to evolution, then we should also teach the stork theory as an alternative to biological reproduction."
> — *Judith Hayes*

5

"In the Beginning...

...God created the heaven and the earth.**"**
— *Hebrew [Genesis 1:1]*

...was the Word, and the Word was with God, and the Word was God.**"**
— *Christian [John 1:1]*

...were Spider Woman (the earth goddess) and Tawa (the sun god) who lived in Spider Woman's lair, Under-the-World.**"**
— *Hopi [American Indian]*[48]

...there was darkness everywhere and the creator, Karora, lay sleeping...**"**
— *Arandan Aborigines [Northern Australia]*[49]

...there was the great goddess Eurynome, who emerged naked from chaos and divided the waters from the sky so she could dance lonely upon the waves.**"**
— *Pelasgian [Greece — before the Greeks]*[50]

...was the void, chaos, from which sprang Gaia, "wide-bosomed Earth," a firm foundation for Mount Olympus and the gods who would live there."

    — *Greece, circa eighth century* BCE[51]

...Shuzanghu lived alone with his wife, Zumaing-Nui. Tired of having nowhere to set their feet, they made love and gave birth to a girl (Earth) and a boy (Sky.)"

    — *Dhammai [Northeastern India (non-Hindu)]*[52]

...Akongo lived with us [humans] in the sky, but he got so tired of human quarrels that he left and has not been seen since."

    — *Ngombe [Zaire]*[53]

...there was only water and twilight everywhere and the island place of the gods."

    — *Fiji Islands*[54]

...after water and bulrushes came about, there was Mbir the worm slithering about in the rushes. Eventually he became a man...."

    — *Guarani [Bolivia]*[55]

...then even nothingness was not, nor existence.
There was no air then, nor the heavens beyond it.
What covered it? Where was it? In whose keeping?
Was there then cosmic water, in depths, unfathomed?
Then there were neither death nor immortality,
nor was there then the torch of night and day.
The One breathed windlessly and self-sustaining.
There, was that One then, and there was no other."

    — *Hindu, from the Rig Veda*[56]

The Stories of Creation

When I visited Ayres Rock in central Australia, I learned the Anangu Aborigines' story of creation — the central focus being how Uluru (Ayres Rock) came into being. What struck me, though, was what was *missing:* there was no mention of the sea.

The absence of a sea is also a feature of other inland peoples' creation stories, like those of the Ute (Colorado) and Winnebago Indians (Midwest).[57]

Not surprising, you might think, given that for each of these peoples the nearest ocean beach is thousands of kilometers away.

Several creation myths are unspecific, or "generic." Like Genesis ("In the beginning God created the heaven and the earth") or the Hindu's *Rig Veda* ("Then even nothingness was not, nor existence"), they could be talking about anywhere or everywhere.

But others have clearly local references, naming geographic or climactic features, animals or plants showing that *this* story could only have happened in *this* place. This is most strikingly obvious in the stories of creation from *island* societies.

For the Ainu (the original inhabitants of Japan) the world was just a mixture of mud and water until the Creator sent a bird to make earth. The bird flapped its wings until a few dry spots emerged — the islands the Ainu call home.

The Japanese have several creation myths; two of them (although both far more complicated) have similarities with Ainu's. In one, Heaven and Earth are joined until Heaven decides to lift himself up, creating islands in the process. In another, the ancestors thrust a jeweled spear into the waters and when they lifted it up the island of "Onogoro-jima (Spontaneously Conceived Island)" came into being.

In the Fiji islanders' story, Rokomautu brings up the islands from beneath the waters (and the home of the Fijian gods, naturally enough, was another island); while to the Kodiak islanders (near Alaska) the first son of the first man and the first woman played with a stone which became Kodiak Island.

There are many other examples. Herewith, just a few:

> *Greece:* the first feature to come into existence after the creation of Gaia (the world) from the void of chaos was Mount Olympus, the home of the gods.

> The *Incas'* predecessors believed that Pachacamac (the sun — also an Inca god) rose from Lake Titicaca and then created everything else.

> *Ngurunderi (southeastern Australia):* Ngurunderi (the great ancestor) canoed along a small stream chasing his runaway wives. Ahead of him was a giant fish which turned the stream into the Murray River as it swam.

> *Aymara (Bolivia):* the main deity is Kun, the snow god.

> *Kukulik Eskimos (Bering Strait):* a man visited the sun to ask for reindeer. Instead, he was given pebbles and told to throw them in the sea, whereupon they turned into whales.

> *Norse/Icelandic:* the Creator is Ymir (or Imir), the Frost or Ice Giant (who, unusually in creation myths, is evil).

> *Arandan (Northern Australia):* playing a major role in the Arandan's story of creation are bandicoots (still sacred to some tribes), wallabies and kangaroos, and the bullroarer.

> *Pomo (Californian Indians):* to create the sun, Old Man Madumda smoked his pipe for a while and then

threw it into the sky — where it still burns today.

➢ *Netsilik Eskimos (Greenland):* the world was free of ice and icebergs until an old witch-woman became angry with a man, Kivioq. While trying to kill him she created sea ice.

➢ *Keraki (Papua New Guinea, where there are more languages per square mile than anywhere else on earth):* humans grew inside a palm tree. While they were still inside the creator, Gainji, heard them talking in many different languages. When they emerged they dispersed into different language groups — and so it still is today.

"Families" of Creation Myths

What also becomes clear is that, like languages, creation myths evolve and *change.* Or *did* when they could only be passed on orally, becoming "frozen" only when written down (though, as we've seen with the Bible, that's no guarantee of stability).

While the *details* of creation stories from different tribes of Australian Aborigines differ from each other markedly, they all share the common theme of what Europeans call (inaccurately, according to the Aborigines) the *Dreamtime:* a long-ago time when the walkabouts of gods, spirits or ancestors resulted in the creation or birth of plants, animals, humans, mountains, valleys, rivers and seas and sacred places, rituals and taboos.

A recurring figure in the creation stories of American Indian tribes as geographically distant as Sioux (the Dakotas) and the Navaho (Arizona/Utah), is the "Trickster," usually named Coyote or simply the "Old Man." Other common figures are the Great Spirit, Beaver and Raven. Raven (as Creator) also figures in the myths of the Kukulik Eskimos in the Bering Strait, and appears (as Trickster) in the Chuckchee (north eastern Siberia) creation myth, suggesting that American Indian creation myths evolved from one or two common ancestors in the same way (and, presumably, simultaneously with) the evolution of the different Amerindian languages from their original Siberian ancestors.

Another feature demonstrating evolution/adaptation is the inclusion of anachronisms. For example, according to the Pima Indians, on his second try at creating people "Earthmaker made two figures, but Coyote urged him to take them out of the oven too soon and they were underdone. These were sent away as white people to other lands." [A similar story, that white people were under-cooked, is also found in the Philippines.]*

A "Non-Creation" Creation Myth

Perhaps the most unusual — and most rational pre-scientific — account of the beginning of everything is found in the ancient Indian religion of Jainism (which dates from at least six centuries *before* Christ).

The Jains believe the world has neither beginning nor end, and (along with heaven and hell) simply exists.

In a Hopi Indian creation myth recorded in 1905, Spider Woman creates *Spaniards* — and teaches them to speak Spanish!

The Konos of Guinea (west Africa) tell the story of Alatangana, who eloped with a daughter of Sa. They gave birth to seven boys and seven girls, eight of them white and six black. Each child spoke a different language, so they couldn't understand each other and nor, for that matter, could their

---

* Could this "ancestral memory" account for the uniquely Caucasian fetish of getting a suntan?

parents understand them. Sa ordered that white children marry only whites and blacks only blacks, hence the separation of the "races."

Unlike the American Indians, who never saw white people before the Vikings, the Kono were prob-bably acquainted

"*I* know how you can get him to notice you."

with whites far earlier — primarily in the form of Arab slave traders.

But the Bulo people of Cameroon have a creation story which is clearly influenced by Islam or Christianity. In the beginning, Mambe's son Zambe created two humans, one white and one black. He gave them many things including fire and a book. Some time later Zambe returned to ask what they'd done with his gifts. The white man said he'd spent his time reading the book, while the black man replied he'd been too busy tending the fire to even look at the book. So Zambe decreed they would both continue to do what they'd been doing — but that the black man would have to look after the white man, who had only book knowledge.

Unsurprisingly, tobacco, native to North America, plays a part in many American Indian myths. But tobacco is mentioned by the Dogon (Mali): Ogetemmeli, before setting out to create the world, takes a pinch of tobacco saying it "makes for right thinking."

Another feature common to *all* creation myths, regardless of tribe, location, original language or religion, is that they are products of revelation: anyone who actually witnessed the creation left no written or otherwise permanent record. The "record," such as it is, has been passed by word of mouth from generation to generation — for *thousands* of generations.

The "Whispering Game"

Did you ever play the "whispering game" as a kid? If so you'll recall how it works: a group of children sit in a circle; one of them is given a simple phrase which he or she has to *whisper* — just *once* — to the next child, who then whispers it to the next and so on until it goes all around the circle. Even a simple phrase like "the cat sat on the mat" can quickly mutate, through the errors of transmission, to "the card saddled the man" or worse. When the last child announces what message he or she received it's usually greeted with riots of laughter when the original phrase is revealed.

So what are the chances of a *complex* story, taking perhaps an hour (or in the case of the Navaho, nine *days)* to tell, being passed from teacher to student for two or three *thousand*-odd generations and surviving intact? Or, indeed, having *any* resemblance to the original story?

"They Can't All Be True"

In Vietnam, I came across a collection of Vietnamese Buddhist tales and sent it to my godson, then about seven years old. Not long afterwards he commented that Christians, Buddhists, Hindus, Aborigines, Indians and others all have different accounts of the creation. "They can't *all* be true," was his conclusion — and he further decided that *none* of them could be true.

Given that most religions insist that if you're an unbeliever you will end up in their hell; given that — *at most* — only *one* of the thousands of creation and related stories could be true; what are the chances that the one believed to be true from, for example, the lottery of birth, actually *is* the true one?

Keeping in mind, of course, the penalty for making the *wrong* choice!

Where Do Myths Come From?

Whatever else myths may be, they are *stories.* If they're well-told and memorable, they're easier to pass on from father to son, from mother to daughter.

But where do they come from?

At 7:17AM on the morning of June 30, 1908, near the Podkamennaya (Lower Stony) Tunguska River northwest of Lake Baikal in Siberia, a large meteorite exploded at an altitude of six kilometers (3.75 miles), turning into a ball of fire which started a brushfire in the forest below. The shockwave flattened trees for miles around, threw people 60 km (40 miles) away to the ground, and broke windows hundreds of miles away. Seismic stations across Eurasia, some 1,000 km (600 miles) from the impact zone, recorded the earth's tremors as 5.0 on the Richter scale.

We now know that the cause was a meteorite or small asteroid, estimated to be around 30 meters in diameter and travelling at about 5,400 kilometers per hour (3,400 MPH) — about five times the speed of sound. Friction with the earth's atmosphere heated it up, and it disintegrated in an explosion equivalent to some 500 kilotons — or 27 times the force of the Hiroshima bomb.[58]

But if you knew nothing about space, planets, gravity, orbits, asteroids, or atmospheric friction, how would you explain this catastrophic event?

The local Tungus people *immediately* knew the cause, long before the scientists had figured out the details: it was a battle between two shamans which probably heralded the end of the world.

Had science not intervened, it's easy to imagine the local storytellers weaving a fascinating tale of how battling shamans had caused a giant ball of fire — a second sun — to suddenly appear, magically, in the sky and of what human evils had caused the gods/demons/spirits/ancestors to become angry enough to cause such widespread devastation.

Consider, then, the following legend from the opening chapter of Elizabeth Barber's and Paul Barber's fascinating analysis of ancient myths: *When They Severed Earth from Sky: How the Human Mind Shapes Myth.*[59] Could it be describing an actual event?

> A long time ago, so long you cannot count it...the Chief of the Below World came up from his home inside the earth and saw Loha, a beautiful maiden who was the daughter of the tribal chief. He fell in love with her and asked her to return with him to his lodge where she would live forever and ever.
>
> Loha refused, and the wise men of the council would not command her to go.
>
> The Chief of the Below World was very angry. In a voice like thunder, he swore he would have revenge on the people of Loha, that he would destroy them with the Curse of Fire. Raging and thundering, he rushed up through the opening and stood upon the top of his mountain.
>
> Then he saw the face of the Chief of the Above World shining among the stars that surrounded his home. Slowly

the mighty form of the chief descended from the sky and stood on the top of Mount Shasta. From the mountaintops the two spirit chiefs began a furious battle....

Mountains shook and crumbled. Red-hot rocks as large as the hills hurled through the skies. Burning ashes fell like rain. The Chief of the Below World spewed fire from his mouth. Like an ocean of flame it devoured the forests on the mountains and in the valleys. On and on the Curse of Fire swept until it reached the homes of the people. Fleeing in terror before it, the people found refuge in the waters of Klamath Lake.

After much discussion, two medicine men of the Klamath people climbed to the top of the cliff which hung over the entrance to the Below World...and jumped into the fiery pit [as sacrifice].

The Chief of the Above World saw the brave deed of the medicine men. He saw that it was good. Once more the mountains shook. Once more the earth trembled on its foundations. This time the Chief of the Below World was driven into his home, and the top of the mountain fell upon him. When the morning sun rose, the high mountain was gone....

Then the rain fell in torrents and filled the great hole that was made when the mountain fell upon the Chief of the Below World. The Curse of Fire was lifted....[60]

This tale, recorded in 1865, comes from the Klamath Indians of southwest Oregon, and refers to Crater Lake, which lies between Mount Shasta (mentioned in the story) and Mount St. Helens (which erupted in 1980, ending 1,200 feet *shorter* with a 1,200 foot deep crater at the top).

"Geologists have reconstructed that a volcano dubbed Mount Mazama formerly towered 14,000 feet high"[61] where Crater Lake now lies — just 8,159 feet above sea level. They ice-dated the eruption, which left a crater 4,000 feet deep, to around 5760 BCE — over 7,500 years ago.

With this added information, parts of the story — "Red-hot rocks as large as the hills hurled through the skies. Burning ashes fell like rain. The Chief of the Below World spewed fire from his mouth. Like an ocean of flame it devoured the forests on the mountains and in the valleys..." — now sound like a *description* of a volcanic explosion, its *cause* attributed, in the story, to a battle between gods.

That this is the case becomes clear when we know that this "story was related as answer to a young soldier at Fort Klamath when he inquired why the native people *never went to this breathtakingly beautiful spot,*"[62] and when we read the *last* paragraph of this story, which I have withheld until now:

> Now you understand why my people never visit the lake. Down through the ages we have heard this story. From father to son has come the warning, "Look not upon the place. Look not upon the place, for it means death or everlasting sorrow."

This memorable story is a *warning.* Told again and again around the campfire, the teller could *point* to Crater Lake as he concluded, "Look not upon the place, for it means death or everlasting sorrow."

One purpose of myths, then, could be to *pass on information* — exactly as this legend has done for over *seven millennia.*

But — what would have happened to this legend if the Kalmath Indians had migrated *away* from Crater Lake? Storytellers would no longer *point* as they said, "Look not upon the place...." Having lost its *context,* the story would no longer have any information value.

So what might it become?

If we replace the Chiefs of the Above and Below Worlds with God and Satan, and the medicine men who sacrificed

The Man God in the Moon?

On a clear night when the moon is full, look up into the sky and you'll see *"The Man in the Moon."*

We know that the moon's "smiling face" is simply the pattern its mountains, valleys and shadows make when viewed from 240,000 miles away.

Our ancestors didn't know that.

One can imagine them *seeing* the face in the sky.

Plainly in sight was the incontrovertible *evidence* that an unknown being was *watching over them.*

Surely, they would then ask questions like:

➤ *Who* is this being?

➤ *Why* is he there?

➤ *What* is his (or her) intent — and powers? (Being completely out of reach, quite probably enormous.)

Could this sight of "the Man in the Moon" be the origin of the beliefs in powerful, immaterial beings that *all* human cultures share?

themselves with priests or prophets, then this narrative could fit seamlessly into the Bible. It would now be a *morality tale,* yet another example of how God (who is, after all, Chief of the Above World) comes to our rescue to save us from the evil Lucifer of the Below World.

Before the invention of writing, there was only one way to pass information from one generation to the next: word of mouth. But a simple warning, "stay away from Crater Lake," hardly conveys the possible peril of being caught in a volcanic explosion. The dramatic *story* of a battle between the Chiefs of the Above and Below Worlds — with memorable but irrelevant details like the beautiful maiden — *does.* And there's an added benefit to the story format: the Klamath people will heed the warning in case the Chief of the Below World is *still* angry with them.

It never pays to provoke the gods.

The result: for an amazing 7,500+ years (to 1865, when it was first recorded), the Klamath Indians kept away from Crater Lake. The warning worked.[*]

"I'll let your people go as soon as they've performed their community service."

---

[*] This is just one of the many myths Elizabeth and Paul Barber analyze in *When They Severed Earth from Sky: How the Human Mind Shapes Myth* — showing that some have quite clearly survived for *as long as twenty thousand years!* They also identify 51 different principles and processes that our ancestors applied in the creation, remembrance and passing on of what we, today, call myths.

6

"In the Name of God"

"Men never do evil so completely and cheerfully as when they do it from religious conviction.**"**

— *Blaise Pascal*

"Herein we see God's great mercy...for the slaughter was in all 5,517, *but ten of the enemy's side were slain to one of ours.***"**

— *Nehemiah Wallington*

"More people have been killed in the name of God than for any other reason.**"**

— *George Carlin*

"For good people to do evil things it takes religion.**"**

— *Steven Weinberg, Nobel Prize Winner, Physics*

Massacres From the Bible —

Massacres Carried Out By God Himself

Passage	Number	Offence
1 Chronicles 2:3	1	Er who was "evil in the sight of the LORD"
Leviticus 24:10-16	1	God orders Moses to have the congregation stone a blasphemer to death
Numbers 3:4	2	Two sons of Aaron who offered fire before the LORD — against the LORD's instructions
Numbers 16:35	250	Men who offered incense
Numbers 16:49	14,700	Plague — for "the children of Israel murmured against Moses and against Aaron"
Numbers 25: 9	24,000	God sends a plague because the Israelites "commit whoredom with the daughters of Moab"
1 Samuel 6:19	50,070	For looking into the ark of the LORD
1 Samuel 25:38	1	The Lord smote Nabal, for being rich, churlish, and saying "Who is [King] David?"
2 Samuel 6:6-7	1	Uzzah, for touching the ark
2 Samuel 12:15	1	David and Bathsheba's child — because David had taken Bathsheba from the Hittites
2 Samuel 24:15	70,000	David "sinned against the LORD" by taking a census so...pestilence
1 Kings 13:26	1	Disobedient prophet, slain by a lion "according to the word of the LORD."
1 Kings 20:35-36	1	For not killing the prophet (another lion)
1 Kings 20:29-30	27,000	God causes a wall to fall on Syrians who'd claimed he was God of the hills but not the valleys
2 Kings 1:9-12	102	Soldiers sent by the king of Samaria who ignored Elijah's instructions from God
2 Kings 2:23-24	42	Children who made fun of Elisha's bald head.
2 Kings 7:17-19	1	An unbeliever
2 Kings 9:33-37	1	Jezebel, "this cursed woman." "Dogs shall eat the flesh of Jezebel" saith the Lord.
1 Chronicles 10:13-14	1	Saul, because of his transgression against the LORD
2 Kings 19:35	7,080	Assyrians killed by an angel of the LORD — mainly because their king had blasphemed against Him.
2 Chronicles 21:14-19	1	Jehoram wrought "evil in the eyes of the LORD," so God kills him by making his bowels fall out.
2 Chronicles 28:6	150,000	In Judah, because they had forsaken the LORD.
Job 1:19	10	Job's 7 sons and 3 daughters — to test Job's faith
Ezekiel 24:15-18	1	Ezekiel's wife, for no apparent reason
Acts 12:23	1	Herod, because he didn't glorify God
TOTAL	*343,269*	

With Number Killed *(as given in the Bible!)*

Massacres By Men — at God's Order

Passage	Number	Offence
Exodus 14:8-28	601	Moses closes the waters on the Egyptians, drowning the Egyptian army (601 named — plus the rest)
Exodus 32: 27-28	3,000	For worshipping the golden calf
Numbers 15: 32-36	1	Moses ordered the congregation to stone to death a man who gathered firewood on the sabbath day
Joshua 8:1-26	12,000	God gives Joshua the land of Ai — so he sets the city of Ai on fire
Joshua 10:23-26	5	Joshua and his men beheaded and hanged the heads of the five kings of his enemies on the trees
Judges 1: 3-4	10,000	LORD delivered the Canaanites and Perizzites into Judah's and Simeon's hands.
Judges 3: 14-22	1	Ehud, an Israelite, killed the Moab king Eglon, oppressor of the Israelites, with a knife in his belly saying: "I have a message from God unto thee"
Judges 3:28-29	10,000	Moabites, Israelites' enemies
Judges 7:25	2	The Midianite army fled before Gideon's men, thanks to the aid of God. Two Midianite princes (and unknown others) killed
Judges 14:19	30	The spirit of the LORD came upon Samson and he killed 30 men
Judges 15:14-15	1,000	The Spirit of the LORD came mightily upon Samson and he slew the Philistines
Judges 20:35-37	25,100	Benjamites — for "wickedness"
Judges 20:44-46	25,000	More Benjamites
1 Samuel 14: 12-14	20	The LORD delivered the Philistines into the hands of Jonathan and his armourbearer
1 Samuel 15: 32-33	1	Samuel hewed Agag in pieces before the LORD in Gilgal
1 Kings 20:28-29	100,000	Syrians, Israelites' enemies
2 Chronicles 13:15-17	500,000	Israel had forsaken the LORD — so God delivered them to Abijah and the people of Judah who slew them
TOTAL	*686,761*	
GRAND TOTAL	**1,030,030**	

> **"**Almost everyone who has read history in a more than casual manner knows that when the great figure of God appears in a controversy, the shooting cannot be far off.**"**
> — *Stewart H. Holbrook*

Massacres From the Bible:

Massacres Carried Out By God Himself

Passage	Offence
Genesis 7:23	Flood kills everyone except Noah & family
Genesis 19:24	Sodom and Gomorrah razed — for their sinfulness
Numbers 11:1	The fire of the Lord burnt among those who complained
Numbers 11:31	When the Israelites complained about food, God sent them a great plague
Numbers 21:6	"And the Lord sent fiery serpents among the people, and they bit the people; and much people of Israel died"
Exodus 9:25	The Pharaoh would not let Moses' people go, so the Lord smote the land of Egypt with hail
Exodus 12:29-30	God kills every Egyptian firstborn child including the Pharaoh's son — because "the Lord hardened the Pharaoh's heart, so that he would not let the children of Israel go"
Exodus 32:35	The Lord plagued the people — because of the calf Aaron made
Leviticus 10:1-3	Nadab and Abihu, sons of Aaron, offered fire before the Lord — "which he commanded them not". So "fire went out from the Lord" and devoured them
2 Kings 17:25-26	God sent lions to kill the people in Samaria "who know not the manner of the God of the land"
Numbers 14:35-37	*Despite* all God's miracles (like killing all Egyptian firstborns) many children of Israel still "murmur against Him" — so he sends a plague to kill them
Numbers 16:27-32	The earth opened its mouth and swallowed people and the earth closed (the children of Israel *still* aren't convinced!)
Deuteronomy 2:14-16	God kills the entire Israelite army "for indeed the hand of the Lord was against them"
Joshua 10:11	God helped the Israelites flee to Bethhoron by casting down great stones from heaven to kill the Israelites' enemies
2 Samuel 21:1	3 years of famine — because Saul's "bloody house slew the Gibeonites"
2 Chronicles 14:9-14	Asa, Abijah's son, sought God's help to overthrow the Ethiopians — so the Lord smote them

No Numbers Specified
Massacres By Men — at God's Order

Passage	Offence
Exodus 17:13	God helps Joshua kill Amalekites
Joshua 10:32-37	Joshua and the Israelites kill "all the souls" in Lachish, Eglon and Hebron — as the Lord God of Israel commanded
Joshua 11:8	The Lord delivers the Amorites unto Joshua — who kills them all
1 Kings 18:22-40	Elijah slays the prophets of Baal
Numbers 21:34-35	God delivers the Amorites unto Moses who kills them "until there was none left alive." "Thus Israel dwelt in the land of the Amorites"
Judges 11:30-32	The Lord delivers the children of Ammon to Jephthah — who "smote them with a very great slaughter"
2 Kings 10:30	Jehu kills the worshippers of Baal — blasphemers all
2 Chronicles 36:16-17	The Israelites incite the Lord's wrath by polluting the house of the Lord and mocking God's messengers — so God causes the Chaldees to slay them all

How Many Did *Satan* Kill?

Just *ten* are enumerated! — Job's seven sons and three daughters (Job 1:18-19). Add to that most of Job's slaves and servants and Satan's total reaches a mere 50 to 100 (Job 1).

Satan killed these people *with God's permission* — if not at his order. So they should rightly be attributed to God, not Satan. Ten is *nothing* compared to the 1,030,030 *God* killed — and that's not counting the God's *unnumbered* massacres: thirty million in the flood just for starters.

Note: These lists ONLY include God's killings and massacres — and may be incomplete. Steve Wells, for example, counts 2,301,417 deaths in the Bible attributed to God himself, and estimates God's other massacres to total 32,358,793 — *34,660,210 people in all!*[63] Not considered are passages where the Israelites or others go on killing sprees on their own initiative.

Religious Wars and Massacres

A partial list (with estimated deaths where available)
Read it and weep.

Roman Empire, 64 to 313 CE
Persecution of Christians
Romans killing Christians

Omayyad Caliphate, 680
Karbala Massacre
Sunni Muslims killing Shiite Muslims

Byzantium, 726 to 842
Iconoclastic Controversy
Christians killing Christians

Spain and other European countries, 772-804
Forced Conversions of Saxons
(led by Charlemagne, Holy Roman Emperor!)
Christians killing Pagans

Medieval times to 20th century
Russian Pogroms
Christians killing Jews

Middle East spreading to other countries, 1095-1291
The Crusades
Christians killing Muslims

Germany, 1096
The German "Crusades"
Christians killing Jews (*on the way* to the Crusades)

Jerusalem, 1099
Siege and Massacre at Jerusalem
(Part of the First Crusade)
Christians killing Jews and Muslims

Byzantium, 1204
Sack of Constantinople
(Part of the Fourth Crusade)
Roman Catholics killing Orthodox Christians

Languedoc, France, 13th century
"Cathar Crusade"
Catholics killing heretics ("Cathars")

13th through 15th centuries
Teutonic Knights and their Crusades
Christians killing Pagans and other Christians

Bohemia/Moravia, 1420-1436
Hussite Wars
Roman Catholics killing Hussites (followers of Jan Huss)

Spain and other countries, 1478-1834
Spanish Inquisition
Christian torturing and killing Jews, Muslims and heretics
(Between 3,000 and 5,000 people were executed)

France, 1562-1598
"The Religious Wars"
Catholics killing Protestants

Lyon, France, 1572
St. Bartholomew's Day Massacre
Catholics killing Protestants
7,000 to 12,000 dead

Germany, 1618 to 1648
Thirty Years War
Catholics and Protestants killing each other

Salem, Massachusetts, 1692
Salem Witch Trials
Christians killing imperfectly orthodox Christians
(25-plus people executed as witches)

Ireland, 1916-1921
Irish War of Independence
Catholics and Protestants killing each other

Ireland, 1922
Irish Civil War
Catholics and Protestants killing each other

Palestine, 1929-1948
Arabs protest Jewish immigration
Muslims killing Jews — and *vice versa*

Germany, 1933-1945
The Holocaust
Christians killing Jews*
6 million Jews (and 3 to 5 million non-Jews)

India-Pakistan, 1947
Massacres of Indian Independence
Hindus and Muslims killing each other

Israel-Palestine, 1948 to present day
Middle East/Israeli wars
Jews and Muslims killing each other

Sudan, 1955-1972; 1983-2005
Sudanese Civil War
Muslims vs. Christians and Animist rebels
1.9 million civilian casualties.

---

* Some people (in addition to Holocaust deniers) might object to including the Holocaust in this list on the basis that Hitler was an atheist. Hitler was born a Roman Catholic — and never renounced that religion. Furthermore, in Mein Kampf he wrote: *"I believe today that my conduct is in accordance with the will of the Almighty Creator."* In 1936 he said, in the Reichstag: *"I believe today that I am acting in the sense of the Almighty Creator. By warding off the Jews I am fighting for the Lord's work."* After all, Hitler's anti-Semitism was firmly based in the 2,000-year-old Christian tradition of labelling *all* Jews "Christ killers" — and Hitler was doing *exactly* what the Catholic Church had done over the centuries, albeit it on a grander and better-organized scale.

Northern Ireland, 1969 to present day
"The Troubles"
Catholics killing Protestants
3,554 deaths

East Timor, 1970s to present day
Jemaah Islamiyah
Muslims mainly killing Christians

Punjab, India, 1981
Sikhs and Hindus killing each other
14,000 dead

Beirut, Lebanon, 1982
Sabra and Chatila Massacre
Christians or Jews killing Muslims
700 to 3,500 dead

Sri Lanka, 1983 to present
Sri Lankan Civil War
Hindus mainly killing Buddhists
65,000 dead

Bosnia, 1990s
Bosnian Civil War
Orthodox Christians killing Muslims and Roman Catholics
250,000 dead

Indonesia, 1990s to present
Muslims killing Christians

Mindanao, Philippines, 1991 to present day
Abu Sayyaf
Muslims killing Catholics — and *vice versa*
197+ dead

Middle East, present day
Al Qaeda *et. al.*
Muslim fanatics killing westerners and innocent Muslims
Thousands dead! — and dozens more every day

Southern Thailand, 2004 to present day
Muslim Separatist Insurgency
Buddhists and Muslims killing each other
2,400 dead

Ivory Coast, present day
Civil War
Christians killing Muslims

"Hey, buddy! — This happens
to be a *Protestant* cloud!"

"I was walking across a bridge one day, and I saw a man standing on the edge, about to jump off. So I ran over and said "Stop! don't do it!"

"Why shouldn't I?" he said.

I said, "Well, there's so much to live for!"

He said, "Like what?"

I said, "Well...are you religious or atheist?"

He said, "Religious."

I said, "Me too! Are you Christian or Buddhist?"

He said, "Christian."

I said, "Me too! Are you Catholic or Protestant?"

He said, "Protestant."

I said, "Me too! Are you Episcopalian or Baptist?"

He said, "Baptist!"

I said, "Wow! Me too! Are you Baptist church of god or Baptist church of the lord?"

He said, "Baptist church of god!"

I said, "Me too! Are you original Baptist church of god, or are you reformed Baptist church of god?"

He said, "Reformed Baptist church of god!"

I said, "Me too! Are you reformed Baptist church of god, reformation of 1879, or reformed Baptist church of god, reformation of 1915?"

He said, "Reformed Baptist church of god, reformation of 1915!"

I said, "Die, heretic scum," and pushed him off."

— *Emo Philips*

From Deuteronomy Chapter 7, verses:1-2:
"When the LORD thy God shall bring thee into the land whither thou goest to possess it, and hath cast out many nations before thee, the Hittites...Girgashites...Amorites... Canaanites... Perizzites...Hivites, and the Jebusites, *seven nations greater and mightier than thou;* And when the LORD thy God shall deliver them before thee; thou shalt smite them, and utterly destroy them...nor shew mercy unto them:"

Atheist Wars and Massacres

Wars and massacres in the cause of the "True," "Reformed" or "Revealed" Atheism, Agnosticism, Humanism, Rationalism, Skepticism, and their sects and factions

A complete list:

Or, to put the issue another way: when was the last time two groups of scientists went to war to settle their theoretical differences?

7

"One Nation Under God"?

"If the liberties of the American people are ever destroyed, they will fall by the hands of the clergy.**"**

— *General Marquis De Lafayette [1789]*

"Those people on the secular left, they say, 'We think you're a threat.' You know what? They're right.**"**[64]

— *Bill Donohue, president of the Catholic League for Religious and Civil Rights [2005]*

"We have enough votes to run the country. And when the people say, 'We've had enough,' we are going to take over.**"**[65]

— *Pat Robertson [1980]*

Religious fundamentalism is politically powerful in the Muslim world, where the Sharia *is the law of several countries... and in the United States, where Christian Evangelicals are a powerful force in (though do not — yet — dominate) the Republican Party.*

"The U.S. is a Christian Nation"

"The Republican Party of Texas affirms that the United States of America is a Christian nation, and the public acknowledgement of God is undeniable in our history. Our nation was founded on fundamental Judeo-Christian principles based on the Holy Bible....

"Our party pledges to exert its influence to...dispel the 'myth' of the separation of church and state."

— *Platform of the*
Republican Party of
Texas, 2004

And here's a great idea...

"We should invade their [Muslim] countries, kill their leaders and convert them to Christianity."

— *Ann Coulter,* National Review,
13 September 2001

Hmm. Christians tried that before. Four times, in fact (the Crusades). Nothing like proposing a policy with a proven record of failure to win friends and influence people in government.

But, then again, the Crusaders didn't have nukes.

"Reclaiming America for Christ"

"Our job is to reclaim America for Christ, whatever the cost. As the vice regents of God [*appointed by...?*], we are to exercise godly dominion and influence over our neighborhoods, our schools, our government, our literature and arts, our sports arenas, our entertainment media, our news media, our scientific endeavors — in short, over every aspect and institution of human society."[66]

> — *James Kennedy, founder,*
> *Coral Ridge Ministries,*
> *February 2005, and an*
> *advisor to George W. Bush*

The Dominionists

"Meet the Dominionists — biblical literalists who believe God has called them to take over the U.S. government. As the far-right wing of the evangelical movement, Dominionists are pressing an agenda that makes Newt Gingrich's Contract With America look like the Communist Manifesto. They want to rewrite schoolbooks to reflect a Christian version of American history, pack the nation's courts with judges who follow Old Testament law, post the Ten Commandments in every courthouse and make it a felony for gay men to have sex and women to have abortions."[67]

— *Bob Moser,* Rolling Stone

" ON THE BRIGHT SIDE, WHEN YOU FALL ASLEEP IN CREATION SCIENCE CLASS, THE TEACHER THINKS YOU'RE PRAYING!"

World Conquest?

"Christians have an obligation, a mandate, a commission, a holy responsibility to reclaim the land for Jesus Christ — to have dominion in civil structures, just as in every other aspect of life and godliness.

"But it is dominion we are after. Not just a voice.

"It is dominion we are after. Not just influence.

"It is dominion we are after. Not just equal time.

"It is dominion we are after.

"World conquest. That's what Christ has commissioned us to accomplish. We must win the world with the power of the Gospel. And we must never settle for anything less...."

— *George Grant*[*]

"Fundamentalism isn't about religion. It's about power."
— *Salman Rushdie*

---

[*] From *The Changing of the Guard: Biblical Principles for Political Action*, by George Grant, former executive director of D. James Kennedy's Coral Ridge Ministries:

Reconstructionism

R. J. Rushdoony was the founder of the Chalcedon Institute, an organization based in California dedicated to furthering the ideas of "reconstructionism," which calls for government by a *theonomy* — rule by the literal word of god. Reconstructionism supports a postmillennialist eschatology, meaning the idea that Christ will only return to earth when biblical law reigns over every corner of the globe.

In his book *The Institutes of Biblical Law* — a "bible" for the evangelical movement — Rushdoony supported the reinstatement of the Mosaic law's penal sanctions. Under such a system, the list of civil crimes which carry a death sentence would include homosexuality, adultery, incest, lying about one's virginity, bestiality, witchcraft, idolatry or apostasy, public blasphemy, false prophesying, kidnapping, rape, and bearing false witness in a capital case.

Well, at least it's better than the Sharia: he doesn't propose cutting off the hands of thieves.

Faith-based initiatives

"[T]hose who question whether or not faith-based grassroots leadership works...they say where's the evidence. No one ever asks the secular programs for their success, but all of the sudden they want the data. Well, I tell you the data that I use is the experience that the blind man had in the book of Matthew, when he was healed by Jesus of his blindness."[68]

— *Robert L. Woodson, Sr.* *

---

* Head of the National Center for Neighborhood Enterprise [which received $1.8 million from the Compassion Capital Fund, established by the Bush administration as part of Bush's "faith-based initiative"] speaking at a conference on Capitol Hill on April 25, 2001.

"Higher rates of belief in and worship of a creator correlate with higher rates of homicide, juvenile and early mortality, STD infection rates, teen pregnancy, and abortion in the prosperous democracies."[69]

— *Gregory S. Paul in the* Journal of Religion and Society

"A disturbing fact continues to surface in sex abuse research. The first best predictor of abuse is alcohol or drug addiction in the father. But the second best predictor is conservative religiosity, accompanied by parental belief in traditional male-female roles. This means that if you want to know which children are most likely to be sexually abused by their father, the second most significant clue is *whether or not the parents belong to a conservative religious group with traditional role beliefs and rigid sexual attitudes.* "[70]

— *Carolyn Holderread Heggen, from* Sexual Abuse in Christian Homes and Churches

Just the facts, ma'am...?

"Does it [abstinence education] work? You know what? Doesn't matter. Cause guess what. My job is not to keep teenagers from having sex. The public schools' job should not be to keep teens from having sex.

"Our job should be to tell kids the truth!

"People of God, can I beg you to commit yourself to truth, not what works! To truth! I don't care if it works, because at the end of the day I'm not answering to you, I'm answering to God."[71]

— *Pam Stenzel**

© 2010 baloocartoons.com

© 2010 www.baloocartoons.com / Reproduced by permission

"Don't look now, but Cain and Abel really blew your 'Family Values' thing."

---

* Pam Stenzel [appointed by president Bush as a member of the Department of Health and Human Services task force to help implement abstinence education; founder of Enlightenment Communications, a non-profit organization specializing in abstinence education, which received grants from Bush's faith-based initiative] speaking at the 2003 "Reclaiming America for Christ" conference.

"Contrary to expectations, we found no significant differences in STD infection rates between [abstinence] pledgers and nonpledgers, despite the fact that they transition to first sex later, have less cumulative exposure, fewer partners, and lower levels of nonmonogamous partners. Examination of the point estimates revealed small or nonexistent differences between pledgers and others, with the exception of white respondents....

"[M]arried pledgers test positive [for STDs] at the same rates as married nonpledgers. The biomarker data we have analyzed in this article cannot tell us whether pledgers had a lower risk of STD infection as young adolescents. By the end of their teenage years, at the time of wave 3, however, these advantages, if any, have vanished. As a social policy, pledging [abstinence] does not appear effective in stemming STD acquisition among young adults.[72]

— *Hannah Brückner and Peter Bearman,*
in the Journal of Adolescent Health

No wonder Pam Stenzel doesn't want to
know anything about the facts!

"Where knowledge ends,
religion begins.**"**
— *Benjamin Disraeli*

Was the U.S. established as a Christian Nation?

The truth is easy to establish simply by looking at the source documents: the Declaration of Independence, the U.S. Constitution, and what the Founding Fathers actually said at the time.

The Declaration of Independence

These famous words from the Declaration of Independence seem "self-evidently" clear:

> We hold these truths to be self-evident, that all men are created equal, that they are endowed by their Creator with certain unalienable Rights, that among these are Life, Liberty and the pursuit of Happiness— That to secure these rights, Governments are instituted among Men, deriving their just powers from the consent of the governed.

But to the Evangelical Right, the word "Creator" is *proof* that the U.S. was established as a Christian nation.

Really?

While a Creator (and, note, *not* God or Jesus — nor, for that matter, Allah, Buddha, or Shiva) is said to be the *source* of man's "unalienable Rights," governments "derive their just power from the consent of the *governed"* — *not* any Creator.

Furthermore, the whole basis of the American Revolution was to overthrow an unjust (British) government and establish a just one — "just" being defined as a government that secures man's "unalienable Rights."

Logically, the evangelicals who wish to rewrite American history should read the *rest* of the paragraph.

But logic isn't their strong point.

The U.S. Constitution

In the U.S. Constitution, there is no mention of a "Creator," and religion is only referred to twice.

Article VI reads, in part:

> The Senators and Representatives before mentioned, and the members of the several state legislatures, and all executive and judicial officers, both of the United States and of the several states, shall be bound by oath or affirmation, to support this Constitution; **but no religious test shall ever be required as a qualification to any office or public trust under the United States**.

Then, of course, there is the First Amendment:

> **Congress shall make no law respecting an establishment of religion, or prohibiting the free exercise thereof;** or abridging the freedom of speech, or of the press; or the right of the people peaceably to assemble, and to petition the government for a redress of grievances.

Historical Note

When the U.S. Constitution was ratified in 1789, most of the States had various religious tests and restrictions on who could vote or hold office. For example:

Georgia: only Protestants could vote.

Massachusetts: the Governor had to be a Christian.

Maryland: uttering "profane words concerning the Holy Trinity" was punishable by torture and branding.

New York: oaths could only be made on the Bible.*

North Carolina: only Protestants (though which sect was not specified) could hold state office.

Massachusetts, New Hampshire, Connecticut, Maryland, South Carolina, and **Georgia** had "established" churches — which, at the time, meant that aid was provided to various churches: Protestant ones, in three states, and to "those of the Christian religion" in the other three.

The U.S. Constitution (until after the Civil War) only restricted the power of the *Federal* government. So, for example, the provision that "no religious test shall ever be required as a qualification to any office or public trust under the United States" did *not* then apply to holding office in *State* governments.

Nevertheless, many of the State governments — which had all voted *for* the Constitution *and* the First Amendment, otherwise they would never have been ratified — proceeded to abolish their religious qualifications for office.

In 1818, the Congregational church was "disestablished" in Connecticut; and in 1833, Massachusetts (home of the Salem witch trials) disestablished *all* its churches... by *popular referendum*. The vote: ten to one *in favor of*

---

* That the first US President, George Washington, took his oath of office on the Bible is cited by some people as evidence that he believed in God. But he took his oath in New York; for it to be a legal oath, at the time, it had to be taken on the Bible.

disestablishment.

Clearly, while most Americans at the time were probably Christians of one flavor or another, they had absolutely no interest in *living in* a "Christian Nation."

"Organized religion is making Christianity political rather than making politics Christian."
— *Laurens van der Post*

The Treaty with Tripoli

For those who need a more direct official statement of whether the United States was founded as a Christian nation, consider the text of the U.S. treaty with Tripoli.

In November, 1796 — while George Washington was President — the United States negotiated a treaty, known as "The Barbary Treaties," with the Bey and Subjects of Tripoli and Barbary.

Known as the "Treaty of Peace and Friendship," article 11 reads:

> **As the government of the United States of America is not in any sense founded on the Christian Religion**, — as it has in itself no character of enmity against the laws, religion or tranquility of Musselmen, — and as the said States never have entered into any war or act of hostility against any Mehomitan nation, it is declared by the parties that no pretext arising from religious opinions shall ever produce an interruption of the harmony existing between the two countries.[73]

The treaty was ratified by the U.S. Senate in 1797 and signed by John Adams, Washington's successor as president.

What America's Founding Fathers actually said

George Washington

"[Every man] ought to be protected in worshipping the Deity according to the dictates of his own conscience."[74]

"In the Enlightened Age and in this Land of equal Liberty it is our boast, that a man's religious tenets will not forfeit the protection of the Laws, nor deprive him of the right of attaining and holding the highest Offices that are known in the United States."[75]

Thomas Jefferson

"Question with boldness even the existence of a god."[76]

"A professorship of Theology should have no place in our institution [the University of Virginia]."[77]

"I have examined all the known superstitions of the world, and I do not find in our particular superstition of Christianity one redeeming feature. They are all alike founded on fables and mythology. Millions of innocent men, women and children, since the introduction of Christianity, have been burnt, tortured, fined and imprisoned. What has been the effect of this coercion? To make one half the world fools and the other half hypocrites; to support roguery and error all over the earth."

"In every country and every age, the priest had been hostile to Liberty."

"And the day will come when the mystical generation of Jesus, by the supreme being as his father in the womb of a Virgin Mary, will be classed with the fable of the generation of Minerva in the brain of Jupiter.... But we may hope that the dawn of reason and freedom of thought in these United States will do away [with] all this artificial scaffolding."[78]

Benjamin Franklin

"The way to see by faith is to shut the eye of reason."

"I have found Christian dogma unintelligible. Early in life, I absented myself from Christian assemblies."

"When a Religion is good, I conceive it will support itself; and when it does not support itself, and God does not take care to support it so that its Professors are obliged to call for the help of the Civil Power, it is a sign, I apprehend, of its being a bad one."[79]

James Madison

"The civil rights of none shall be abridged on account of religious belief or worship, nor shall any national religion be established, nor shall the full and equal rights of conscience be in any manner, or on any pretence, infringed."[80]

"During almost fifteen centuries has the legal establishment of Christianity been on trial. What has been its fruits? More or less, in all places, pride and indolence in the clergy; ignorance and servility in the laity; in both, superstition, bigotry, and persecution."

John Adams

"This would be the best of all possible worlds if there were no religion in it."

"The United States of America have exhibited, perhaps, the first example of governments erected on the simple principles of nature; and if men are now sufficiently enlightened to disabuse themselves of artifice, imposture, hypocrisy, and superstition, they will consider this event as an era in their history.... It will never be pretended that any persons employed in that service had interviews with the gods, or were in any degree under the influence of Heaven, more than those at work upon ships or houses, or laboring in merchandise or agriculture; it will forever be acknowledged that these governments were contrived merely by the use of reason and the senses." [81]

"The divinity of Jesus is made a convenient cover for absurdity."

"Thirteen governments [of the original states] thus founded on the natural authority of the people alone, without a pretence of miracle or mystery, and which are destined to spread over the northern part of that whole quarter of the globe, are a great point gained in favor of the rights of mankind." [82]

Even the clergy agreed!...

Reverend Timothy Dwight
[President of Yale College, 1812]

"The nation has offended Providence. We formed our Constitution without any acknowledgement of God; without any recognition of His mercies to us, as a people, of His government or even His existence. The [Constitutional] Convention, by which it was formed, never asked even once, His direction, or His blessings, upon their labours. Thus we commenced our national existence under the present system, without God." [83]

...as did other presidents...

Abraham Lincoln

"The Bible is not my book, and Christianity is not my religion. I could never give assent to the long, complicated statements of Christian dogma."

"My earlier views of the unsoundness of the Christian scheme of salvation and the human origin of the scriptures have become clearer and stronger with advancing years, and I see no reason for thinking I shall ever change them."

Ulysses S. Grant

"Leave the matter of religion to the family altar, the Church, and the private schools, supported entirely by private contributions. Keep the church and state forever separate."

"I would suggest the taxation of all property equally whether church or corporation."

James A. Garfield

"The divorce between church and state ought to be absolute. It ought to be absolute. It ought to be so absolute that no church property anywhere, in any state, or in any nation, should be exempt from taxation, for if you exempt the church property of any church organization, to that extent you impose tax upon the whole community."

John F. Kennedy

"I believe in an America where the separation of church and state is absolute — where no Catholic prelate would tell the President (should he be Catholic) how to act, and no Protestant minister would tell his parishioners for whom to vote — where no church or church school is granted any public funds or political preference — and where no man is denied public office merely because his religion differs from the President who might appoint him or the people who might elect him.

"I believe in an America that is officially neither Catholic, Protestant nor Jewish — where no public official either requests or accepts instructions on public policy from the Pope, the National Council of Churches or any other ecclesiastical source — where no religious body seeks to impose its will directly or indirectly upon the general populace or the public acts of its officials — and where religious liberty is so indivisible that an act against one church is treated as an act against all....

"Finally, I believe in an America where religious intolerance will someday end — where all men and all churches are treated as equal — where every man has the same right to attend or not attend the church of his choice — where there is no Catholic vote, no anti-Catholic vote, no bloc voting of any kind — and where Catholics, Protestants and Jews, at both the lay and pastoral level, will refrain from those attitudes of disdain and division which have so often marred their works in the past, and promote instead the American ideal of brotherhood."

> **"One of the embarrassing problems for the early nineteenth-century champions of the Christian faith was that not one of the first six Presidents of the United States was an orthodox Christian."**
> — *Mortimer Adler*[84]

But things have changed since 1776...

George W. Bush

"God told me to strike at al Qaida and I struck them, and then he instructed me to strike at Saddam, which I did, and now I am determined to solve the problem in the Middle East."[85] *[June, 2003]*

"Tyrants and dictators will accept no other gods before them. They require disobedience to the First Commandment. They seek absolute control and are threatened by faith in God. They fear only the power they cannot possess — the power of truth. So they resent the living example of the devout, especially the devotion of a unique people chosen by God."[86] *[April 25, 2001]*

"This crusade, this war on terrorism is going to take a while."[87] *[September 16, 2001]*

It was a family affair...

George H.W. Bush...

"No, I don't know that atheists should be considered as citizens, nor should they be considered as patriots. This is one nation under God."[88] *[1987, while vice-president]*

Hmmm. Please refresh my memory...which article of the Constitution (which he took an oath to protect) is he referring to?

"At the time of its Founding, the United States seemed to be an infertile ground for religion. Many of the nation's leaders — include George Washington, Thomas Jefferson, and Benjamin Franklin — were not Christians, did not accept the authority of the Bible, and were hostile to organized religion. The attitude of the general public was one of apathy: in 1776, only 5 percent of the population were participating members of churches.**"**

— *Ian Robertson*[89]

8

Life Without God?

"If there were a god, there would be no need for religion. If there were not a god, there would be no need for religion."

— *Ron Barrier*

"Those who will not reason, are bigots, those who cannot, are fools, and those who dare not, are slaves."

— *Lord Byron*

"An atheist is someone who chooses to be moral, rather than simply giving in to fear of divine wrath."

— *Anonymous*

"Christians, like slaves and soldiers, ask no questions."

— *Jerry Falwell, American Evangelist*

"If you believe in eternity then life is irrelevant."

— *Author Unknown*

"Pandora's Box"

If you believe in a god and you're reading this book, then perhaps you're beginning to doubt your life-long beliefs.

That's scary.

Quite possibly, you just don't want to think about it. That's understandable.

Maybe you share the reaction of one reader of an earlier draft who said: "I feel cheated and *angry:* the church has been *lying* to me all my life!"

Or, you read a few pages and put the book down for a while, scared that "If I keep reading, I'll be *alone.*"

Just the thought of giving up something that's been a central part of you for as long as you can remember — and everything that goes with it — of possibly losing friends and even being rejected by your own family simply doesn't bear thinking about.

The inevitable result: an emotional state of *high anxiety.* A natural reaction to such anxiety is to run away from its source. But — like the injunction, *don't* think of a pink hippopotamus — dipping into this book can be rather like unlocking Pandora's Box which, once open, can never be closed again.

> **"When I was young I used to pray for a bicycle. Then I realized that God doesn't work that way, so I stole a bike and prayed for forgiveness."**
>
> — *Emo Philips*

So here are some things to think about, a few suggestions of things you might like to do or try, a variety of options to consider — and a few techniques that will help alleviate anxiety. Let's first address some common reactions, beginning with the prospect that...

"I'll Become A Bad Person"

If you stopped believing in God, would you suddenly be a bad person? Would you start killing people, stealing from them, defrauding your employers, abusing children or worse — without a second thought? With no sense of guilt, remorse, or shame?

If not, why not?

On the other hand, why are the world's prisons filled with murderers, thieves and rapists and other scoundrels —

> **"**I am a humanist, which means, in part, that I have tried to behave decently without any expectation of rewards or punishments after I'm dead.**"**
> — *Kurt Vonnegut*

"bad people" *beyond all reasonable doubt* — who devoutly believe in God, some even claiming God *commanded* them to commit their crimes?

And I bet you know *at least* one person *you* wouldn't trust with the time of day — and you make sure your wallet's still intact when they've gone. Yet *other* people think that *same person* is a fine, upstanding, God-fearing citizen.

God certainly seems to work

© 2010 baloocartoons.com

"Atheists I can put up with —
it's those wishy-washy
agnostics I can't stand!"

in mysterious ways. Consider the saying: "God helps those

who help themselves."*

Speaking as two atheists who have achieved comfortable success in life — and who both know many other atheists and agnostics who have done as well if not better than us, both George and I can say that if God *does* help those who help themselves, it seems he does so whether they believe in him or not!

"I'll Be Alone"

Are you thinking that to even *voice* any doubts about your beliefs would result in *rejection* or worse by friends and family?

Well, if you've become a bit skeptical about religion's claims, there's no need to shout it from the rooftops. Test the waters with your friends and family by making a few vague comments — or just keep everything to yourself for the time being.

After all, when you come right down to it, how often do you discuss your religious beliefs with anyone?

"Oh, I understand — with the 'coveting' part, we can get *everybody!*"

---

* This saying is not to be found in the Bible. It was popularized by Benjamin Franklin (a skeptic!) in the 1736 edition of *Poor Richard's Almanack*.

Occasionally, I imagine, but not all that often. So if you don't talk about it, who will notice?

Perhaps you know a few people who hardly ever go to church but haven't necessarily given up their beliefs (would you know if they had?).

> **"**An atheist doesn't have to be someone who thinks he has a proof that there can't be a god. He only has to be someone who believes that the evidence on the god question is at a similar level to the evidence on the werewolf question.**"**
> — *John McCarthy*

Others *change* their re-ligion — that happens all the time.

If, say, a Catholic becomes a Pentecostal or a Methodist, not too many people mind. After all, he or she is still a *Christian.*

Becoming a Zoroastrian, Bahá'í or Buddhist would certainly raise more eyebrows. But that person still believes in *a* god — which, to most believers, is better than believing in no god at all.

"There's *Some* Kind of God"

One step before atheism is *Deism* (which was the belief system of most of America's Founding Fathers, and is similar to Aristotle's "Unmoved Mover").

The Deist believes that there *is* a god who created the universe with its natural laws — but hasn't taken much interest in his creation since. There's not much point in praying to the Deist god — he's not listening.

A less radical belief is: "There's *some* kind of God, Creator or Higher Power. I'm not sure exactly what he, she or it is like — but I pray to him/her/it anyway."

So if you've been thinking atheism is the only alternative to the God of Christianity, it's not.

What Atheists Don't Have

But in case you've ever wondered what it's like to be an atheist, there are (as with everything else) pluses and minuses. For example, there are certain things that believers (of *all* faiths) *have,* that atheists and agnostics *don't.*

1.   We Don't Have Anywhere To Go

The world is full of churches, mosques, synagogues and temples. There, you can be with hundreds of other people who feel the same way you do. It's an easy place to make new friends — but even if you never talk to anyone else, you still feel a powerful sense of community, belonging — and spiritual uplift.

> **"I am what you might call a practicing atheist. I'm quite happy to be an atheist because I think, actually, God likes atheists better. We never ask for anything, we're not bothering him all the time saying "Oh God please help me I want this-'n-this-'n-this...."**
>
> — *Dave Allen*

Of course, there are lots of other places where people of like minds meet — clubs, associations, political parties, professional bodies, special interest groups, hobbyist societies, and so on. But — other than in the bosom of your family — in none of them will you experience the same kind of attachment.

They just don't compare, do they?

2.   No One's Looking Out For Us

We've got no one to pray to. We don't believe there's anyone Up There who's on our side (or anyone Down There who's against us, either). As psychologist Nathaniel Branden puts it: "Nobody's Coming" [to the rescue].

Branden said that so often that one of his clients crocheted a sign, NOBODY'S COMING, which he hung on the wall of his office.

One day, one of his clients pointed to the sign and said: "But *you* came, Nathaniel."

"That's true," Branden replied. "But I came to tell you that *nobody's coming.*"

> **"**Give a man a fish, and you'll feed him for a day; give him a religion, and he'll starve to death while praying for a fish.**"**
>
> — *Author Unknown*

If nobody's coming to our rescue, we're on our own.

That sounds scary. And, sure, it can be. If we don't have a god to rely on, what *do* we have?

Only the people who love us, our true friends — and ourselves.

Ultimately, the people who make the most of their lives are those who pull themselves up by their own bootstraps — regardless of their beliefs.

3. We Don't Feel Guilty At Being Alive

We weren't born with Original Sin; we weren't born *evil;* we feel no guilt at just being on this earth. What a relief!

When you think about, it becomes obvious that no woman could have come up with the idea of "Original Sin" (unless she was certifiably insane).

No — it could *only* have come from a man (which it did: in the early years of Christianity, there were many Church Fathers — preeminently, St. Augustine — but no Church *Mothers).*

© 2010 baloocartoons.com

"You knew when you took this job that there's no rest for the wicked!"

No woman can hold a newborn baby in her arms and say, *with total conviction: "You* are *evil."*

Nor, I submit, can *you,* whatever your gender (try it sometime).

When a baby is baptized, supposedly the "Original Sin" is washed away. But in what observable way has the infant changed?

None at all. And the child doesn't even *know* it was born sinful — until he or she learns it from adults.

That's when the child starts to feel "Original Guilt." Not before.

> **"All I know is that if God loves me only half as much as my mother does, he will not send me to Hell."**
> — *Lin Yutang*

Do atheists still feel guilt? Of course — when we transgress one of our *own* moral rules. Yes, atheists *do* have moral rules which, by and large, are surprisingly similar to every religions': "Thou shalt not kill; thou shalt not steal; thou shalt not bear false witness" and so on.

There's even *one* of the Ten Commandments atheists and agnostics follow better that all Catholics and many other Christians: we faithfully observe the Commandment "Thou shalt not make thee any graven image" — and certainly never *worship* any!

4. We're Not Afraid...

...because we don't believe in Hell (or Heaven for that matter).

I've yet to meet a believer who thinks he or she is destined for Hell. On the contrary, *everyone* who believes in God is confident *they* (unlike their neighbors) are in God's good graces.

Yet, deep down inside they can't be sure; deep down they're scared legless that, come Judgement Day, God might hold them accountable for some sin they committed years and years ago — and send them to Hell after all. The result is a life lived in uncertainty and fear.

That said, for *you* to stop believing in God without being *sure* there's no God would make you feel worse, not better: you'd then be *certain* you're destined for Hell.

5. We Don't Much Care What Other People Believe

That might come as a surprise, especially from the authors of a book like this!

But think about it: What organizations send people out knocking on doors on Sundays? What organizations send missionaries to every corner of the globe to convert people to their beliefs? What organizations have TV and radio stations all around the world dedicated to marketing *their* values?

How many of them are atheist? Well...none.*

©2008 baloocartoons.com

© 2010 www.baloocartoons.com / Reproduced by permission

Baloo

"In compliance with Federal full-disclosure laws, I'm required to tell you that I'm really not all that sure about some of this stuff."

---

* There was one once: the Communist Party. Though atheists, Communists weren't out there selling *atheism* but a glorious future — like all other religions. The major difference: while *you* could enter the Christian Paradise *after you die,* the Communist Paradise is to be enjoyed by your great-great-grandchildren.

There are a few well-known proselytizers for atheism, most notably Christopher Hitchens and Richard Dawkins.[*] They and the many others who have written books and articles on the subject have inspired many atheists to "come out of the closet." But I'm having trouble adding to that list of just *two* atheists who are out there "actively hustling for atheism" — in competition with the hundreds of thousands of door-knockers and television evangelists selling one brand of God or another.

> **"**If I were not an atheist, I would believe in a God who would choose to save people on the basis of the totality of their lives and not the pattern of their words. I think he would prefer an honest and righteous atheist to a TV preacher whose every word is God, God, God, and whose every deed is foul, foul, foul.**"**
>
> — *Isaac Asimov*

For atheists, by and large, other people's religious beliefs are simply a non-issue. Sure, if you want to argue with us we'll argue back. Otherwise, though, few of us feel any impulse whatsoever to "save your soul."

All atheists have friends who are firm believers in God (and, by the same token, *they* have friends who are atheists). How do we stay friends?

We agree to disagree.

This attitude of "live and let live" is the foundation of a peaceful society. We agree to settle our differences peacefully — or simply ignore them.

But the fundamentalist believer won't buy into that agreement. Whether he's an Islamic suicide bomber, a Hindu

---

[*] Authors of the best-selling books *God Is Not Great: How Religion Poisons Everything* and *The God Delusion* respectively. For more see www.hitchensweb.com and www.richarddawkins.net.

"Thou Shalt Not Kill": Hardwired?

In the First and Second World Wars, only 15%-20% of American frontline soldiers fired their rifles — *even when the enemy was shooting at them.* Most who did fire their rifles aimed to miss!

The US Army got the average firing rate up to 55% in the Korean war, and 95% in Vietnam (which doesn't mean the *aiming* rate had gone up. "Over 50,000 bullets [were] fired for every [Vietcong/North Vietnamese] enemy killed"[90]).

How? The US Army changed its training methods.

To quote from *On Killing* by Lt. Col. Dave Grossman: "Since World War II, a new era has quietly dawned in modern warfare: an era of psychological warfare — psychological warfare conducted not upon the enemy, *but upon one's own troops.*"[91]

This "psychological warfare" involves **Desensitizing** soldiers to the idea of killing, **Conditioning** them *using techniques lifted straight from Pavlov and Skinner* to produce an "automatic killing *reflex,*" and teaching them **"Prepackaged" Denial Defence Mechanisms** so soldiers can (partially) convince themselves they're shooting at a target, not another human being.

Grossman presents an enormous body of evidence — detailed research from recent wars, corroborated by data going back as long ago as the Greek "phalanx" — that human beings have a natural, inborn *resistance* to taking another person's life.

It would seem the Commandment "Thou Shalt Not Kill" is hard-wired into humankind.

who does "Shiva's will" by killing innocent Muslims, or the born-again Christian who goes around shooting doctors who perform abortions, the fundamentalist is a danger to us all — believers and non-believers alike.

Does God Make People Happy?

The available evidence across 50 countries suggests there's a strong link between *wealth* and *happiness:* richer people are, *on average,* happier than poorer people, regardless of their religious beliefs.

Meanwhile, there appears to be no link whatsoever between religious belief and happiness *or* wealth: rich atheists are generally happier than poor believers, and *vice versa.*

For more detail see Appendix I, page 310.

Most believers are peaceful people who read the passages their Holy Book — like "He that loveth not knoweth not God; for God is love." (John 4:8) or "These things I [Jesus] have spoken unto you, that in me ye might have peace" (John 16:33) — that accord with their peaceful nature.

The fundamentalist reads the same Holy Book — with a different focus. *He* comes away, his mission of "death to infidels" reinforced by passages like: "He that sacrificeth unto any god, save unto the LORD only, he shall be utterly destroyed" (Exodus 22:20) and "...whosoever would not seek the LORD God of Israel should be put to death, whether small or great, whether man or woman" (2 Chronicles 15:13).

Both read the same book, the same source...selectively.

Can you have one side of the coin without the other?

The answer would seem to be *Yes, you can* — as an individual.

For all of us, though, the answer is *No,* since if *you* can choose the kind of God Yahweh is, then so can everyone else — including the fanatics and fundamentalists.

Coping With Anxiety

Finally, here are a few ideas and techniques you might like to try to help relieve any anxiety you might feel (regardless of where it came from).

Comedy: Do you have a favorite comedy program? Get a DVD of past episodes and watch it (or browse

> **"**Every prayer reduces itself to this: Great God, grant that twice two be not four.**"**
> — *Ivan Turgenev*

through the comedy selections on YouTube). It's pretty hard to feel anxious, depressed or stressed out while you're laughing your head off.

Exercise: Aside from being good for you, exercise, if vigorous enough, releases endorphins that lift your mood. People who exercise regularly feel "withdrawal" symptoms

"Are you sure we should do all this praying on Sunday? — I thought it was God's day off."

when they miss a couple of days or stop. You'll also improve your health and live longer (although to someone who's *really* depressed that's hardly something to look forward to!).

> **"**Believe nothing, no matter where you read it, or who said it, no matter if I have said it, unless it agrees with your own reason and your own common sense.**"**
> — *Buddha*

Shop Around: Have you ever gone to a church of a *different* "brand" of Christianity — or even to a service of some other faith? Have a look around, see what other believers are saying and broaden your mind.

In the same vein, do you know anyone who's an atheist/agnostic/skeptic/non-practicing believer? What are they like? How are they different from you? Think about it.

If you're wondering what atheists, agnostics and skeptics talk about, well, the same sorts of things you mostly talk about. The *really* important things in life: wine, women, song, money — and who's sleeping with whom.

Try Meditation which results in a mental state similar to prayer (see "Altered States," page 300).

How meditation works is simple: you get comfortable, close your eyes, and repeat a "mantra" — which is simply a sound like *Om man padre hum* which has no meaning to you. So it can be any sound.

Repeating the sound fills your mind with that sound — and so excludes all the normal internal chatter, fleeting thoughts and worries that normally intrude into your consciousness. Meditation, then, is the *reverse* of *"don't* think about a pink hippopotamus": by focusing on one thought, the mantra, all *other* thoughts are excluded, resulting in a relaxed *mental* state.

Repetition gives that meaning-less sound meaning. The "meaning" in this case becomes *the meditative state itself.*

Prayer is much the same mental process, except that the words you say *do* have meaning — so your mind focuses on *those* thoughts while excluding all others.

If you'd like to investigate this idea, you'll find more information on meditation and how to do it at www.marktier.com/meditate, plus links to other sites and programs you can download such as *Breathe To Relax,* which will help you reach a relaxed state and reduce stress and anxiety.

"It's not atheism, agnosticism, or Protestantism, Patrick — our true enemy is *golf.*"

"Surprisingly, recent research suggests that a religious person is more likely to commit a crime than a non-religious person. One can even argue that the more religious the society, the more likely it is to have high crime rates."
— Lisa Conyers and Philip D. Harvey[92]

"It's for Sunday School, Mom —
I googled 'Adam and Eve.'"

"Believe those who are
seeking the truth.
Doubt those who find it."
— *Andre Gide*

9

"Sacred Cows Make the Best Hamburger"
— *Mark Twain*

Life in Lubbock, Texas, taught me two things: One is that God loves you and you're going to burn in hell. The other is that sex is the most awful, filthy thing on earth and you should save it for someone you love.
— *Butch Hancock*

All religions are the same: religion is basically guilt, with different holidays.
— *Cathy Ladman*

We must respect the other fellow's religion, but only in the same sense and to the extent that we respect his theory that his wife is beautiful and his children smart.
— *H.L. Mencken*

In Heaven all the interesting people are missing.
— *Friedrich Nietzsche*

Shoes and minds must be left at the gate.
— *Sign at the entrance of the ashram of Bhagwan Sri Rajneesh, Poona, India*

Philosophy is questions that may never be answered. Religion is answers that may never be questioned.

> — *Anonymous*

What a queer thing is Christian salvation! Believing in firemen will not save a burning house; believing in doctors will not make one well, but believing in a savior saves men. Fudge!

> — *Lemuel Washburn*

RELIGION, *n.* A daughter of Hope and Fear, explaining to Ignorance the nature of the Unknowable.

> — *Ambrose Bierce,* The Devil's Dictionary

One good thing about religion is that it is reliable. You can figure to get the same results whether you pray to Jehovah, Jesus, St. Paul, Buddha, Mohammed or Vishnu.

> — *From* Heavenly Humor

The most ridiculous concept ever perpetrated by Homo Sapiens is that the Lord God of Creation, Shaper and Ruler of the Universes, wants the saccharine adoration of his creations, that he can be persuaded by their prayers, and becomes petulant if he does not receive this flattery. Yet

© 2010 baloocartoons.com

"I didn't get a wink of sleep — my descendants were holding séances all night!"

> Religion has actually convinced people that there's an invisible man — living in the sky — who watches everything you do, every minute of every day. And the invisible man has a special list of ten things he does not want you to do. And if you do any of these ten things, he has a special place, full of fire and smoke and burning and torture and anguish, where he will send you to live and suffer and burn and choke and scream and cry forever and ever till the end of time.
>
> But he loves you!
>
> — *George Carlin*

this ridiculous notion, without one real shred of evidence to bolster it, has gone on to found one of the oldest, largest and least productive industries in history.

> — *Robert Heinlein*

Every path of Natural Science is closed with the sign: NO THOROUGHFARE, MOSES.

> — *T. H. Huxley*

We have fought long and hard to escape from medieval superstition. I, for one, do not wish to go back.

> — *James Randi*

All religions are ancient monuments to superstition, ignorance, ferocity; and modern religions are only ancient follies.

> — *Paul Henri Thiry*

Scientific research can reduce superstition by encouraging people to think and view things in terms of cause and effect.

> — *Albert Einstein*

Your religion says we were created in God's image. Well, that's ridiculous, of course — God would have no need for a belly button.

> — *Robert J. Sawyer*

Man is the only animal that believes God sits up nights thinking about him.

> — *Mark Twain*

A myth is a religion in which no one any longer believes.

> — *James Feibleman*

God has given us the Papacy — let us enjoy it.

> — *Pope Leo X (formerly Cardinal Giovanni de' Medici)*

Politics has slain in its thousands, but religion has slain in its tens of thousands.

> — *Sean O'Casey*

Nothing can be more contrary to religion and the clergy than reason and common sense.

> — *Voltaire*

The Christian church, in its attitude toward science, shows the mind of a more or less enlightened man of the Thirteenth Century. It no longer believes that the earth is flat, but it is still convinced that prayer can cure after medicine fails.

> — *H.L. Mencken*

The nice thing about citing God as an authority is that you can prove anything you set out to prove. It's just a matter of

"Wait — what if the Canaanites want to *convert?*"

selecting the proper postulates, then insisting that your postulates are "inspired." Then no one can possibly prove that you are wrong.

> ## The "Money Tree"
>
> **"**If a man really wants to make a million dollars, the best way would be to start his own religion.**"**
> — *L. Ron Hubbard,*
> *founder of Scientology,*
> *in 1949 when he was a science fiction*
> *writer making just a penny a word*

— *Robert A. Heinlein*

I do not believe in the creed professed by the Jewish church, by the Roman church, by the Greek church, by the Turkish church, by the Protestant church, nor by any church that I know of. My own mind is my own church.

— *Thomas Paine*

The two principal mono-manias of modern man: monotheism and monogamy.

— *Thomas Szasz*

When lip service to some mysterious deity permits bestiality on Wednesday and absolution on Sunday — cash me out.

— *Frank Sinatra*

Wouldn't it be interesting if somebody found hard scientific evidence that God exists — and that He is a product of evolution?

— *Stanley Schmidt*

Religion is an insult to human dignity. With or without it you'd have good people doing good things and evil people doing evil things. But for good people to do evil things it takes religion.

— *Steven Weinberg, Nobel Prize Winner, Physics*

Well, I believe there's somebody out there who watches over us. Unfortunately, it's the government.

— *Woody Allen*

Hell is an outrage on humanity. When you tell me that your deity made you in his image, I reply that he must have been very ugly.

— *Victor Hugo*

Religion — the greatest disease of mankind.

— *Ayn Rand*

What is the function that a clergyman performs in the world? Answer: he gets his living by assuring idiots that he can save them from an imaginary hell. It is a business almost indistinguishable from that of a seller of snake-oil for rheumatism.

— *H.L. Mencken*

I give money for church organs in the hope the organ music will distract the congregation's attention from the rest of the service.

— *Andrew Carnegie*

"...And any of you tribes that don't like it can get lost!"

It has been often said, very truly, that religion is the thing that makes the ordinary man feel extraordinary; it is an equally important truth that religion is the thing that makes the extraordinary man feel ordinary.

— *Charles Dickens*

In a heated controversy over the wisdom of giving the Bible to slaves, [Frederick Douglass] asserted that it would be "infinitely better to send them a pocket compass and a pistol."

— *Benjamin Quarles*

> ## "If *You* Were God...?"
>
> Robert G. Ingersoll, asked how he would improve the world if he were God, said:
>
> "Why, I'd make good health catching instead of sickness."

Religion is comparable to a childhood neurosis.

— *Sigmund Freud*

Religious liberty might be supposed to mean that everybody is free to discuss religion. In practice it means that hardly anybody is allowed to mention it.

— *G.K. Chesterton*

Education and intelligence as a whole are contradictory to faith and belief.

— *Vexen Crabtree*

I believe it because it is absurd.

— *Tertullian*

Hearing nuns' confessions is like being stoned to death with popcorn.

— *Fulton Sheen*

If there is no Hell, a good many preachers are obtaining money under false pretences.

— *William Sunday*

All religions are cruel, all founded on blood; for all rest principally on the idea of sacrifice — that is, on the perpetual immolation of humanity to the insatiable vengeance of divinity.

— *Mikhail Bakunin*

If triangles had a God, He'd have three sides.

— *Old Yiddish Proverb*

Say what you will about the ten commandments, you must always come back to the pleasant fact that there are only ten of them.

— *H.L. Mencken*

On the surface, [holy scriptures] may appear to have been composed as conscientious history. In depth they reveal themselves to have been conceived as myths: poetic readings of the mysteries of life from a certain interested point of view. But to read a poem as a chronicle of fact is — to say the least — to miss the point. To say a little more, it is to prove oneself a dolt.

— *Joseph Campbell*

If I had been the Virgin Mary, I would have said "No."

— *Margaret "Stevie" Smith*

The "Power" of God

Religion is regarded by the common people as true, by the wise as false, and by the rulers as useful.

— *Seneca the Younger*

A tyrant must put on the appearance of uncommon devotion to religion. Subjects are less apprehensive of illegal treatment from a ruler whom they consider god-fearing and pious. On the other hand, they do less easily move against him, believing that he has the gods on his side.

— *Aristotle*

Religion is what keeps the poor from murdering the rich.

— *Napoleon Bonaparte*

Whoever talks to me of God has designs on my liberty or on my purse.

— *Proudhon*

There can be but little liberty on earth while men worship a tyrant in heaven.

— *Robert G. Ingersoll*

Religion is excellent stuff for keeping common people quiet.

— *Napoleon Bonaparte*

Man is a Religious Animal. He is the only Religious Animal. He is the only animal that has the True Religion — several of them. He is the only animal that loves his neighbor as himself and cuts his throat if his theology isn't straight. He has made a graveyard of the globe in trying his honest best to smooth his brother's path to happiness and heaven.

— *Mark Twain*

Businesses may come and go, but religion will last forever, for in no other endeavor does the consumer blame himself for product failure.

> If a God needs our worship then at least to that extent he is inferior to us.
> — *John Zube*

— *Harvard Lampoon*

It is the position of some theists that their right to freedom *of* religion is abridged when they are not allowed to violate the rationalists' right to freedom *from* religion.

— *James T. Green*

On the other hand, the Bible contains much that is relevant today, like Noah taking forty days to find a place to park.

— *Curtis McDougall*

I still say a church steeple with a lightning rod on top shows a lack of confidence.

— *Doug McLeod*

To die for a religion is easier than to live it absolutely.

— *Jorge Luis Borges,* Labyrinthes

Christian fundamentalism: the doctrine that there is an absolutely powerful, infinitely knowledgeable, universe spanning entity that is deeply and personally concerned about my sex life.

— *Andrew Lias*

Christianity preaches only servitude and dependence. Its spirit is so favorable to tyranny that it always profits by such a regime. True Christians are made to be slaves, and they know it and do not much mind: this short life counts for too little in their eyes.

— *Jean Jacques Rousseau*

©2007 baloocartoons.com

Baloo

"If this is Good Friday, I'd hate to see a *bad* one!"

Religion supports nobody. It has to be supported. It produces no wheat, no corn; it ploughs no land; it fells no forests. It is a perpetual mendicant. It lives on the labors of others, and then has the arrogance to pretend that it supports the giver.

— *Robert G. Ingersoll*

An Inuit hunter asked the local missionary priest: "If I did not know about God and sin, would I go to hell?" "No," said the priest, "not if you did not know." "Then why," asked the Inuit earnestly, "did you tell me?"

— *Annie Dillard*

God split himself into a myriad parts that he might have friends. This may not be true, but it sounds good — and is no sillier than any other theology.

— *Robert A. Heinlein*

SCRIPTURES, *n:* the sacred books of our holy religion, as distinguished from the false and profane writings on which all other faiths are based.

— *Ambrose Bierce,* The Devil's Dictionary

If we assume that man actually does resemble God, then we are forced into the impossible theory that God is a coward, an idiot and a bounder.

— *H.L. Mencken*

Religions are not revealed: they are evolved. If a religion were revealed by God, that religion would be perfect in whole and in part, and would be as perfect at the first moment of its revelation as after ten thousand years of practice. There has never been a religion which fulfills those conditions.

— *Robert Blatchford*

Generally speaking, the errors in religion are dangerous; those in philosophy only ridiculous

— *David Hume*

Why should we take advice on sex from the pope? If he knows anything about it, he shouldn't.

— *George Bernard Shaw*

I don't know if God exists, but it would be better for His reputation if He didn't.

— *Jules Renard*

That God cannot lie, is no advantage to your argument, because it is no proof that priests can not, or that the Bible does not.

— *Thomas Paine*

INFIDEL, *n*: In New York, one who does not believe in the Christian religion; in Constantinople, one who does.

— *Ambrose Bierce,* The Devil's Dictionary

I wonder why the so-called acts of God are always catastrophes.

— *Poul Anderson*

God has no religion.

— *Mahatma Gandhi*

Such a thing as a truly enlightened Christian is hard to imagine. Either he is enlightened or he is Christian, and the louder he protests that he is the former the more apparent it becomes that he is really the latter.

— *H.L. Mencken*

If a man would follow, today, the teachings of the Old Testament, he would be a criminal. If he would follow strictly the teachings of the New, he would be insane.

— *Robert G. Ingersoll*

"Now, let me get this straight — You got this blonde hair on your shoulder by wrestling an *angel?*"

I sometimes think that God, in creating man, somewhat overestimated His ability.

— *Oscar Wilde*

Christ died for our sins. Dare we make his martyrdom meaningless by not committing them?

— *Jules Feiffer*

There is not sufficient love and goodness in the world to permit us to give some of it away to imaginary beings.

— *Friedrich Nietzsche*

A celibate clergy is an especially good idea because it tends to suppress any hereditary propensity toward fanaticism.

— *Carl Sagan*

I prayed for twenty years but received no answer until I prayed with my legs.

— *Frederick Douglass, escaped slave*

Top 10 reasons why
Beer is better than Religion

10. No one will kill you for not drinking Beer.

9. Beer doesn't tell you how to have sex.

8. Beer has never caused a major war.

7. They don't force Beer on minors who can't think for themselves.

6. When you have a Beer, you don't knock on people's doors trying to give it away.

5. Nobody's ever been burned at the stake, hanged, or tortured over his brand of Beer.

4. You don't have to wait 2,000+ years for a second Beer.

3. There are laws saying Beer labels can't lie to you.

2. You can prove you have a Beer.

1. If you've devoted your life to Beer, there are groups to help you stop.

— *Author Unknown*

A dogma is a set of beliefs accepted on faith; that is, without rational justification, or against rational evidence. A dogma is a matter of blind faith.

— *Ayn Rand*

A long and wicked life followed by five minutes of perfect grace gets you into Heaven. An equally long life of decent living and good works followed by one outburst of taking the name of the Lord in vain — then have a heart attack at that moment and be damned for eternity. Is that the system?

— *Robert A. Heinlein*

If I owe Smith ten dollars, and God forgives me, that doesn't pay Smith.

— *Robert G. Ingersoll*

God is dead.

> — *Friedrich Nietzsche*

God is dead! But don't worry, Mary is pregnant again.

> — *Gegenschein*

To hear many religious people talk, one would think God created the torso, head, legs and arms, but the devil slapped on the genitals.

> — *Don Schrader*

God is believed in because no one can see Him.

> — *Japanese proverb*

Religion, like poetry, is simply a concerted effort to deny the most obvious realities.

> — *H. L. Mencken*

If you talk to God, you are praying. If God talks to you, you have schizophrenia.

> — *Thomas Szasz*

"What? — All that work, and now they don't even believe in evolution?"

> It has been said that few people doubted the existence of god until philosophers attempted to prove it.
> — *George H. Smith,* Atheism: The Case Against God

The clergy know that I know that they know that they do not know.
— *Robert G. Ingersoll*

Those people who tell me that I'm going to hell while they are going to heaven somehow make me very glad that we're going to separate destinations.
— *Martin Terman*

A Christian is a man who feels
Repentance on a Sunday
For what he did on Saturday
And is going to do on Monday.
— *Thomas Russell Ybarra,* The Christian

A converted cannibal is one who, on Friday, eats only fishermen.
— *Emily Lotney*

"God is truth" does not make any sense to me. But "Truth is my God" is a statement with which I can sympathize.
— *John Zube*

> If someone tells me the earth is less than ten thousand years old, in my opinion he should see a psychiatrist.
> — *Francis Crick*

God is intellectually superfluous...emotionally dispensable...and morally intolerable.
— *Antony Flew*

I am amused by the puzzled look on the faces of those who ask: "Do you believe in God?" when the response is: "What do you mean?" — I have yet to meet any "believer" who knows what, in reality, the word "God" denotes.
— *Judith M. James*

Forgive, O Lord, my little jokes on Thee
And I'll forgive Thy great big one on me.
— *Robert Frost*

To command the professors of astronomy to confute their own observations is to enjoin an impossibility, for it is to command them not to see what they do see, and not to understand what they do understand, and to find what they do not discover.
— *Galileo Galilei*

It is only the savage, whether of the African bush or of the American gospel tent, who pretends to know the will and intent of God exactly and completely.
— *H. L. Mencken*

"There are no atheists in foxholes" isn't an argument against atheism, it's an argument against foxholes.
— *James Morrow*

God being everything, the real world and man are nothing. God being truth, justice, and infinite life, man is falsehood, inequality, and death. God being master, man is the slave.
— *Michael Bakunin*

A man without God is like a fish without a bicycle.
— *Graffiti*

"You realize, these are going to lead inevitably to the legal profession."

Religion...is the opium of the people.

— *Karl Marx*

Religion is no longer the opiate of the masses. It is the speed of the masses.

— *Akbar Ahmed*

Marx was wrong. Religion is not the opiate of the people. Opium suggests something soporific, numbing, dulling. Too often religion has been an aphrodisiac for horror, a Benzedrine for bestiality. At its best it has lifted spirits and raised spires. At its worst it has turned entire civilizations into cemeteries.

— *Phillip Adams*

Anyone who can worship a trinity and insist that his religion is a monotheism can believe anything — just give him time to rationalize it.

— *Robert A. Heinlein*

A man is accepted into a church for what he believes and he is turned out for what he knows.

— *Mark Twain*

An apology for the Devil: It must be remembered that we have only heard one side of the case. God has written all the books.

— *Samuel Butler*

It is interesting that every time God gives direct orders to anyone, it is always "Thou shalt kill."

— *Newsweek magazine*

Proof of God would be fatal to religion: a God susceptible of proof would have to be finite and limited; He would be one entity among others within the universe, not a mystic omnipotence transcending science and reality.

— *Leonard Peikoff*

The idea that God is an oversized white male with a flowing beard who sits in the sky and tallies the fall of every sparrow is ludicrous. But if by "God" one means the set of physical laws that govern the universe, then clearly there is such a God. This God is emotionally unsatisfying...it does not make much sense to pray to the law of gravity.

> — *Carl Sagan*

The Gods take no thought for our happiness, but only for our punishment.

> — *Tacitus*

Theologians had to introduce Satan, or there wouldn't be any story value in the Bible.

> — *John W. Campbell*

For every complex problem, there is a solution that is simple, neat, and wrong.

> — *H. L. Mencken*

PRAY, *v.* To ask that the laws of the universe be annulled in behalf of a single petitioner, confessedly unworthy.

> — *Ambrose Bierce,* The Devil's Dictionary

"There goes Methuselah again, cackling about all his lifetime subscriptions."

Jesus preached, although he rarely practiced, the tactic of turning the other cheek, loving one's enemies and praying for them, and forgiving those who wrong you seventy times seven times (which should lead any opponent to capitulation)....

Typically with adversaries, such as the scribes and Pharisees who criticized him, Jesus not only answered criticism with criticism but reviled and threatened them.... In fact, Jesus never forgave anyone who wronged or criticized him, although he forgave those who had wronged others.

— *Jay Haley,* **The Power Tactics of Jesus Christ**

Belief means not wanting to know what is true.
— *Friedrich Nietzsche*

I have little confidence in any enterprise or business or investment that promises dividends only after the death of the stockholders.
— *Robert G. Ingersoll*

Lighthouses are more helpful than churches.
— *Benjamin Franklin*

If Jesus had been killed twenty years ago, Catholic school children would be wearing little electric chairs around their necks instead of crosses.
— *Lenny Bruce*

So far as religion of the day is concerned, it is a damned fake.... Religion is all bunk.
— *Thomas Edison*

I can't say I believe in god. If, in fact, I ever find out that he does indeed exist, I think I'll stay away from him, because if he's responsible for half the things he gets credit for, he's got to be one mean son of a bitch.
— *Peter Gethers*

Insofar as faith is possible, it is irrational; insofar as faith is rational, it is impossible.

— *George H. Smith,* Atheism: The Case Against God

The essence of science is that it is always willing to abandon a given idea, however fundamental it may seem to be, for a better one; the essence of theology is that it holds its truths to be eternal and immutable.

— *H.L. Mencken*

Science has proof without any certainty. Creationists have certainty without any proof.

— *Ashley Montague*

If people are good only because they fear punishment, and hope for reward, then we are a sorry lot indeed.

— *Albert Einstein*

History does not record anywhere or at any time a religion that has any rational basis. Religion is a crutch for people not strong enough to stand up to the unknown without help. But, like dandruff, most people do have a religion and spend time and money on it and seem to derive considerable pleasure from fiddling with it.

— *Robert A. Heinlen*

"Don't look now, Newton, but that Einstein kid is finding loopholes."

Belief in gods and belief in ghosts is identical. God is taken as a more respectable word than ghost, but it means no more.

— *E. Haldeman-Julius*

The Jews, the Muslims and the Christians,
They've all got it wrong.
The people of the world only divide into two kinds,
One sort with brains who hold no religion,
The other with religion and no brain.

— *Abu-al-Ala al-Marri,
10th century Syrian poet*

The biggest advantage to believing in God is you don't have to understand anything, no physics, no biology.

— *James Watson*

Every day people are straying away from the church and going back to God.

— *Lenny Bruce*

If religion were true, its followers would not try to bludgeon their young into an artificial conformity; but would merely insist on their unbending quest for truth, irrespective of artificial backgrounds or practical consequences.

— *H.P. Lovecraft*

The Church says that the Earth is flat, but I know that it is round. For I have seen the shadow on

Baloo

"The trouble with monotheism is that you can never get a second opinion."

Some of you say religion makes people happy. So does laughing gas.

— *Clarence Darrow*

The fact that a believer is happier than a skeptic is no more to the point than the fact that a drunken man is happier than a sober one.

— *George Bernard Shaw*

The believer is happy; the doubter is wise.

— *Hungarian proverb*

The widely-held assumption that believers are happier is contradicted by the evidence. See Appendix I, "Happiness and God," page 310.

the moon and I have more faith in the shadow than in the Church.

— *Attributed to Ferdinand Magellan*

To explain the unknown by the known is a logical procedure; to explain the known by the unknown is a form of theological lunacy.

— *David Brooks,* The Necessity of Atheism

God has always resembled his creatures. He hated and loved what they hated and loved and he was invariably found on the side of those in power.

— *Robert G. Ingersoll*

I believe in God, only I spell it Nature.

— *Frank Lloyd Wright*

Prayers never bring anything... They may bring solace to the sap, the bigot, the ignorant, the aboriginal, and the lazy — but to the enlightened it is the same as asking Santa Claus to bring you something for Xmas.

— *W. C. Fields*

PURITANISM, *n.*: The haunting fear that someone, somewhere, may be happy.

— *H.L. Mencken*

[As a young man] I came to the conclusion that the church was just a bunch of fascists that supported Franco. I stopped going on Sunday mornings and watched the birds with my father instead.

— *James Watson*

God is the only being who does not have to exist in order to reign.

— *Charles Baudelaire*

The Bible is a book that has been read more and examined less than any book that ever existed.

— *Thomas Paine*

Fantastic doctrines (like Christianity or Islam or Marxism) require unanimity of belief. One dissenter casts doubt on the creed of millions. Thus the fear and the hate; thus the torture chamber, the iron stake, the gallows, the labor camp, the psychiatric ward.

— *Edward Abbey*

We are here to unlearn the teachings of the church, state, and our educational system. We are here to drink beer. We are here to kill war. We are here to laugh at the odds and live our lives so well that Death will tremble to take us.

— *Charles Bukowski*

Baloo

"'Promised Land"? — You mean we're going to *California?*"

So, What's the Difference?

I accompanied a Filipina friend who was visiting Thailand to several Roman Catholic masses. I enjoyed the walk to the church, and found the ceremonies relaxing, often providing me with an opportunity to gently snooze.

After one of them, she asked me what I thought. I told her a lot of the ceremonies were boring to me with the priest droning on endlessly repeating the same thing. But the occasional personal anecdotes of hardship and persecution were very interesting.

"I have two questions that have been bothering me about the ceremonies. Do you mind if I ask?" "No, please do," she answered.

"Well," I said, "If god is a good god, kind, and loving, why do people stand in fear and trembling in his presence? What are they afraid of?"

There was silence from my friend, and I went on ...

"And Supunsa, Jiraporn, and Aun," I asked, naming three mutual friends of ours, "they're good people aren't they?" "Well, yes," she said.

"So why is god going to torture them, burn them for a thousand years, just because they were born Buddhist? Does that sound like something a good person would do? If someone tied Supunsa down and tortured her with flames day after day for weeks, you'd think that was terrible, wouldn't you? You'd hate the torturer, wouldn't you?"

Silence.

"So why is it different, why is it good when god does it?"

Silence.

— *Dan Rosenthal*

> If I were to speak your kind of language, I would say that man's only moral commandment is: Thou shalt think. But a "moral commandment" is a contradiction in terms. The moral is the chosen, not the forced; the understood, not the obeyed. The moral is the rational, and reason accepts no commandments.
>
> — *Ayn Rand,* **Atlas Shrugged**

Gods are fragile things; they may be killed by a whiff of science or a dose of common sense.

— *Chapman Cohen*

An intelligent hell would be better than a stupid paradise.

— *Victor Hugo*

We would be 1,500 years ahead if it hadn't been for the church dragging science back by its coattails and burning our best minds at the stake.

— *Catherine Fahringer*

It is clear that the individual who persecutes a man, his brother, because he is not of the same opinion, is a monster.

— *Voltaire*

I realized early on that it is detailed scientific knowledge which makes certain religious beliefs untenable. A knowledge of the true age of the earth and of the fossil record makes it impossible for any balanced intellect to believe in the literal truth of

"A Crusade? — But that might offend Muslims!"

every part of the Bible in the way that fundamentalists do. And if some of the Bible is manifestly wrong, why should any of the rest of it be accepted automatically?

> — *Francis Crick*

The beauty of religious mania is that it has the power to explain everything. Once God (or Satan) is accepted as the first cause of everything which happens in the mortal world, nothing is left to chance...logic can be happily tossed out the window.

> — *Stephen King*

To die for an idea; it is unquestionably noble. But how much nobler it would be if men died for ideas that were true!

> — *H.L. Mencken*

The more I study religions the more I am convinced that man never worshipped anything but himself.

> — *Sir Richard Francis Burton*

The God of the Christians is a father who is a great deal more concerned about his apples than he is about his children.

> — *Diderot*

> Faith is believing what you know ain't so.
> — *Mark Twain*

With soap, baptism is a good thing.

> — *Robert G. Ingersoll*

I never yet have seen the person who could withstand the doubt and unbelief that enter his mind when reading the Bible in a spirit of inquiry.

> — *Etta Semple*

A myth is a religion in which no one any longer believes.

> — *James Feibleman*

Science is the record of dead religions.

> — *Oscar Wilde*

The Good Book — one of the most remarkable euphemisms ever coined.

— *Ashley Montagu*

I don't believe in God because I don't believe in Mother Goose.

— *Clarence Darrow*

There are no sects in geometry.

— *Voltaire*

It vexes me when they would constrain science by the authority of the Scriptures, and yet do not consider themselves bound to answer reason and experiment.

— *Galileo Galilei*

The religion of one age is, as a rule, the literary entertainment of the next.

— *Fridtjof Nansen*

What is it the Bible teaches us? — raping, cruelty, and murder. What is it the New Testament teaches us? — to believe that the Almighty committed debauchery with a woman engaged to be married, and the belief of this debauchery is called faith.

— *Thomas Paine*

Baloo

"If you're omnipresent, why do I always have to climb way up *here?*"

I do understand what love is, and that is one of the reasons I can never again be a Christian. Love is not self denial. Love is not blood and suffering. Love is not murdering your son to appease your own vanity. Love is not hatred or wrath, consigning billions of people to eternal torture because they have offended your ego or disobeyed your rules. Love is not obedience, conformity, or submission. It is a counterfeit love that is contingent upon authority, punishment, or reward. True love is respect and admiration, compassion and kindness, freely given by a healthy, unafraid human being.

— *Dan Barker,* Losing Faith in Faith

I was thinking about how people seem to read the Bible a whole lot more as they get older — then it dawned on me... they're cramming for their finals!

— *George Carlin*

By Doubting we are led to questions, questioning we arrive at truth.

— *Peter Abelard*

We are here because one odd group of fishes had a peculiar fin anatomy that could transform into legs for terrestrial creatures; because the earth never froze entirely during an ice age; because a small and tenuous species, arising in Africa a quarter of a million years ago, has managed, so far, to survive by hook and by crook. We may yearn for a "higher answer" — but none exists.

— *Stephen J. Gould*

Why is it, when a patient lives the family thanks Jesus, but when the patient dies, the family sues the doctors?

— *Author Unknown*

It is time the Arabs and the Jews sat down and settled this dispute in the true Christian spirit.

— *Senator Warren Austin*

We owe it to ourselves as respectable human beings, as thinking human beings, to do what we can to make humanity more rational....

Humanists recognize that it is only when people feel free to think for themselves, using reason as their guide, that they are best capable of developing values that succeed in satisfying human needs and serving human interests.

— *Isaac Asimov*

All religions are inconsistent with mental freedom.

— *Robert G. Ingersoll*

My bible thumping cousin once claimed that Jesus must have risen from the dead since thousands of people saw him after the resurrection. I simply pointed out that if that was the case then Elvis should be deified because thousands of people have seen him in McDonalds since 1977.

— *Rand Race*

Not All There
I turned to speak to God
About the world's despair
But to make bad matters worse
I found God wasn't there.

— *Robert Frost*

Where it is a duty to worship the sun, it is pretty sure to be a crime to examine the laws of heat.

— *John Morley*

Science is the great antidote to the poison of enthusiasm and superstition.

— *Adam Smith*

To one who has faith, no explanation is necessary. To one without faith, no explanation is possible.

— *St. Thomas Aquinas*
Shouldn't it be the other way around? [Think about it.]

How happy can you be when you think every action and thought is being monitored by a judgmental ghost?

— *Dan Barker,* Losing Faith in Faith

When science and the Bible differ, science has obviously misinterpreted its data.

— *Henry Morris, Institute for Creation Research*

Go to Heaven for the climate, Hell for the company.

— *Mark Twain*

The Christian God is a being of terrific character — cruel, vindictive, capricious, and unjust.

— *Thomas Jefferson*

In Christianity neither morality nor religion come into contact with reality at any point.

— *Friedrich Nietzsche*

The Old Testament is responsible for more atheism, agnosticism, disbelief — call it what you will — than any book ever written; it has emptied more churches than all the counter-attractions of cinema, motor bicycle and golf course.

— *A.A. Milne*

"We'd better speed up the Eve project — Adam's got himself an imaginary playmate."

It was, of course, a lie what you read about my religious convictions, a lie which is being systematically repeated. I do not believe in a personal God and I have never denied this but have expressed it clearly. If something is in me which can be called religious then it is the unbounded admiration for the structure of the world so far as our science can reveal it.

> — *Albert Einstein*

Belief in a cruel God makes a cruel man.

> — *Thomas Paine*

Two hands working do more than a thousand clasped in prayer.

> — *Author Unknown*

During many ages there were witches. The Bible said so. The Bible commanded that they should not be allowed to live. Therefore the Church, after doing its duty in but a lazy and indolent way for 800 years, gathered up its halters, thumbscrews, and firebrands, and set about its holy work in earnest. She worked hard at it night and day during nine centuries and imprisoned, tortured, hanged, and burned whole hordes and armies of witches,

"But we've got laws on the books *now* that we can't enforce!"

> According to literal Christianity, Jesus was God and the son of Mary; the Holy Ghost was God and the husband or at least the impregnator of Mary. Therefore, God is his own father. But God is also the father of all humanity, including Mary, so God is the father of his mother, and thus his own grandfather.
>
> — *Robert Anton Wilson*

and washed the Christian world clean with their foul blood. Then it was discovered that there was no such thing as witches, and never had been. One does not know whether to laugh or to cry.

— *Mark Twain*

All Bibles are man-made.

— *Thomas Edison*

"Creation science" has not entered the curriculum for a reason so simple and so basic that we often forget to mention it: because it is false, and because good teachers understand exactly why it is false.

— *Stephen Jay Gould*

Civilization has come about by going to school more than to church.

— *Lemuel K. Washburn*

It's been suggested that if the supernaturalists really had the powers they claim, they'd win the lottery every week. I prefer to point out that they could also win a Nobel Prize for discovering fundamental physical forces hitherto unknown to science. Either way, why are they wasting their talents doing party turns on television?

— *Richard Dawkins*

It is surely harmful to souls to make it a heresy to believe what is proved.

— *Galileo Galilei*

You will notice that in all disputes between Christians since the birth of the Church, Rome has always favored the doctrine which most completely subjugated the human mind and annihilated reason.

— *Voltaire*

Ministers say that they teach charity. That is natural. They live on hand-outs. All beggars teach that others should give.

— *Robert G. Ingersoll*

In spite of all the yearnings of men, no one can produce a single fact or reason to support the belief in God and in personal immortality.

— *Clarence Darrow*

A dogma is the hand of the dead on the throat of the living.

— *Lemuel K. Washburn*

All through the centuries scholars and scientists have been imprisoned, tortured and burned alive for some discovery which seemed to conflict with a petty text of Scripture. Surely the immutable laws of the universe can teach more impressive and exalted lessons

"You always talk about robbing Peter to pay Paul, but you never mention *Mary.*"

The "Feminism" of the Bible

Susan B. Anthony:

To no form of religion is woman indebted for one impulse of freedom.

H.L. Mencken:

It is now quite lawful for a Catholic woman to avoid pregnancy by a resort to mathematics, though she is still forbidden to resort to physics or chemistry.

Arianna Huffington:

Well, you could become a Southern Baptist. I mean, instead of having to obey the Pope, you could just obey your husband.

Robert G. Ingersoll:

As long as woman regards the Bible as the charter of her rights, she will be the slave of man. The bible was not written by a woman. Within its leaves there is nothing but humiliation and shame for her.

Elizabeth Cady Stanton:

The whole tone of Church teaching in regard to women is, to the last degree, contemptuous and degrading.

The religious superstitions of women perpetuate their bondage more than all other adverse influences.

The Bible and the Church have been the greatest stumbling blocks in the way of women's emancipation.

Lemuel K. Washburn:

The foolish and cruel notion that a wife is to obey her husband has sent more women to the grave than to the courts for a divorce.

than the holy books of all the religions on earth.
— *Elizabeth Cady Stanton*

Everything has a natural explanation. The moon is not a god but a great rock and the sun a hot rock.
— *Anaxagorus, ca. 475 BCE*

Two recent surveys rate the United States at the top among Western nations in belief in God and at the bottom among six major countries in school kids' understanding of science and math. This could be dismissed as chance, but it shouldn't be. While our economic competitors' schools are teaching students advanced math and science, many of our schools are wasting energy debating whether to teach evolution or creationism, which maintains that God created the universe over a six-day period about 6,000 years ago.
— *Bill Mandel*

They say [a candidate for sainthood] cured a nun's lupus. A miracle. Now I'm not a doctor, but I know lupus goes into remission. It's not always fatal. Have Ray Charles and Stevie Wonder play ping-pong together. *That's* a miracle.
— *Mick LaSalle*

Kill one man and you are a murderer. Kill millions and you are a conqueror. Kill all and you are God.
— *Jean Rostand*

Baloo

"We were sort of hoping that the Promised Land would be somewhere *outside* the Middle East."

> The night of December 25, to which date the Nativity of Christ was ultimately assigned, was exactly that of the birth of the Persian savior Mithra, who, as an incarnation of eternal light, was born the night of the winter solstice (then dated December 25) at midnight, the instant of the turn of the year from increasing darkness to light.
>
> — *Joseph Campbell,* The Mythic Image

Reality is that which, when you stop believing in it, doesn't go away.

— *Philip K. Dick*

One of the proofs of the immortality of the soul is that myriads have believed it — they also believed the world was flat.

— *Mark Twain*

Prayer has no place in the public schools, just like facts have no place in organized religion.

— *"The Simpsons"*

It is wonderful how much time good people spend fighting the devil. If they would only expend the same amount of energy loving their fellow men, the devil would die in his own tracks of ennui.

— *Helen Keller*

The book, called the Bible, is filled with passages equally horrible, unjust and atrocious. This is the book to be read in schools in order to make our children loving, kind and gentle! This is the book they wish to be recognized in our Constitution as the source of all authority and justice!

— *Robert G. Ingersoll*

Power tends to corrupt and absolute power corrupts absolutely. That unalterable rule applies both to God and man.

— *Lord Acton*

> If God made us...then presumably our sense of right and wrong comes from him. If that's the case, there is no other true sense of right and wrong but his. If he does something wrong, then he is culpable by the very standards of judgment that he has given us as sentient human beings. And murdering babies, starving masses, and allowing — or causing — genocides are wrong.
>
> — *Bart D. Ehrman,* God's Problem

OCEAN, *n.:* A body of water occupying ⅔ of a world made for man — who has no gills.

— *Ambrose Bierce,* The Devil's Dictionary

The very concept of sin comes from the bible. Christianity offers to solve a problem of its own making! Would you be thankful to a person who cut you with a knife in order to sell you a bandage?

— *Dan Barker,* Losing Faith in Faith

A guy says: "I hate Jews," and I said: "Why?" He goes: "Because they killed my God." They believe that. If I believed that the Jews killed my God, I'd worship the Jews, 'cause shit, there's some badasses on that team, man.

— *Bill Hicks*

"They're not going to take these commandments seriously unless You carve them in stone or something."

If God is love, and if God is also omnipresent, then

the Devil cannot exist. If the Devil exists, God cannot be love and also be omnipresent. Yet, an omnipresent God of love and the Devil are both said to exist. It doesn't take Sherlock Holmes to figure that there is something wrong here!

— *Donald Morgan*

I'm completely in favor of the separation of Church and State. My idea is that these two institutions screw us up enough on their own, so both of them together is certain death.

— *George Carlin*

The central problem of Christianity is: if the Messiah has come, why is the world so evil? For Judaism, the problem is: if the world is so evil, why does the Messiah not come?

"Could you tone down your humility a bit, Brother Jerome — Some of the other monks are getting jealous."

— *Seymour Siegel*

Citing the Bible as evidence for anything is like saying that the sun is in fact a chariot of fire that races across the sky because we read about it in Greek mythology.

— *Stephen Ban*

SUNDAY, *n.:* A day given over by Americans to wishing that they themselves were dead and in Heaven, and that their neighbors were dead and in Hell.

— *H.L. Mencken*

God says do what you wish, but make the wrong choice and you will be tortured for eternity in hell. That sir, is not free will. It would be akin to a man telling his girlfriend, do what you wish, but if you choose to leave me, I will track you down and blow your brains out. When a man says this we call him a psychopath and cry out for his imprisonment/execution. When god says the same we call him "loving" and build churches in his honor.

— *William C. Easttom*

My young son asked me what happens after we die. I told him we get buried under a bunch of dirt and worms eat our bodies. I guess I should have told him the truth that most of us go to Hell and burn eternally but I didn't want to upset him.

— *Jack Handey*

Why should I hate someone on the basis of their religion, when I can take a little time to get to know them and hate them for a myriad of *real* reasons.

— *Dennis Miller*

Never before have I encountered such corrupt and foul-minded perversity! Have you ever considered a career in the Church?

— *Black Adder*

According to that Holy Book, Jehovah was a believer in witchcraft, and said to his chosen people: "Thou shalt not suffer a witch to live." (Exodus 22:18). This one commandment — this simple line — demonstrates that Jehovah was not only not God, but that he was a poor, ignorant, superstitious savage. This one line proves beyond all possible doubt that the Old Testament was written by men, by barbarians.

— *Robert G. Ingersoll*

Bolo

"Which would be more Zen — a pizza with
nothing, or a pizza with everything?"

Organized religion is like organized crime; it preys on peoples' weaknesses, generates huge profits for its operators, and is almost impossible to eradicate.

— *Mike Hermann*

I like your Christ, I do not like your Christians. Your Christians are so unlike your Christ.

— *Mahatma Gandhi*

The only thing wrong with being an atheist is that there's nobody to talk to during an orgasm.

— *Anonymous*

MOSLEMS, *n.:* people who believe suicide is a good way to get laid.

— *Scott Adams*

You keep accusing me of blasphemy all of the time, but I cannot be convicted of a victimless crime.

— *Dan Barker,* Losing Faith in Faith

Let the gods avenge themselves.

— *Roman law maxim on blasphemy*

Gods are immortal but not eternal.

— *Ancient Greek saying*

It is a lot better to come from an evolved monkey than from a fallen angel.

— *Marcellin Boule*

It is impossible that there should be inhabitants on the opposite side of the Earth, since no such race is recorded by Scripture among the descendants of Adam.

— *St. Augustine*

I am an agnostic; I do not pretend to know what many ignorant men are sure of.

— *Clarence Darrow*

The sense of spiritual relief which comes from rejecting the idea of God as a supernatural being is enormous.

— *Sir Julian Huxley*

When you believe in an imaginary figure that only you can see or hear, it's called a psychological problem. If you believe in an imaginary figure that even you can't see or hear, it's a religion.

— *Author Unknown*

© 2010 baloocartoons.com

"Hey, why don't You make the Sabbath on Saturday, and then on Sundays we can play *golf!*"

All national institutions of churches, whether Jewish, Christian, or

> The God of the Old Testament is arguably the most unpleasant character in all fiction: jealous and proud of it; a petty, unjust, unforgiving control-freak; a vindictive, bloodthirsty ethnic cleanser; a misogynistic, homophobic, racist, infanticidal, genocidal, filicidal, pestilential, megalo-maniacal, sadomasochistic, capriciously malevolent bully.
> — *Richard Dawkins*

Turkish, appear to me no other than human inventions set up to terrify and enslave mankind, and monopolize power and profit.
— *Thomas Paine*

There's a Bible on that shelf there. But I keep it next to Voltaire — poison and antidote.
— *Bertrand Russell*

If only God would give me a clear sign! Like making a large deposit in my name at a Swiss bank.
— *Woody Allen*

In nature there are neither rewards nor punishments; there are consequences.
— *Robert Ingersoll*

If the lord had meant us to have faith, he'd have given us lobotomies.
— *Zlatko*

Fundamentalism means never having to say "I'm wrong."
— *Author Unknown*

A mythology is someone else's religion, different enough from your own for its absurdity to be obvious.
— *Anonymous*

I believe in karma.... That means I can do bad things to you all day long and assume you deserve it.
— *Scott Adams*

> Take from the church the miraculous, the supernatural, the incomprehensible, the unreasonable, the impossible, the unknowable, the absurd, and nothing but a vacuum remains.
> — *Robert G. Ingersoll*

You can cite a hundred references to show that the biblical God is a bloodthirsty tyrant, but if they can dig up two or three verses that say "God is love," they will claim that *you* are taking things out of context!
— *Dan Barker,* Losing Faith in Faith

Theology is the effort to explain the unknowable in terms of the not worth knowing.
— *H.L. Mencken*

Give me chastity and continence, but not yet.
— *St. Augustine*

When did I realize I was God? Well, I was praying and I suddenly realized I was talking to myself.
— *Peter O'Toole*

"Nobody's leaving till I get the offering plate back!"

It was only when I finally undertook to read the Bible through from beginning to end that I perceived that its depiction of the Lord God — whom I had always viewed as the very embodiment of perfection — was

The Sight of Hell

The Sight of Hell was a Catholic *children's* book written in the late nineteenth century. After giving a detailed description of hell (an actual place, according to this book, at the center of the earth) — of the dungeons, floods of burning pitch and sulphur, never-ending fire, red-hot ovens and the awful shrieking of tormented souls — it tells the fate of an eight-year-old child who had committed a mortal sin and died before going to confession:

The little child is in the red-hot oven, hear how it screams to come out, see how it turns and twists itself about in the fire, it beats its head against the roof of the oven, it stamps its little feet on the floor.

God was very good to this little child.

Very likely God saw that it would become a worse sinner and never repent, and so it would have to be punished more severely in hell. So God in his mercy called it out of the world in early childhood. *[Emphasis added.]*

From *The Sight of Hell* by the Reverend Joseph Furniss.[93]

actually that of a monstrous, vengeful tyrant, far exceeding in bloodthirstiness and insane savagery the depredations of Hitler, Stalin, Pol Pot, Attila the Hun, or any other mass murderer of ancient or modern history.

— *Steve Allen*

If you want to get together in any exclusive situation and have people love you, fine — but to hang all this desperate sociology on the idea of The Cloud Guy who has The Big Book, who knows if you've been bad or good — and *cares* about any of it — to hang it all on that, folks, is the chimpanzee part of the brain working.

— *Frank Zappa*

"Nice try, Dante, but no cigar."

If absolute power corrupts absolutely, where does that leave God?

— *George Deacon*

Communism, like any other revealed religion, is largely made up of prophecies.

— *H.L. Mencken*

As a freethinking human being, I have come not to favor or fear religion, but to face and fight it as an impediment to civilized advancement.

— *Steve Benson*

Freedom of religion includes freedom from religion.... Why don't we celebrate living, instead of worrying about damnation and sin?

— *Ed Schempp*

Atheism leaves a man to sense, to philosophy, to natural piety, to laws, to reputation; all of which may be guides to an outward moral virtue, even if religion vanished; but religious superstition dismounts all these and erects an absolute monarchy.

— *Francis Bacon, Sr.*

Not only is there no God, but try getting a plumber on weekends.

— *Woody Allen*

No religion has ever given a picture of deity which men could have imitated without the grossest immorality.

— *George Santayana*

> There is in every village a torch — the teacher; and an extinguisher — the clergyman.
>
> — *Victor Hugo*

Religion is the most malevolent of all mind viruses. We should get rid of it as quick as we can.

— *Arthur C. Clarke*

FAITH, *n.*: Belief without evidence in what is told by one who speaks without knowledge, of things without parallel.

— *Ambrose Bierce,* **The Devil's Dictionary**

Religions are like glow worms; they shine only when it's dark. A certain amount of ignorance is the condition of all religions, the element in which alone they can exist.

— *Arthur Schopenhauer*

I venture to ask whether the Creator is or is not? If He is not, how can He create things? If He is, then (being one of those things), He

© 2010 baloocartoons.com

"Forty years wandering in the desert? — Couldn't you find a god who knows a short cut?"

is incapable of creating the mass of bodily forms.... The creating of things has no Lord; everything creates itself. Everything produces itself and does not depend on anything else. This is the normal way of the universe.

— *Kuo Hsiang [died 312 CE]*

Faith is a cop-out. It is intellectual bankruptcy. If the only way you can accept an assertion is by faith, then you are conceding that it can't be taken on its own merits.

— *Dan Barker,* Losing Faith in Faith

The only way to reconcile science and religion is to create something which isn't science or something which isn't religion.

— *H.L. Mencken*

"Okay, who spilled the beans to that Darwin guy?"

When I think of all the harm [the Bible] has done, I despair of ever writing anything to equal it.

— *Oscar Wilde*

A man who is a merchant can seldom if ever please God

— *St. Jerome*

Religions are the great fairy tales of conscience.

— *George Santayana*

> Ministers ask: Is it possible for God to forgive man? And when I think of what has been suffered — of the centuries of agonies and tears, I ask: Is it possible for man to forgive God?
> — *Robert G. Ingersoll*

The Christian God was once a Jew. Now he is an anti-Semite.
— *Anatole France [1905]*

We are in the world to laugh. In purgatory or in hell, we shall no longer be able to laugh. And in heaven it would not be proper.
— *Jules Renard*

Cult: a small unpopular religion.
Religion: a large popular cult.
— *Anonymous*

Religions are founded on the fear of the many and the cleverness of the few.
— *Stendhal*

Devout believers are safeguarded in a high degree against the risk of certain neurotic illnesses; their acceptance of the universal neurosis spares them the task of constructing a personal one.
— *Sigmund Freud*

"My wives found out about my girlfriends!"

What is Atheism?

Testimony to the Supreme Court of the United States in the case of Murray v. Curlett, 374 U.S. 203, 83 S. Ct. 1560, 10 L.Ed.2d (MD, 1963), to remove reverential Bible reading and oral unison recitation of the Lord's Prayer in the public schools.

Your petitioners are Atheists and they define their beliefs as follows. An Atheist loves his fellow man instead of god. An Atheist believes that heaven is something for which we should work now — here on earth for all men together to enjoy.

An Atheist believes that he can get no help through prayer but that he must find in himself the inner conviction, and strength to meet life, to grapple with it, to subdue it and enjoy it.

An Atheist believes that only in a knowledge of himself and a knowledge of his fellow man can he find the understanding that will help to a life of fulfillment.

He seeks to know himself and his fellow man rather than to know a god. An Atheist believes that a hospital should be built instead of a church. An Atheist believes that a deed must be done instead of a prayer said. An Atheist strives for involvement in life and not escape into death. He wants disease conquered, poverty vanquished, war eliminated. He wants man to understand and love man.

He wants an ethical way of life. He believes that we cannot rely on a god or channel action into prayer nor hope for an end of troubles in a hereafter.

He believes that we are our brother's keepers; and are keepers of our own lives; that we are responsible persons and the job is here and the time is now.[94]

The act of worship, as carried on by Christians, seems to me to be debasing rather than ennobling. It involves grovelling before a Being who, if He really exists, deserves to be denounced instead of respected.

— *H.L. Mencken*

"'Creationism'? — Those little twerps are *always* trying to shift the blame!"

If there is a God, atheism must seem to Him as less of an insult than religion.

— *Edmond de Goncourt*

I am an atheist because there is no evidence for the existence of God. That should be all that needs to be said about it: no evidence, no belief.

— *Dan Barker,* Losing Faith in Faith

The truths of religion are never so well understood as by those who have lost the power of reasoning.

— *Voltaire*

Mankind will only really be free, once the last king is strangled with the entrails of the last priest.

— *Robert A. Heinlein*

There is no difference between someone who eats too little and sees Heaven and someone who drinks too much and sees snakes.

— *Bertrand Russell*

Christianity is the strangest religion ever set up, for it committed a murder upon Jesus in order to redeem mankind from the sin of eating an apple.

— *Thomas Paine*

"Mythology" is what we call someone else's religion.

— *Joseph Campbell*

As a Roman Catholic, I thank God for the heretics. Heresy is only another word for freedom of thought.

— *Graham Greene*

It's hard to be religious when certain people are never incinerated by bolts of lightning.

— *Bill Waterson*

The best cure for Christianity is reading the Bible.

— *Mark Twain*

The being cannot be termed rational or virtuous who obeys any authority but that of reason.

— *Mary Wollstonecraft*

Atheism is the vice of a few intelligent people.

— *Voltaire*

Once there was a time when all people believed in God and the church ruled. This time is called the Dark Ages.

— *Ruth Hurmence Green*

Talking to god is crazy.
Hearing god is schizophrenia.
Acting on it is insanity.

— *Robert Patterson*

Is man one of God's blunders, or is God one of man's blunders?

— *Friedrich Nietzsche*

[Former US Attorney-General John] Ashcroft went on to say that our way of life is being threatened by a group of radical religious fanatics who are armed and dangerous. And then he called for prayers in the schools and an end to gun control.

— *Jay Leno*

If atheism is a religion, then bald is a hair color.

— *Mark Schnitzius*

I respect faith, but doubt is what gets you education.

— *Wilson Mizner*

Religion began when the first scoundrel met the first fool.

— *Voltaire*

So far as I can remember, there is not one word in the Gospels in praise of intelligence.

— *Bertrand Russell*

"But if He's omniscient, wouldn't praying just *annoy* Him?"

When I told the people of Northern Ireland that I was an atheist, a woman in the audience stood up and said, Yes, but is it the God of the Catholics or the God of the Protestants in whom you don't believe?

— *Quentin Crisp*

A church is a place in which gentlemen who have never been to heaven brag about it to persons who will never get there.

— *H.L. Mencken*

It only stands to reason that where there's sacrifice, there's someone collecting the sacrificial offerings. Where there's service, there is someone being served. The man who speaks to you of sacrifice is speaking of slaves and masters, and intends to be the master.

— *Ayn Rand*

"Here you go — Don't say I
didn't warn you."

Imagine...

Imagine, with John Lennon, a world with no religion. Imagine

no suicide bombers,
no 9/11,
no 7/7,
no Crusades,
no witch-hunts,
no Gunpowder Plot,
no Indian Partition,
no Israeli/Palestinian wars,
no Serb/Croat/Muslim massacres,
no persecution of Jews as "Christ-killers,"
no Northern Ireland troubles,
no honor killings,
no shiny-suited bouffant-haired televangelists fleecing gullible people of their money (God wants you to give till it hurts).

Imagine no Taliban to blow up ancient statues, no public beheadings of blasphemers, no flogging of female skin for the crime of showing an inch of it.

— *Richard Dawkins in* The God Delusion

Mad Mullahs With Nukes?

Kingdom Coming: the Rise of Christian Nationalism by Michelle Goldberg is a horror story. It chronicles the growing political power of the proto-totalitarian fundamentalist evangelical Christian right in the United States. They're smart, unified, politically savvy, flush with cash, have superb marketing; and their political influence is based on their ability to worm their way into and bring out the vote for...the Republican Party.

Their aim is simple: turn the United States into a Christian nation, which — aside from teaching creationism in schools and making homosexuality illegal — would inevitably mean the persecution of "heretics" and the repeal (or, more likely, "reinterpretation") of the First Amendment...should they ever gain firm possession of the White House, Congress, and the Supreme Court.

Sounds far-fetched? It seems so — especially now the Democrats are in power and the Republican party is in disarray...for the moment. But as Ayn Rand put it: "The battle of human history is fought and determined by those who are predominantly *consistent*"[95] — and the fundamentalists' message is *very* consistent and *very* simple, while those who would stand in their way hardly realize they present a threat!

And if they eventually succeed...Mad Mullahs in *Washington* with Nukes!

The God Strategy

The rise of faith-based politics in the US is chronicled in *The God Strategy: How Religion Became a Political Weapon in America.* The authors, David Domke and Keven Coe, analyze how many times American presidents referred to God, Christianity or faith in their speeches and found a dramatic rise in the Reagan to Bush Jr. years (1980 to 2006, halfway through Bush Jr.'s second term) compared to their predecessors, from Roosevelt to Carter. There was also a change in *tone* from earlier presidents' references to the Creator, now alluding to or invoking the authority of the Declaration of Independence.

The "God Strategy" was developed and used with great success by the Republican party (and Clinton). It involves appearing at religious events and making statements which signal "I'm one of you" to evangelical Christians — while being bland enough to pass over the heads of moderate Christians and non-believers.

Under Clinton, and again in the 2006 (congressional) and 2008 (presidential) elections, the Democrats rebounded by...also adopting the "God Strategy."

The authors note that even though no non-Christian could be elected to national office (for the immediate future, at least), since 2006 more moderate Christian groups are fighting back by proclaiming their faith as fervently as the evangelicals — while saying, in effect, that it is a mistake "to render unto Caesar that which is God's."

The History of Christianity

The Closing of the Western Mind: The Rise of Faith and the Fall of Reason by Charles Freeman tells the story of how Christianity, hand-in-hand with the power of the State once the Emperor Constantine made it an official religion of the Roman Empire, caused the suppression of reason, science and knowledge. All other religions, including Christian sects which refused to follow the church-state line, were now deemed heretical and violently suppressed with the full force of Roman law.

The result: Europe entered the "Dark Ages" until Greek thought was rediscovered with the invasion of Muslim Spain in the eleventh century. The consequent retreat of Christianity in the face of reason — and how and why it happened — is chronicled in *The Rise of Early Modern Science: Islam, China and the West,* by Toby E. Huff.

Arab scholars preserved and extended Greek thought — yet Plato, Aristotle, Pythagoras and other Greek thinkers had no impact in the Islamic *or* Byzantine Empires (where the language of Aristotle was the language of everyday life).

Huff exhaustively establishes the reasons why western Europe was *different.* There were many factors, the most significant being:

The Christian doctrine of free will, and the corollary that man has a conscience, which has no counterpart in Islam. In Christianity, the human being is free to choose his own destiny — admittedly, between the narrow choices of heaven or hell. A corollary is the principle of *secondary causation:* when you hit the white billiard ball which strikes a red one, the movement of the red ball is caused *(secondarily)* by the action of the white. In Islam, there is no secondary causation: *everything,* including the movement of the red billiard ball, is caused by Allah.

The separation of state and church: After the collapse of the western Roman Empire, Europe still had its monopoly Catholic church, centered in Rome, which was occasionally divided by dissension; but political power was *fragmented* between dozens of kingdoms and tiny principalities. Thus, temporal and spiritual power were *separated,* and competed for power. In Islam (and the Byzantine Empire) the Caliph was the ruler of both church *and* state, and the law of the state was the law of the church, and *vice versa.*

The "universitas" and the rediscovery of Roman Law: The rediscovery of Roman Law led to the *idea* of regular, universal laws, the codification of civil and canon (church) law, and the *universitas,* or corporation. Unlike today's corporation, the *universitas* was a cross between a guild and a mini-state: it could make laws binding its members which had equal force with the laws of the state and church. One profession that established the *universitas* was that of *teachers,* the result being the University, which became yet another center of power, jealously guarding its *legal* privileges against both church *and* state. No equivalent to the flourishing universities of Oxford, Paris, and Bologna existed anywhere else on earth. They became *transmitters of knowledge:* a *certificate* from one university was recognized by others. In the Islamic world, a student could learn from an individual teacher, but if he changed teachers he would usually have to begin again. In any event, to Muslims *everything* was (and still is) to be found in the Koran, so any other source of knowledge was seen to be unnecessary, if not *dangerous* to the health of state and society. Such independent scholars as did exist did so on sufferance, or thanks to the (usually temporary) protection of a relatively-open-minded ruler.

The European universities of the time offered just four courses: Natural Philosophy (mainly Aristotle), Medicine, Law, and Theology. Natural Philosophy was the *prerequisite* for any of the other three schools. One result: Catholic theologians were all steeped in the methods of *reason* they learned studying the Greek philosophers. The greatest of these was Thomas Aquinas who, so to speak, turned Augustine on his head. (Another consequence, the reaction, was the Inquisition.)

This is a very abbreviated summary of just a few of the highlights of Toby Huff's work. If you read just one other book related to our subject, I highly recommend this one.

Aristotle's Children by Richard E. Rubenstein also analyzes the intellectual revolution the Greeks wrought (via the Arabs) on western civilization, focusing on the turmoil it caused within the church; and Edward Grant's *The Foundations of Modern Science in the Middle Ages* shows how the roots of modern science began not with Kepler, Copernicus, Galileo, and the Renaissance but with the influx of Greek thought in the eleventh century — and that the seeds of a revival of reason had sprouted even earlier.

Who Wrote the Bible?

Old Testament scholar Richard Friedman addresses this question in his book *Who Wrote the Bible?* Focusing on the Bible's first five books, he shows us how the Bible has been analyzed for clues to the original authors. He compares various passages with what is known from history and archeology, and analyzes different styles within the same book, to give just two examples, that have led scholars to conclude that certain books were compiled from different original documents — most of which, of course, are now lost to history and are known as "E," "J," "D," and "P." An excellent survey and introduction to the conclusions — and controversies — of biblical scholarship.

Asimov's Guide to the Bible by Isaac Asimov, originally published in two volumes (Old and New Testaments respectively) is now available in one. Written in his inimitable style, Asimov takes us through every book of the Bible, adding history and geography to the stories, the meanings of words, as well as the probable antecedents to various Biblical stories.

To take just one example, of Noah and the flood he says: "A tidal wave plus rain, in other words." He tells of ancient Assyrian tablets from the royal Assyrian library, deciphered in 1872 but long pre-dating Christianity, which tell the story of a man who saves himself and his family, plus some animals, from a flood.

Misquoting Jesus The Story Behind Who Changed the Bible and Why by Bart D. Ehrman is a fascinating survey of how and why errors crept into the books of the Bible, resulting in manuscripts of the same book which are quite different — and often opposite in meaning.

In high school, Ehrman became a "born-again," fundamentalist Christian which led him to become a Biblical scholar, focusing in part on the textual analysis of the Bible — comparing various editions and accounting for their differences.

To read the Bible in their original languages, he learnt Greek and Hebrew — plus Latin, French and German. What turned him into a skeptic was *studying the Bible in detail* — and finding all manner of errors and differences. A few examples:

Simple copyist errors where a copyist mispelt a word as he wrote it or, perhaps half-asleep, skipped a whole line by mistake. These were especially prevalent in the early years of Christianity when most copyists were volunteers rather than professionals.

Some changes, however, were not accidental but *intentional*. Sometimes, a copyist felt he could clarify or "improve" the meaning of a verse — and did, so changing it. Less innocent were changes inspired by theological "wars." In their battles with the Gnostics, Marcionites, and the various other Christian sects, Jews, the pagans of the Roman empire and, later, Muslims, Bible verses — including the words of Jesus — were changed, deleted or inserted so the winning sect (which became "orthodox" with the aid of Constantine) could "prove" that the Bible supported their view and not the "heretics'."

Ehrman spins a fascinating tale of how the Bible changed over the eons, but there is nothing unscholarly about his work

— except that it's highly readable, and so the most *accessible* introduction to Biblical analysis.

In the end, all the changes and errors he found convinced him that — as he put it — "Even if God had inspired the original words [of the Bible], we don't have the original words."

Why Do We Suffer?

In *God's Problem: How the Bible Fails to Answer Our Most Important Question — Why We Suffer,* Bart D. Ehrman examines the "problem of suffering."

This is hardly a new topic. The question "If God is good why does he permit suffering [and evil]?" has been debated since the time of the Ancient Greeks, if not before.

What makes Ehrman's approach so absorbing is how he weaves *the differing views of suffering found in the Bible itself* into his search for *his* answer to that question.

To give just one example: he devotes one chapter — *Does Suffering Make Sense?* — to comparing the "nature of suffering" as expressed in the books of Job and Ecclesiastes.

We learn that the book of Job was written by at least *two different authors* — whose views of suffering are contradictory. "The story begins and ends," Ehrman writes, "with the prose narrative of the righteous suffering of Job, whose patient endurance under duress is rewarded by God, [which] stands at odds with the poetic dialogues that take up most of the book, in which Job is not patient but defiant, and in which God does not reward the one he has made to suffer but overpowers him and grinds him into submission."

Ecclesiastes, in contrast, is "contrary to the traditional views of a book like Proverbs, which insists that life is basically meaningful and good, that evil is punished and right behavior rewarded. Not so for the author of Ecclesiastes, who calls himself the Teacher (Hebrew: *Qoheleth).* On the contrary, life is often meaningless, and in the end, all of us — wise and foolish, righteous and wicked, rich and poor — all of us die. And that's the end of the story."

These two short extracts merely hint at the depth of analysis Ehrman brings to his work. He concludes, much as the Greek philosopher Epicurus did some 2,500 years ago (see page 120):

> God knows all things and can do all things. That's why he is God. To say that he can't cure cancer, or eliminate birth defects, or control hurricanes, or prevent nuclear holocaust is to say that he's not really God — at least not the God of the Bible and of the Judeo-Christian tradition. Believing in a God who stands beside me in my suffering, but who cannot actually do much about it, makes God a lot like my mother or my kindly nextdoor neighbor, but it doesn't make him a lot like GOD.

Did God *Evolve?*

When Moses led the Israelites from Egypt, they brought their monotheistic God, Yahweh, with them and proceeded to wipe out the Canaanites and occupy their lands.

That's the standard story.

But to go by Robert Wright's exposition in his book, *The Evolution of God,* it's wrong on every count.

First, there is no archeological or other evidence to suggest that the Exodus from Egypt ever occurred (certainly not on the *scale* depicted in the Bible). Rather, the available evidence suggests the Israelites were once Canaanites — and *poly*theistic too boot.

Second, Yahweh was originally a Warrior God — one of the many *Canaanite* gods. Slowly, over time, Yahweh evolved into the gods' "chairman of the board" (rather like

Jupiter/Zeus of the Roman/Greek pantheon), becoming the *sole* Israelite god only in the second century BCE — *God* instead of *a god* (see, for example, Psalm 82).

Thirdly, Yahweh was originally anthropomorphic, like most pagan gods: he walks in the Garden of Eden looking for Adam and Eve after they had eaten the forbidden fruit; he has "human" characteristics, showing anger and jealousy; he made "garments of skins" for Adam and Eve; met Jacob "face to face" and he even met Moses and 70 elders of Israel who "saw the God of Israel"; later, he becomes non-anthropomorphic and no longer shows himself.

Wright convincingly amasses verification from history, archeology and even the Bible itself which still contains traces of polytheism (see *"For I Am A Jealous God,"* page 104, for some samples).

Then he goes further, showing how Yahweh's very personality changes depending on circumstances. To simplify his analysis, when Israel is ascendant over its neighbors, the vengeful, wrathful Yahweh of the Old Testament comes to the fore to smite Israel's enemies. When Israel is at peace and the Israelites perceive it to be in their interests to be friendly trading partners with their neighbors, the kindly side of Yahweh rules. When the Israelites are oppressed and persecuted, they take comfort in how Yahweh will take revenge on their enemies — sometime in the unspecified future.

Wright detects the same pattern in Christianity and Islam (and, to a lesser extent, in other, non-monotheistic religions), and his analysis of how Paul took Jesus' obscure Jewish sect and turned it into a world-wide religion is riveting, as is his study of Mohammed and the beginnings of Islam.

As with evolution in nature, the evolution of God (and gods) continues — a never-ending story.

Jesus: A Pagan God?

In *The Jesus Mysteries: Was the Original Jesus a Pagan God?*, Timothy Freke and Peter Gandy demonstrate that Christian doctrines like the virgin birth were common in many of the religions that pre-dated the time of Jesus — and that the origins of Christianity are *very* different from what most people have been led to believe.

The Power Tactics of Jesus Christ by Jay Haley shows that, based on the New Testament, Jesus never *himself* "turned the other cheek" or *otherwise* practiced what he preached. The other essays in this collection are on the subject of therapy (Haley was a therapist), and include advice on how to succeed as a schizophrenic despite your therapist's best efforts, how to fail as a therapist and "How To Have An Awful Marriage." Lots of fun.

Everything You Know About God is Wrong, edited by Russ Kick, is a wonderful collection of articles on a wide range of topics. My personal favorite is *"Irish Gulags for Women":* in Ireland the Catholic Church ran "Magdalene Asylums" for "fallen women." They had another name: "Magdalene Laundries," since the Church used the women as unpaid labor to run very profitable laundry businesses. But the "fallen women" — who also came to include orphans and others picked off the streets — weren't just unpaid: they were effectively *slaves,* locked up "for their own good." This practice — which died with the advent of the washing machine — only came to light in 1993 when a developer found a mass grave on the grounds of a Catholic nunnery: 155 female bodies, most of whom had been buried with*out* the legally-required death certificate! (So much for idea that belief in God is a prerequisite for *moral behavior!)*

It's also worth browsing the *Catholic Encyclopedia* (www.newadvent.com) to appreciate the torturous rationalizations necessary to accommodate a supposedly unchanging faith with the constantly expanding knowledge of reality (see, for example, the section on Infallibility which is almost incomprehensible). Similarly, check out the "word of God's representative" in his Papal Encyclicals (www.papalencyclicals.net and www.vatican.va).

Take, for example, Pope Pius XII's 1 November, 1950 encyclical *Munificentissimus Deus: Defining the Dogma of the Assumption* where he "infallibly" establishes the doctrine of the Assumption — that the Virgin Mary ascended into heaven *body and soul* (as did her son).*

Speaking with the authority of God, and imbued with the Holy Spirit, Pope Pius writes 47 paragraphs in support of his/God's decision. However, *34* of those 47 paragraphs — 72% of the entire encyclical — refer to pleas and petitions received from bishops, other church officials and the laity, corroborating opinions of past theologians including Pope Pius IX's 1854 declaration of Mary's "Immaculate Conception," the Catholics' veneration of the Virgin Mary and the feast days and churches dedicated to her name.

It's hard to read this encyclical without concluding — from the Pope's own words — that he's promulgating this doctrine as a result of *pressure from below* rather than inspiration from above.

Atheism

Arguments for atheism are nothing new. What *is* new is that books like *The End of Faith, Letter to a Christian Nation,* both by Sam Harris, *The God Delusion* by Richard Dawkins, and *God is Not Great* by Christopher Hitchens have all hit the bestseller lists. Each is an excellent exposé of the nature

---

* www.vatican.va/holy_father/pius_xii/apost_constitutions/documents/hf_p-xii_ apc_19501101 _munificentissimus-deus_en.html

and absurdity of religion — *all* religions — and paeans to the benefits and virtues of non-belief which I found highly convincing (though, of course, I didn't need to be convinced).

Excellent and wide-ranging as those books are, my personal favorite remains *Atheism: the Case Against God* by George H. Smith, which I found so personally persuasive that, for over thirty years, I had no desire to read anything else on the subject until a friend lent me one of Sam Harris' books.

Islam

Paradoxically, it you want to *understand* Islam, and why the Muslim world is so different from the West, the best choice is Toby Huff's *The Rise of Early Modern Science: Islam, China and the West* (see above).

In books by two British Muslims you'll find insiders' perspectives on the complexity, limitations — and the horrors — of the Muslim world.

In *The Islamist,* Ed Husain recounts how he was attracted to radical Islam as a teenager in Britain, and rose in its hierarchy until, when a fellow Islamist drew a knife and killed another student, he finally realized that radical Islamists *really meant what they said* about killing infidels. He turned to Sufism, and went to Syria to learn Arabic where, to his surprise, he found you could be a good Muslim *without* the total segregation of the sexes, veiling and locking up women, and all the other practices he'd preached as a radical. In many respects, the highlight of his book is his sojourn in Saudi Arabia, a society closed to a non-male, non-Arab, non-Arabic speaker. Husain takes us inside this culture which is far worse than living under apartheid or communism. For Husain, actually *seeing* the society idealized by the Islamists was the final nail in the coffin of his radical beliefs. Indeed, he condemns the country as possibly the most racist, sexist, and inhumane place on earth. Furthermore, Husain's Saudi acquaintances, "many of them university graduates, argued strongly that...it was the veil and other social norms that were responsible for such widespread sexual frustration among Saudi youth." One result:

> I heard from an Asian taxi driver about a Filipino who had brought his new bride to live with him in Jeddah. After visiting the prominent Bahad shopping district, the couple caught a taxi home. Some way through their journey, the Saudi driver complained that the car was not working properly and perhaps the man could help push it. The passenger obliged. Within seconds, the Saudi driver had sped off with the man's wife in his car and, months later, there was still no clue as to her whereabouts. [96]

It's not hard to imagine what happened to the poor Filipino's wife!

In *Desperately Seeking Paradise: Journeys of a Sceptical Muslim,* Ziauddin Sardar takes us on a guided tour through the world of Islam in his search for "paradise." He is trying to find — and becomes involved in attempting to create — a society which is at once Islamic, modern, and free. Along the way we are introduced to a variety of spiritual figures, some likeable, some not, and some who seem to be a fellow spirit but turn into mini-Ayatollahs. (One, the director of an institute Sardar had helped create, told him: "If you come here again, I will have your legs broken.")

At each turn, he becomes disillusioned — but doesn't give up. One example: the revolution in Iran which overthrew the Shah fills him with hope. He visits Iran a number of times — but on his last visit he gets no further than Teheran airport, and is deported as a potential "counterrevolutionary."

He and like-minded friends formed a group they called *Ijmalis* ["the root word *jml* conveys the idea of beauty on the one hand and wholeness on the other"] with the aim of "liberating Islam from a fossilized tradition and religious obscurantism." However, the book concludes with the final meeting of the *Ijmalis* whose members scatter disheartened with the feeling of failure. Sardar, however, makes it clear that he has not abandoned his search.

Why I Am Not A Muslim by Ibn Warraq, is a penetrating dissection and devastating critique of the history and theology of Islam. Warraq conclusively demonstrates that Islam is incompatible with the concepts of democracy and human rights; that it is a *closed mental system,* meaning that its ideology is resistant to change, that Islam presents an *either/ or* choice: either you're a Muslim — which means believing and following the literal word of the Koran and the law of the Sharia — or you're an infidel. As we've seen Christian theology is *flexible,* so Christianity is an umbrella for many different and often opposing beliefs. It's much harder (though not impossible) for Muslims to believe their Holy Book *selectively* — and still be considered Muslim.

That the writer, a former Pakistani zealot, had to publish under a pseudonym *for his own safety* is powerful proof of his arguments.

Infidel by Ayaan Hirsi Ali is at once horrifying — and inspiring. Horrifying, because she tells us *exactly* what it's like to be brought up female and Muslim; inspiring, as we follow her slow transformation into a free-thinking individual. Reading her story also dramatically reaffirms the crucial importance of many features of the western world, like freedom of speech, freedom of conscience, and the separation of church and state that most of us take for granted.

The Origin of Myths

When They Severed Earth from Sky: How the Human Mind Shapes Myth, by Paul T. Barber, and Elizabeth Wayland Barber is highly recommended (see *Where Do Myths Come From?,* page 173).

Altered States

Fire in the Brain: Clinical Tales of Hallucination, by Ronald K. Siegel, is an eye-opening study of how our own brains can *mis*interpret the data of the senses, leading us to believe we've *seen* or *experienced* things that simply ain't so. Siegel, an associate professor at the UCLA School of Medicine when he wrote this book (1992) begins with an investigation of hallucinations caused by drugs from marijuana to mescaline. With student volunteers he calls "psychonauts," Siegel studies hallucinations under controlled conditions, showing how the brain *structures* them from a handful of similar units, mostly simple geometric shapes. He finds that even the tunnel with the light at the end reported in "near death" experiences are similar mental constructs, which can also be caused by factors such as severe stress or oxygen deprivation.

The remaining two-thirds of his book are case studies of people who came to him for help. With the expertise of a Sherlock Holmes, Siegel shows how the brain is the cause of a wide range of different so-called psychic phenomena. A few examples: the succubus (waking up "knowing" that some intruder is sitting on you and you're about to die), channelling, escaping pain during torture by "leaving" your body, and invisible playmates. Perhaps the most fascinating of these are his investigations of how an otherwise sober-minded man was convinced he'd seen a UFO and been abducted by aliens, a nurse who saw swastikas on her patients, a man who, now and then, was haunted by a black hole which was about to swallow him, and a piano teacher who had to quit because she couldn't turn off the music in her own head. In each of these cases, Siegel manages to eliminate these phenomena in his clients' minds by persuading them to change the behaviors or avoid the stimuli that caused them.

Meditation: At one level, *Freedom in Meditation* by Patricia Carrington is a "how to meditate" book — with no religious or mystical content. In the process, however, Carrington (a psychologist and lecturer in the Department of Psychology at Princeton University) investigates the similarities and differences between meditation and others mental states like prayer (similar) and hypnosis (different). She finds that meditation has demonstrable beneficial psychological and even physical effects like a slower metabolic rate (and a portion of smokers who meditate regularly quit without even *intending* to).

Ironically, she began her independent research because she could not get cooperation from instructors of Transcendental Meditation. Not surprisingly, some of her scientifically-reached conclusions contradict the mysticism-based instructions of TM. For example, some TM students found meditation an unpleasant, even unnerving, experience. They were simply told to persevere, that they had "issues" to work through. Carrington found that giving them a different mantra changed the experience to a pleasant one — in other words, in one of those scientific conclusions that are startlingly obvious once they've been stated, that different sounds have dramatically different mental and emotional effects (think of fingernails grating on a blackboard versus Vivaldi playing softly in the background).

Time Distortion and Hypnosis: At one time or another we've all had the experience that the *subjective* sense of time can seem to flow at a different rate from the "world time" as measured by a clock. How often have you made a comment like, "I just don't know where the day has gone"? while at other times — waiting for the dentist, for example — the second hand of the clock seems to take forever to make each *click.*

The intentional induction of such "Time Distortion," under hypnosis, was first demonstrated by Linn Cooper in 1948. His researches were extended in cooperation with psychiatrist and hypnotherapist Milton H. Erickson (see the section on "Time Distortion" in *The Collected Papers of Milton H. Erickson on Hypnosis, Volume II**).

With dozens of subjects, Cooper and Erickson demonstrated the subjective sense of time could consistently be distorted in any direction under hypnosis. A subject could come out of trance, unable to understand why an hour had passed according to the clock when her subjective experience had been just a few minutes. Others could "watch" a vaguely-remembered movie or football game and vividly recall every detail — even though the clock had advanced just ten seconds.

Also included are case studies of Erickson's therapeutic use of time distortion. One woman was "trained as a hypnotic subject for the delivery of her first child. No suggestions of any sort had been given her concerning her perception of time except that she would 'have a good time' and would 'enjoy having her baby'."

She later reported that time had speeded up — the "minute hand of the bedside clock appeared to move with the speed of a second hand," that nurses and the obstetrician "dashed in and out of the room" and "everybody apparently spoke with the utmost rapidity."

Another woman sought treatment for severe headaches that would incapacitate her for hours or even days. But she paradoxically and dictatorially insisted that no "psychological investigative procedures" be employed, and demanded that the headaches continue in a fashion that would meet "her hidden personality needs" [which were to *stay* hidden from

---

* See *Time Distortion*, Part IV of *Hypnotic Alteration of Sensory, Perceptual and Psychophysiological Processes: The Collected Papers of Milton H. Erickson on Hypnosis, Volume II*, edited by Ernest L. Rossi [New York: Irvington Publishers, 1989], pp221-298.

both herself and Erickson].

Erickson trained her in time distortion so that she could have the *subjective* experience of a three to four hour headache, while just ten seconds of clock time passed.

Time distortion is just one of many hypnotic procedures Milton Erickson used with therapeutic effects that often seem "miraculous"[*] — until you realize that they usually came only after his client had spent hours learning how to go into a deep hypnotic trance, and Erickson had (usually) gathered voluminous data about the client's background so he could tailor an appropriate treatment.

In summary, "mystical" experiences result from the brain's misinterpretation of external stimuli, or can be induced by oneself or others. Indeed, Erickson states that common, everyday trance experiences are natural: being so absorbed in a book or a movie that you don't know you're dying to go to the bathroom until you come to the end or are otherwise interrupted, or driving on "autopilot" so that only when you get home do you remember that you meant to stop at the grocery store.

So when people report "visions" — like St. Paul's epiphany on the road to Damascus — the most likely explanation is that they are seeing internal mental images constructed by their own minds.

Psychic "Powers": In "Psychic for a Day"[†] Michael Shermer, publisher of *Skeptic* magazine and founder of the International Skeptics Society, relates his experience of posing as a "psychic" on the PBS TV show, *Eye on Nye*.

---

[*] See all four volumes of Erickson's *Collected Papers*. For a shorter introduction to Erickson's methods, see *Uncommon Therapy* by Jay Haley [W.W. Norton & Company New York, 1986].

[†] Included in *Science Friction* by Michael Shermer [New York: Owl Books, 2005], pp3-18.

He gave "readings" for five "clients." Except for their date and time of birth (to prepare astrological charts) he had no knowledge or contact with any of them until taping began. Shermer refused to take the easy way out by, for example, just being an astrologer for a day. Rather, each of the five "clients" received a different *kind* of "reading": Tarot cards, Palm reading, Astrology, a Psychic reading, and Talking to the Dead. *Each one* of the five clients came away believing Shermer was an expert in his field, though their ratings of his ability varied from mediocre (the "client" had had many other readings she rated as "similar") to absolute conviction in Shermer's psychic abilities.

To achieve these results in five different psychic fields, Shermer spent a total of *one day in preparation!*

Why was he so successful? Because his "clients" all arrived expecting to meet a man with psychic powers, and Shermer's words and actions, however vague (often intentionally so) confirmed their expectations. All five believed he was psychic; only differing on how *good* a psychic he was.

Shermer's experiment is a powerful demonstration that someone who is willing to believe can easily have his or her beliefs confirmed by a person with an appealing or magnetic personality — whether an Indian guru, a television preacher or a charismatic politician.

Morality Without God

Michael Shermer's *The Science of Good & Evil* shows how human ethics and morality can be rationally derived from evolution and the nature of man — *without* resort to some supernatural, invisible source in the sky. And in "The Objectivist Ethics" (an essay included in *The Virtue of Selfishness)* Ayn Rand shows how "ought" can be derived from "is" without the necessity for any superhuman entity.

Santa Claus, the Tooth Fairy, and the Easter Bunny

Did your parents ever lie to you?

Mine did.

As a kid, I was dying to wake up early every Christmas morning to open the presents Santa Claus was going to leave for me in the middle of the night.

Of course, I tried to stay awake to *see* Santa come. And when a baby tooth fell out I'd try to keep my eyes open long enough to *see* the Tooth Fairy replace the tooth under my pillow with some money.

What I didn't realize at the time was that my parents could always stay up longer than I ever could.

When I became a parent myself I'd learnt the truth; now *I* could join the long chain of parents who deceive their innocent, inquisitive — and *trusting* — children. Until I realized what I was doing...resulting in an *extremely* upset five-year-old when she learnt (too bluntly, I admit) that there was no Easter Bunny.

Most parents believe, as I once did, that such an inconsequential deception is just good, innocent fun.

But is it?

The trouble is, our kids weren't in on the joke.

When we told them what *we knew* was a lie, *they believed us.*

And then, one day, they *find out* we lied to them....

"Parents Lie!"

One Christmas eve, Harry, aged four, had seen his father putting out the presents instead of Santa. This had been weighing on his mind and one day he suddenly piped up in his kindergarten class: "Do you believe in Santa Claus?"

The other kids (aged four to six) chorused "Yes!"

Vic (five): "Of course! Santa brought me a bicycle! And the Tooth Fairy too — I just got a dollar from the Tooth Fairy."

"You mean Adam and Eve were *streakers?*"

Harry: "Not true! Santa Claus isn't real. Santa is your Dad! So is the Tooth Fairy."

Vic *(shouting):* "That's not true!"

Harry *(shouting):* "It is so your Dad!"

Kevin (six): "We know that fairies are like Tinkerbell — it's a story. So if a Tooth Fairy is a fairy it's not real too!"

Celia (five): "How does Santa get in? We don't have a chimney!"

Vic *(still shouting): "We* do!"

Harry: "Anyway, the chimney's full of soot. How come Santa's still clean?"

Others: "Yeah." "Where else is Santa coming from?"

Harry *(shouting):* "From inside! He's your Dad!"

Kevin: "Who cares? We still get presents."

Vic, blubbering, shakes his head.

Harry: "Parents Lie!"

Vic: "They don't."

Harry: "You ask your Dad!"

Vic cried for the rest of the class — not, as was later discovered, because Santa might not exist, but because his parents might have lied to him. The next day Vic, still upset — he'd asked his father, who evaded the question — told the teacher: "My Dad wants to talk to you." Apparently, Vic's Dad needed advice on how to handle his distraught son. But the question he was *really* worried about was: "Will my son ever trust me again?"

It's too early to say.[*]

Some parents, however, go to enormous lengths to keep the tissue of lies they've woven from unravelling....

One day, my son came home from school with the following tale:

Miriam, aged five, had seen her mother wrapping the presents that later appeared in her stocking on Christmas morning (so her older sister told my son). She told her mother: "I know *you're* the one who gives the presents, not Santa."

Her mother angrily retorted: "Santa's not coming this year because you've been a bad girl. *I'm* giving you presents instead,

© 2010 baloocartoons.com

"We learned in Sunday School today that God uses illegal surveillance techniques."

---

[*] Personal communication from a kindergarten teacher, name withheld by request.

> **"**If a kid asks where rain comes from, I think a cute thing to tell him is "God is crying." And if he asks why God is crying, another cute thing to tell him is, "Probably because of something you did."**"**
> — *Jack Handey*

so you won't cry."

Needless to say, Miriam was extremely upset. (Great strategy, Mum!)

So don't bitch the next time some two-faced politician (but I repeat myself) opens his mouth and lies spew forth, or when your favorite son or daughter grows up to be a snake-oil salesman. Where do you think they learnt to lie through their teeth?

On Mummy's and Daddy's knees.

If *your* parents deceived you about Santa Claus, the Tooth Fairy, the Easter Bunny, the Sandman, the Bogeyman who'd come and "get you" in the night if you weren't "good" (which, of course, meant "if you don't *obey"*) what *else* did they deceive you about?

At least there was *evidence* (albeit *planted* evidence) for Santa Claus and the Tooth Fairy.

But what about the evidence for God? And by "evidence" I mean what my then-nine-year-old son said whenever someone talked to him about God:

"Don't tell me what you *feel.*

Show me your God.

I want to *see* him."

Try those words yourself, next time one of "God's door-to-door salesmen" ruins your peaceful Sunday morning. It's a great conversation-stopper.

> **"**Religion doesn't come from God. It comes from your parents.**"**
> — *Author Unknown*

One last thing...

We welcome your comments (see www.marktier.com for more) — but rather than send us an email we'd *much* prefer you post your thoughts and reactions (positive *or* negative) on Amazon (www.amazon.com), Barnes & Noble (www.bn.com) or similar websites.

However, if you feel impelled to tell us that we're inevitably going to hell — or that you'd like to put us there yourself — let us save you the trouble by responding here:

Didn't Jesus tell you to "turn the other cheek"? And come Judgement Day, what will he think if you *didn't?*

Are you such a poor believer that *we,* of all people, have to remind you?

And is your God so *weak* and *puny* that he can't look after himself but needs *your help?* If he does, how can he be a God worth worshipping?

And if you feel offended by anything in this book well, what can we say? It's *your* Bible, not ours.

Last night I saw upon the stair
A little man who wasn't there
He wasn't there again today
Oh, how I wish he'd go away
— *Hughes Mearns*

APPENDIX I: **Happiness and God**

It's impossible to tell how happy anyone *else* is. So the only way you can measure "happiness" is *subjectively:* ask people how happy they consider themselves to be.

The "Life Satisfaction" index (which I'm using as a proxy for happiness) was compiled by asking people in 179 countries to rate, on a scale of 0 (dissatisfied) to 10 (satisfied) their answer to the question:

All things considered, how satisfied are you
with your life as a whole these days?

Comparing this database with the 51 countries with available statistics on regular church/mosque/temple attendance (a proxy for religious belief) shows that life satisfaction correlates highly with wealth (GDP), suggesting a causal link, while church attendance has *no* correlation with either wealth *or* happiness. Here's the raw data for the 51 countries, ranked by Life Satisfaction:

THE CORRELATIONS	
Highly Positive Correlation:	
Life Satisfaction with GDP	+0.82
Zero Correlation:	
Church Attendance with GDP	-0.07
Church Attendance with Life Satisfaction	-0.02

Country	Church Attendance	Life Satisfaction	Per capita GDP (US$)
1 Ireland	84%	8.14	$38,505
2 Norway	5%	8.09	$41,420
3 Denmark	5%	8.08	$33,973
4 Finland	4%	8.02	$32,153
5 Canada	38%	7.97	$33,375
6 Australia	16%	7.88	$31,794
7 Sweden	4%	7.85	$32,525
8 United States	44%	7.85	$41,890
9 Iceland	4%	7.84	$36,510
10 New Zealand	15%	7.81	$24,996
11 Austria	30%	7.80	$33,700
12 Mexico	46%	7.72	$10,751
13 Netherlands	35%	7.71	$32,684
14 Switzerland	16%	7.69	$35,633
15 Belgium	44%	7.61	$32,119

Country	Church Attendance	Life Satisfaction	Per capita GDP (US$)
16 Spain	25%	7.60	$27,169
17 Brazil	36%	7.57	$8,402
18 United Kingdom	27%	7.42	$33,238
19 Argentina	25%	7.14	$14,280
20 France	21%	7.06	$30,386
21 Italy	45%	6.93	$28,529
22 Venezuela	31%	6.89	$6,632
23 Czech Republic	14%	6.85	$20,538
24 Japan	3%	6.75	$31,267
25 Uruguay	31%	6.75	$9,962
26 China	9%	6.70	$6,757
27 Poland	55%	6.48	$13,847
28 Croatia	22%	6.41	$13,042
29 Korea	14%	6.31	$22,029
30 Chile	25%	6.29	$12,027
31 Slovakia	47%	6.07	$15,871
32 Romania	20%	5.92	$9,060
33 Peru	43%	5.90	$6,039
34 Russia	2%	5.87	$10,845
35 Portugal	47%	5.85	$20,410
36 Belarus	6%	5.83	$7,918
37 Lithuania	16%	5.76	$14,494
38 Hungary	21%	5.73	$17,887
39 Moldova	10%	5.65	$2,100
40 Estonia	4%	5.64	$15,478
41 Turkey	43%	5.52	$8,407
42 India	42%	5.51	$3,452
43 Philippines	68%	5.47	$5,137
44 Bulgaria	10%	5.47	$9,032
45 Latvia	5%	5.43	$13,646
46 Ukraine	10%	5.30	$6,848
47 Azerbaijan	6%	5.28	$5,016
48 Armenia	8%	5.03	$4,945
49 South Africa	56%	4.95	$11,110
50 Nigeria	89%	4.78	$1,128
51 Georgia	10%	4.26	$3,365
AVERAGE	*27%*	*6.73*	*$19,246*

Countries ranked by "Life Satisfaction"

SOURCES. Church attendance (percent of population who *say* they attend church once or more per week): www.nationmaster.com/graph/rel_chu_att-religion-church-attendance and biblesociety.org.nz; Life Satisfaction and GDP per capita: *The Happy Planet Index 2.0, 2009*, www.happyplanetindex.org

APPENDIX II: The Liturgical Guide of the Catholic Church

Each year, the Catholic Church issues a "Liturgical Guide": a complete list of the Bible passages to be read in mass and other church services for the year. Analysis of the Guide for the "Liturgical Year" December 2007 to November 2008[*] showed:

— a total of 1,184 Bible readings (3.2 per day);

— 147 (12.4%) those 1,184 selections contain verses that could be considered offensive;

— of those 147, 93 (63.3%) came from the Old Testament, 54 (36.7%) from the New;

— in those 147 readings is a total of 318 offensive verses — an average of 2.6 verses per reading (or, of the total 1,184 readings, less than *one verse a day);*

— the shortest of these 147 readings was just two verses long [Judith 13:18-19]; the longest contained 117 verses [Psalm 119:14-131];

— only 30 (20.4%) of the 147 *ended* on an offensive verse; the remainder ending on a more upbeat note.

The 147 readings can be categorized as follows:

Category	No. of readings	Percent
Demonstrations of the Power of God	15	9.5%
Examples of God's Anger & Wrath	28	19.0%
Examples of God's Punishment	40	27.2%
The Fate of Sinners	16	10.9%
What Awaits Sinners on Judgement Day	28	19.7%
Killing (2) & Massacres (1) Ordered by God in Support of his "Chosen People"	3	2.0%
Other	17	11.6%
TOTAL	147	100.0%

which can be expressed as just two "meta" categories:

---

[*] Published by the Catholic Church, Manila, Philippines

Category	No. of readings	Percent
God's Anger & Violence Towards Sinners (*i.e.*, what to expect if you sin)	127	86.4%
Other	20	13.6%

The number of offensive verses in each reading varies considerably:

Number of readings with		Percent	Cumulative Percent
1 offensive verse	71	48.3%	48.3%
2 offensive verses	37	25.2%	73.5%
3 offensive verses	18	12.2%	85.7%
4 offensive verses	9	6.1%	91.8%
5 offensive verses	5	3.4%	95.2%
6 offensive verses	2	1.4%	96.6%
7 offensive verses	1	0.7%	97.3%
8 offensive verses	2	1.4%	98.6%
11 offensive verses	1	0.7%	99.3%
12 offensive verses	1	0.7%	100.0%
TOTAL READINGS	147		
TOTAL VERSES	318		

The average reading has over ten verses. With 85.7% of the 147 readings containing three or fewer *offensive* verses you have to be wide awake and paying *very* close attention to even notice them

This close examination of the "Liturgical Guide" clearly confirms the conclusion of the introduction, *When God Speaks For Himself* (page 7) that the *official* position of the church is to downplay, almost to the point of extinction, the vengeful, wrathful, murderous side of Yahweh in favor of the more comforting message that "God/Jesus is Love."

Defining "Offensive"

The analysis of the Liturgical Guide for offensive verses was done by a lay Catholic. As "offensive" is a *subjective* reaction, it was left to *her* independent judgement to decide what was offensive or not. You can download the list of readings at www.marktier.com/lg — and decide for yourself..

"Abide in My Word"

A second source of readings was a book called *Abide in My Word,* (published in 2002), a collection of scripture readings chosen from the Catholic "liturgical calendar."*

In this book were 1,085 readings (just under three per day), with only 16 (or 1.47%) considered to include offensive verses. For a different perspective, let's take a look at the remaining 1,069 readings — positive or even inspirational. Seventy percent of the readings fall into just 12 major categories:

Category	Readings	Percent of total	Cumulative Percent
Inspirational stories and parables	221	20.67%	20.67%
The greatness of God	118	11.04%	31.71%
In the Kingdom of God	79	7.39%	39.10%
Believing in God and Jesus	56	5.24%	44.34%
Preaching about God & Jesus	55	5.14%	49.49%
Faith and its rewards	50	4.68%	54.16%
The blessings of believing in God	50	4.68%	58.84%
Judgement Day	47	4.40%	63.24%
Rejoicing in God	37	3.46%	66.70%
Obeying God	34	3.18%	69.88%
Words of wisdom	34	3.18%	73.06%
Gathering God's believers	33	3.09%	76.15%

NOTE: The full analysis is available at www.marktier.com/lg

"Over the course of the year," according to the book's introduction, "the entire mystery of Christ and his redeeming work is unfolded to us through the selection."

This selective focus on the inspirational "Words of God," while hardly surprising, is yet another confirmation that the dark, barbarous and murderous side of God is intentionally ignored.

---

* The selection of sources for analysis was purely accidental. A friend gave me a copy of the Catholic Church's Liturgical Guide, and I came across a copy of *Abide in My Word* in a second-hand bookshop.

Acknowledgements

Our thanks are due to the many people who helped in the preparation of this book:

Raquel Narca, whose comments, criticisms, suggestions and support as the manuscript was written were invaluable;

Dan Rosenthal, for his many constructive suggestions, and permission to include his stories;

Heath Motley, whose extensive fund of information added enormously to the text;

John Zube, for access to his library and his collection of pertinent quotations;

Bruce Tier, Don Tier and Robert Forrai, who spotted our many errors, and whose constructive and often challenging comments improved the text immeasurably;

Desiree Samson, who helped enormously with the research;

George Notaras, Neville Kennard, Tim Staermose, Kris Wadia, Lee Holmes, Marby Villerceran, and Don Hauptman, for their valuable comments and corrections;

And to those of various faiths — Angela, Ben, Cecelia, Marion, Julienne, and others who prefer not be named but know who they are — who read earlier drafts: your reactions were both helpful and convinced us of the power of this concept, inspiring us to continue.

Sources and References

Books and Articles:

Abide in My Word: Mass Readings At Your Fingertips (2002), [The Word Among Us Press, Ijamsville MD, 2001].

American Theocracy: The Peril and Politics of Radical Religion, Oil, And Borrowed Money in the 21ˢᵗ Century by Kevin Phillips, [Penguin Books: London, 2006]

Aristotle's Children by Richard E. Rubenstein, [Harcourt: Orlando, 2003]

Asimov's Guide to the Bible: Two volumes in one, by Isaac Asimov, [Wing Books: New York, 1981].

Atheism: the Case Against God by George H. Smith, [Nash Publishing Co.: Los Angeles, 1974].

The Bible Examined and Found Wanting, by D. J. Taylor [Brisbane, 1984].

The Closing of the Western Mind: The Rise of Faith and the Fall of Reason by Charles Freeman [Vintage: New York, 2005].

Desperately Seeking Paradise: Journeys of a Sceptical Muslim, by Ziauddin Sardar [Granta Books: London, 2004].

A Distant Mirror by Barbara W. Tuchman [Knopf: New York, 1978].

"The Effects of the Condemnation of 1277" by Jason Gooch, *The Hilltop Review,* 2006, Volume 2, Western Michigan University.

Encyclopedia Britannica, 15th edition [Encyclopedia Britannica, Inc.: Chicago, 1995].

The End of Faith, by Sam Harris, [W.W. Norton & Company, Inc: New York, 2005].

Everything You Know About God is Wrong, Russ Kick (editor), [disinformation: New York, 2007].

The Evolution of God by Robert Wright [Little, Brown: New York, 2009].

For the New Intellectual by Ayn Rand [NAL: New York, 1963].

The God Delusion by Richard Dawkins [Transworld: London, 2006].

God is Not Great by Christopher Hitchens [Twelve: New York, 2007].

God's Problem: How the Bible Fails to Answer Our Most Important Question — Why We Suffer by Bart D. Ehrman [HarperCollins: New York, 2008].

The God Strategy: How Religion Became a Political Weapon in America by David Domke and Kevin Coe [Oxford University Press: New York, 2008].

The Holy Bible (King James Version), [Cambridge University Press: Cambridge].

Hypnotic Alteration of Sensory, Perceptual and Psychophysiological Processes: Volume II, edited by Ernest L. Rossi, [New York, Irvington Publishers, 1989].

The Islamist by Ed Husain, [Penguin Books Ltd: London, 2007].

The Jesus Mysteries: Was the Original Jesus a Pagan God?, Timothy Freke and Peter Gandy, [Thorsons: London, 1999].

Kingdom Coming: the Rise of Christian Nationalism by Michelle Goldberg, [W.W. Norton: New York, 2007].

Letter to a Christian Nation, by Sam Harris, [Knopf: New York, 2006].

Misquoting Jesus The Story Behind Who Changed the Bible and Why by Bart D. Ehrman [HarperCollins: New York, 2005].

The New American Militarism, by Andrew Bacevich [Oxford University Press: New York, 2005].

On Killing: The Psychological Cost of Learning to Kill in War and Society (revised edition) by Lt. Col. Dave Grossman [Back Bay: New York, 2009].

Online:

astro.wcupa.edu
biblesociety.org.nz
biblia.com
books.google.com
comebackalive.com
duke.edu
en.wikipedia.org
en.wikiquote.org
home.c2i.net
homepage.tinet.ie
journalofbiblicalstudies.org
moses.creighton.edu
news.bbc.co.uk
plato.stanford.edu
thinkexist.com
topics.nytimes.com
whywontgodhealamputees.com
www.abs-cbnnews.com
www.atheists.org
www.biblegateway.com
www.cfr.org
www.christiananswers.net
www.codexsinaiticus.org
www.cogwriter.com
www.creeds.net
www.csmngt.com
www.dailymail.co.uk
www.deadseascrollsfoundation.com
www.english.emory.edu
www.evilbible.com
www.fordham.edu
www.gdargaud.net
www.happyplanetindex.org
www.hrw.org

www.hweb.org.uk
www.infidels.org
www.infoplease.com
www.jewishencyclopedia.com
www.law.umkc.edu
www.lepg.org
www.mechon-mamre.org
www.nag-hammadi.com
www.nationmaster.com
www.newadvent.org *(The Catholic Encyclopedia)*
www.papalencyclicals.net
www.pipeline.com
www.psi.edu
www.positiveatheism.org
www.quotationspage.com
www.quotedb.com
www.reformation.org
www.religion-is-bunk.org
www.rollingstone.com
www.ronaldbrucemeyer.com
www.salemweb.com
www.ship-modelers-assn.org
www.skepticsannotatedbible.com
www.solagroup.org
www.sonofthesouth.net
www.strategos.demon.co.uk
www.time.com
www.tkb.org
www.vexen.co.uk
www.warfareeast.co.uk
www.wikipedia.org
www.wisdomquotes.com
www.yale.edu

The Power Tactics of Jesus Christ, by Jay Haley [The Triangle Press: Rockville, MD, 1986].

The Rise of Early Modern Science: Islam, China and the West, by Toby E. Huff, [Cambridge University Press: Cambridge, 1993].

The Role of Religion in History by George Walsh [Transaction Publishers: New Brunswick, 1998].

Science Friction, by Michael Shermer, [Henry Holt: New York, 2003].

Seven Who Shaped Our Destiny: The Founding Fathers as Revolutionaries, by Richard B. Morris [Harper & Row: New York, 1973].

Sociology, 3rd edition, by Ian Robertson, [New York: Worth Publishing, 1987].

Uncommon Therapy: The Psychiatric Techniques of Milton H. Erickson, M.D., by Jay Haley, [W.W. Norton & Company New York, 1986].

When They Severed Earth from Sky: How the Human Mind Shapes Myth, by Paul T. Barber, and Elizabeth Wayland Barber [Princeton University Press: Princeton, 2004].

Who Wrote the Bible? by Richard Elliott Friedman, [Perennial: New York, 1989].

Why I Am Not A Muslim by Ibn Warraq, [Prometheus Books: Amherst, New York, 1995].

Notes

1 www.timesonline.co.uk/tol/comment/faith/article6964050.ece.

2 www.papalencyclicals.net/Leo13/l13provi.htm

3 www.mechon-mamre.org/e/et/et08a13.htm

4 Ehrman, *Misquoting Jesus*, [New York: HarperCollins, 2005] p84.

5 *ibid*, p88.

6 *ibid*, p211.

7 www.mechon-mamre.org/e/et/et1007.htm

8 Personal communication.

9 www.newadvent.org/bible/1co011.htm#verse2.

10 www.newadvent.org/fathers/101602.htm.

11 www.newadvent.org/bible/psa136.htm.

12 "Mithraism," www.newadvent.org/cathen/10402a.htm.

13 Justin Martyr, *First Apology*, www.newadvent.org/fathers/0126.htm.

14 "Before the Manger," www.solagroup.org/articles/understandingthebible/utb_0001.html.

15 *The Catholic Encyclopedia*, www.newadvent.org/cathen/15448a.htm.

16 www.newadvent.org/cathen/15459a.htm.

17 *Ineffabilis Deus*, Apostolic Constitution issued by Pope Pius IX, 8 December 1854, www.papalencyclicals.net/Pius09/p9ineff.htm.

18 *Munificentissimus Deus: Defining the Dogma of the Assumption*, Pius XII, November 1, 1950, www.vatican.va/holy_father/pius_xii/apost_constitutions/documents/hf_p-xii_apc_19501101_munificentissimus-deus_en.html.

19 *Encyclopedia Britannica*, 1995, Volume 26, p905.

20 Robin Wright, *The Evolution of God* [New York: Little, Brown, 2009] p101.

21 "Saint and Saintliness," *Jewish Encyclopedia*, www.jewishencyclopedia.com/view.jsp?artid=49&letter=S#249.

22 "Beatification and Canonization," *Catholic Encyclopedia*, www.newadvent.org/cathen/02364b.htm.

23 *Catholic Encyclopedia*, www.newadvent.org/cathen/01476d.htm.

24 *ibid*.

25 www.newadvent.org/cathen/05646b.htm.

26 www.newadvent.org/bible/wis002.htm#vrs24. "Wisdom" is one of the books found in the Catholic but not Protestant Bible.

27 en.wikipedia.org/wiki/Cubit.

28 R.P. Philips, *Modern Thomistic Philosophy* [The Newman Press, 1950], pp355-356.

29 Quoted in *A Distant Mirror A Distant Mirror* by Barbara Tuchman, p104.

30 David C. Lindberg, quoted in "The Effects of the Condemnation of 1277" by Jason Gooch, *The Hilltop Review*, Spring 2006, Volume 2, Western Michigan University, p42.

31 Baylor, *Action and Person*, p24, quoted in *The Rise of Early Modern Science* by Toby Huff, [New York: Cambridge University Press, 1993], p109.

32 *ibid*, p100.

33 Quoted in *ibid*, p104.

34 Quoted in Richard E. Rubenstein, *Aristotle's Children*, [Harcourt: Orlando, 2003], p254.

35 Edward Grant, *The Foundations of Modern Science in the Middle Ages* [New York: Cambridge University Press, 1996], p70.

36 "Selections from the Condemnation of 1277," *Philosophy of Nature, Philosophy of the Soul, Metaphysics*, www.fordham.edu/gsas/phil/klima/Blackwell-proofs/MP_C22.pdf.

37 Aristotle, *On the Heavens*, quoted in Grant, *op. cit.*, p74.

38 Rubenstein, *op. cit.*, p210.

39 *ibid*, p229.

40 *ibid*, p225.

41 *ibid*, p236.

42 www1.umn.edu/ships/galileo/library/1616docs.htm.

43 *The Galileo Affair* by Maurice A. Finocchiaro, [Berkley/LA: University of California Press, 1989] pp288-291, at books.google.com/books?id=wKCZFJuMCaQC&printsec=frontcover&dq.

44 www.newadvent.org/library/docs_jp02tc.htm.

45 "The Proofs for the Existence of God in the Light of Modern Natural Science," Address of Pope Pius XII to the Pontifical Academy of Sciences, November 22, 1951, www.papalencyclicals.net/Pius12/P12EXIST.HTM.

46 "Truth Cannot Contradict Truth," *Catholic Encyclopedia*, www.newadvent.org/library/docs_jp02tc.htm.

47 www.newadvent.org/cathen/07790a.htm

48 *A Dictionary of Creation Myths* by David Leeming with Margaret Leeming [New York: Oxford University Press, 1995] p14.

49 *ibid*, p124.

50 *ibid*, p224.

51 *ibid*, p206.

52 *ibid*, p68.

53 *ibid*, p212.

54 *ibid*, p93.

55 *ibid*, p108.

56 *ibid*, pp140-141.

57 Unless otherwise noted, *A Dictionary of Creation Myths* is the source of this and the other references in this section.

58 Sources: www.psi.edu/projects/siberia/siberia.html and en.wikipedia.org/wiki/Tunguska_event.

59 Paul T. Barber, and Elizabeth Wayland Barber, *When They Severed Earth from Sky: How the Human Mind Shapes Myth*, [Princeton and Oxford, Princeton University Press, 2004].

60 Edited from Ellis Clark, *Indian Legends of the Pacific Northwest*, [Berkley, University of

California Press, 1953], pp53-55. Quoted in *ibid*, pp6-7.

[61] *ibid.*, pp7-8.

[62] *ibid.*, p7.

[63] dwindlinginunbelief.blogspot.com/2009/01/how-many-has-god-killed-revised_04.html.

[64] Quoted in Michelle Goldberg, *Kingdom Coming* [New York: W.W. Norton, 2007], p170.

[65] Garrett Epps, "Born-Again Politics Is Still Waiting to Be," *Washington Post*, 30 March, 1980; quoted in *The New American Militarism*, by Andrew Bacevich [Oxford University Press: New York, 2005] p127.

[66] "The Crusaders" by Bob Moser, *Rolling Stone*, 7 April 2005, www.rollingstone.com/politics/story/7235393/the_crusaders/.

[67] *ibid.*

[68] Quoted in Goldberg, *op. cit.*, p117.

[69] Gregory S. Paul, "Cross-National Correlations of Quantifiable Societal Health with Popular Religiosity and Secularism in the Prosperous Democracies," a systematic study of eighteen economically developed countries, *Journal of Religion and Society* (Volume 7, 2005) moses.creighton.edu/JRS/2005/2005-11.html #figures.

[70] Carolyn Holderread Heggen, *Sexual Abuse in Christian Homes and Churches* [Scotdale, PA: Herald Press, 1993] p73.

[71] Quoted in Goldberg, *op. cit.*, pp135-136.

[72] Hannah Brückner, Ph.D., and Peter Bearman, Ph.D., "After the promise: the STD consequences of adolescent virginity pledges," *Journal of Adolescent Health* 36 (2005), p277.

[73] www.yale.edu/lawweb/avalon/diplomacy/barbary/bar1796t.htm, reproduced from *Treaties and Other International Acts of the United States of America*, Volume 2 Documents 1-40 : 1776-1818, Edited by Hunter Miller [Washington : Government Printing Office, 1931].

[74] Letter to the United Baptist Churches in Virginia in May, 1789.

[75] George Washington, letter to the members of the New Church in Baltimore, January 27, 1793. Quoted in Richard B. Morris, *Seven Who Shaped Our Destiny: The Founding Fathers as Revolutionaries*, [Harper & Row: New York, 1973], p269.

[76] Letter to Peter Carr, 10 August 1787.

[77] Thomas Jefferson, letter to Thomas Cooper, October 7, 1814. From Gorton Carruth and Eugene Ehrlich, eds., *The Harper Book of American Quotations*, [New York: Harper & Row, 1988], p492.

[78] Thomas Jefferson, letter to John Adams, 11 April 1823, as quoted by E. S. Gaustad, "Religion," in Merrill D. Peterson, ed., *Thomas Jefferson: A Reference Biography*,

New York: Charles Scribner's Sons, 1986, p287.

[79] From a letter to Richard Price, October 9, 1780.

[80] Original wording of the First Amendment; Annals of Congress 434 (June 8, 1789).

[81] "A Defence of the Constitutions of Government of the United States of America" (1787-88), from Adrienne Koch, ed., *The American Enlightenment: The Shaping of the American Experiment and a Free Society* (1965) p258, quoted in Ed and Michael Buckner, "Quotations that Support the Separation of State and Church," www.infidels.org/library/modern/ed_buckner/quotations.html.

[82] *ibid.*

[83] Quoted in Goldberg, *op. cit.*, p44n.

[84] Mortimer Adler, ed., "Religion and Religious Groups in America," in *The Annals of America: Great Issues in American Life, Vol. II* [Chicago: Encyclopedia Brittanica, 1968] p420.

[85] According to Palestinian Prime Minister Mahmoud Abbas, from minutes acquired by *Haaretz* from cease-fire negotiations between Abbas and faction leaders from the Hamas, Islamic Jihad and the Popular and Democratic Fronts (circa June, 2003), quoted from Arnon Regular, "'Road map is a life saver for us,' PM Abbas tells Hamas" (Haaretz.com:June 27, 2003), quoted from EvilOz (*The Iterative Record*).

[86] George W. Bush, speaking at the National Commemoration of the Days of Remembrance at the U.S. Capitol on April 19, 2001, quoted from Freedom From Religion Foundation, "Bush's Holocaust Remarks Distort History, Scapegoat Freethinkers," April 25, 2001.

[87] Jonathan Lyons, "Bush enters Mideast's rhetorical minefield" (Reuters: September 21, 2001).

[88] Answering a question from American Atheists' reporter Robert Sherman in 1987, while serving as vice-president.

[89] Ian Robertson, *Sociology, 3rd edition* (New York: Worth Publishing, 1987), p410.

[90] *On Killing* by Lt. Col. Dave Grossman [Back Bay: New York, 2009], p12.

[91] *ibid.*, p253.

[92] "Religion and Crime: Do They Go Together?", by Lisa Conyers and Philip D. Harvey, *Free Inquiry*, Summer 1996.

[93] Quoted in *The Role of Religion in History* by George Walsh [New Brunswick: Transaction Publishers, 1998], pp180-181.

[94] www.atheists.org/Atheism/.

[95] Ayn Rand, *For the New Intellectual* [New York: NAL, 1963], p21.

[96] Ed Hussain, *The Islamist* (London: Penguin, 2007), pp243-244.

About the Authors

Mark Tier decided he was an atheist while attending a Church of England high school — and the following year won the only prize in his entire time at school: the Divinity Prize!

A graduate of economics from the Australian National University, he founded and edited the investment newsletter *World Money Analyst,* is author of *The Winning Investment Habits of Warren Buffett & George Soros,* and co-editor (with Martin H. Greenberg) of the science fiction anthologies *Give Me Liberty* and *Visions of Liberty* (reissued in one edition titled *Freedom!)* — which, together, won a Prometheus Award for libertarian fiction in 2005.

George Forrai was born in Budapest, a post-war baby "to make up for the dozens of Jewish relatives murdered by the Nazis." He and his family escaped from Hungary in 1956 and ended up in Australia.

A graduate of Sydney University law school, with a Masters from UC Berkeley, in the 1970s he was one of the founders of the Hong Kong office of a major international law firm, retiring as a partner in 2007 — and still lives in Hong Kong "which I love!"

He says he has his mother, Edith Forrai, to thank for his lack of religion, relating that:

> When I was about twelve, a client of my mother (a beautician) gave me a children's book full of New Testament stories. After reading the book, I began to drive my mother mad saying "God will punish me for this and this and that." I really got scared by some of the stories! One day my mother, tired of my whingeing, took the book from me and ripped it into pieces. She then asked me: "Now, did anything happen? Did God punish us?" — and that was the end of my religious experience! I thank her for being such a good mother as to free me from the nonsensical fear induced in me by that silly book.

www.ingramcontent.com/pod-product-compliance
Lightning Source LLC
Chambersburg PA
CBHW071710120626
46550CB00001B/170